UTAH:
THE STRUGGLE FOR STATEHOOD

For Bob & Nyla —

   With great memories — and
deep appreciation for the special
friendship we share.
   May a little of Utah follow you
through your travels ⟶

Ken Verdoin
1996

UTAH:
THE STRUGGLE FOR STATEHOOD

Ken Verdoia
and
Richard Firmage

1996
University of Utah Press

Library of Congress Cataloging-in-Publication Data

Verdoia, Ken, 1952–
    Utah : the struggle for statehood / Ken Verdoia and Richard Firmage.
        p.   cm.
    Includes bibliographical references and index.
    ISBN 0-87480-506-6
    1. Utah—Politics and government. 2. Statehood (American
politics)   I. Firmage, Richard A., 1946–   . II. Title.
F826.V47   1996
979.2'02—dc20

                                                    95—49921
                                                    CIP

First Edition
ISBN: 0-87480-506-6

Book and jacket design by Richard Firmage
Frontispiece photograph: January 1896—the Salt Lake LDS Tabernacle
decorated for the celebration of Utah statehood. (USHS)

For Amanda and Stephanie
... and the next 100 years.

Acknowledgments

———————————

The publication of this book was made possible in part by a generous grant from the

R. Harold Burton Foundation

Appreciation is also extended to the following organizations for their assistance in locating and granting permission to use photographs and other graphic material:

The Arizona Historical Foundation (AHF)
The Harold B. Lee Library, Brigham Young University (BYU)
The Church of Jesus Christ of Latter-day Saints (LDS)
The Library of Congress (LOC)
The National Archives and Records Administration (NARA)
The Nebraska Historical Society (NHS)
Special Collections, the Marriott Library, University of Utah (UU)
The Utah State Archives and Records Administration (USAR)
The Utah State Historical Society (USHS)

—☆—

Contents

A UNIQUE JOURNEY 1847–1896

UTAH'S PATH TO STATEHOOD IS UNIQUE in the annals of the American experience. No other western territory was carved from the wilderness on the strength of religious conviction. No other territory was initially settled by such a like-minded, homogenous wave of pioneers. No other territory faced the torrent of criticism, conflict, and confrontation that dominated Utah's pre-statehood experience. While other territories waged longer campaigns to enter the Union, none experienced a more pitched battle than Utah's struggle for statehood.

It was a story played out against remarkable times in the nation's history. The Utah Territory came into being when the West was still young, unmapped, and untamed. By the time statehood was achieved, the frontier had been all but formally declared closed, and major cities were emerging throughout the West. At the dawn of the Utah story native tribes lived in delicate balance with the land; by the time the forty-fifth star was sewn onto the flag, almost all of the nation's native people had been driven to reservations after major battles and great loss of life—both of which also scarred the history of Utah Territory.

Below: Main Street, Salt Lake City, 1860s. (USHS)

9

Mormon church president Brigham Young at the time of the Civil War. (USHS)

Although he was governor of Utah Territory for less than a decade, Brigham Young remained the real power in religious and civil affairs in Utah for thirty years, until his death in 1877.

In 1847, when the territory received its first settlers through the overland trek by members of the Church of Jesus Christ of Latter-day Saints, the national debt totaled one dollar for each man, woman and child ... and was considered a scandal. There were no Republicans in political office—Whigs and Democrats dominated the political scene. The New York Knickerbockers captured attention as pretty fair hands at the new game of "base ball." The Industrial Revolution swept across Europe and leapt the Atlantic to the United States. It left in its wake the stirrings of a dislocated society that produced angry revolts in the streets of old Europe, and sharpened the vision of a little-known German economist, Karl Marx, who would describe a changing world in his 1848 work, *The Communist Manifesto*. The sun never set on the British empire, as Queen Victoria celebrated her tenth year on a throne she would occupy for another fifty years.

Beyond the eastern seaboard, America was a rough-hewn, unforgiving land. Heroic explorers would venture into the uncharted wilderness of the heartland to fanfare another generation of Americans would reserve for men walking on the moon. The landscape was vast and ready for the taking, and the nation moved with determination to fill those lands from the Atlantic to the Pacific. European social and economic upheavals, epidemics, and famine drove a tidal wave of humanity to the United States, swamping the scanty immigration checkpoints at Castle Garden, New York, and the Port of New Orleans in Louisiana.

Nineteenth-century life in the nation, while not entirely lawless, could border on a tyranny of the most powerful. Civil liberties and constitutional rights were broad but in the infancy of interpretation, and could often be set aside or applied narrowly to lean with the political winds. A blind eye could be turned to individuals and groups that were considered "unique." The American legislative and judicial systems could identify African-Americans as property, women as political non-beings, and an ardent religious group in Utah Territory as being unworthy of or outside the Constitution's religious protections.

Still, the era remains, on balance, a magnificent chapter in history. It was a time when opportunity called across social, political, and economic lines. A time when passions ran deep, tapping the dark sides of the human experience, or appealing, as Lincoln said, "to the better angels of our nature." Dreams of new beginnings, of justice, and of dignity were nurtured in millions of families whose personal, intimate histories would form the most powerful story lines of the nation in its first one hundred years.

While unique, the story of Utah is also a part of the story of the nation in the mid-nineteenth century. The vision that drove a people to seek refuge in a new homeland had much in common with the vision that carried millions of people to America from foreign shores. The struggle to build a sustainable society that could be passed lovingly to the next generation defines what so many others sought as they merged their lives with the fortunes of the young nation. The emergence of diversity in that society, and the need to balance principled dedication against practical coexistence, led to a redefinition of Utah, its people, and its dreams as the state, and the nation, stepped into the twentieth century.

UTAH: The Struggle for Statehood is offered as a celebration of the people and events that shaped the fifty years of history leading to the state's admission to the Union in 1896. But it is a celebration that honors controversy as well as conviction, courage as well as faith. For in the controversial struggles we can find important lessons—lessons not just for understanding Utah's path to statehood but for discovering the living legacy that graces each day as the state approaches another new century.

In the fall of 1987 I was pushing my way through massive stacks of photographs in the collection of the Utah State Historical Society in Salt Lake City as I researched a public-television documentary on life in relocation

camps during World War II. My eyes kept wandering to the collection's earliest photos—those showing the pioneer days of Utah Territory and the men and women who carved a homeland in the Great Basin. Each picture seemed to tell a story. And each story seemed to have been lost to the ages or relegated to a footnote on the academic side of history. I was struck by a sense that the full, wondrous range of the Utah experience was being lost. Our common understanding of Utahns' epic struggle to create the state of Utah was being streamlined, condensed, homogenized, and filtered to the point that it was easily digested but stripped of relevance. I hoped then that someday I might be able to help bring Utah's history to life for the average person.

In 1993 I received that chance—public-television station KUED provided me an opportunity to work on a documentary project that would seek to explore Utah's history from the perspective of the men and women who lived the conflicts, setbacks, and triumphs of the state's earliest years. By combing through archives, libraries, and even attics we would attempt to reconstruct the story of this unique place from earliest pioneer settlement through the granting of statehood. Through rare photographs and first-person accounts we would attempt a new, more humanized retelling of the Utah experience for a television audience. This endeavor has proved to have been the most rewarding work of my career in journalism.

Above: Workers pause to mark their progress on the Salt Lake Temple, 1870. (USHS)

This book takes its life from the result of that effort: the public-television series *UTAH: The Struggle for Statehood*, developed by KUED-TV of Salt Lake City, Utah, to recognize and help celebrate the state's centennial observance of admission to the Union. Conceived at first as a companion volume, the book soon took on a life of its own—with its own demands, promises, and rewards—to emerge as an illustrated history of Utah's fifty-year path to the forty-fifth star.

In undertaking the research that brought both the documentary series and this book to life, I was able to discover the excellent works of a dedicated group of Utah historians who have chronicled this state and its people so well. Through their scholarship, and even the friendship of some, I was guided and encouraged as I discovered the power and diversity of the story of Utah. While I remain accountable for errors that may be found in this attempt to visualize the territorial years, I want to express my appreciation and respect for those who shared their time and scholarship, and who made any such errors more

Right: Women of the Cedar Fort settlement, Utah Territory, 1880s. (USHS)

Men of Cedar Fort. (USHS)

By the 1880s a second generation had been born in the Utah territory. (USHS)

rare. They include Thomas G. Alexander, D. Michael Quinn, Leonard Arrington, Jan Shipps, Martha Sonntag Bradley, Carol C. Madsen, Jean Bickmore White, Charles Hibbard, Brigham Madsen, Edward Leo Lyman, Fred Gowans, Jessie L. Embry, and Harold Schindler.

As I worked my way through archives, museums, and history collections, I was continually saved by competent hands which would point the right way and often help in unearthing rare photographs or diaries that brought another chapter of Utah history to life. While I am unable to mention each person who made a difference, the following people and/or institutions made substantial contributions to my research: Susan Whetstone (Utah State Historical Society); Bill Slaughter (LDS Church Archives); Special Collections, Marriott Library, University of Utah; the Daughters of the Utah Pioneers Museum; the Utah State Archives and Records Administration; the Library of Congress; and the National Archives and Records Administration.

Attempting to simultaneously produce a television documentary series and author a heavily illustrated book on the same subject is not something a rational person should ever undertake. The sole exception would be if an exceptional partnership could be orchestrated between the broadcast outlet and the publishing house. I am grateful to Jeff Grathwohl of the University of Utah Press for his patient and understanding stewardship of our collaboration. Other staff members of the press—especially Rodger Reynolds—were most helpful in making this book a reality in such a short period of time. The project would not have materialized, in print or on television, without the farsighted support of Fred Esplin and Scott Chaffin of KUED-TV. For their confidence, support, and friendship through the hills and valleys of this project I shall remain forever grateful.

A number of my professional colleagues and friends offered comments, guidance, and input during the writing of this book. I thank them for their support. Cheryl Gustafson deserves thanks for days of legwork in tracking down photographs. Nichole Bywater Coombs did valuable work on the index in a brief amount of time. I reserve special mention for my very special colleague, Nancy Green, who constantly amazed me during the research and writing of this project as she routinely tracked down a missing picture or encouraged a better way to deliver a thought.

I have taken the liberty of dedicating this book to my daughters, Amanda and Stephanie, as a reminder that history is something we should lovingly share with each succeeding generation. While they receive the dedication, anyone who knows me will know that my inspiration flows from another

Cove School, c. 1890. (USHS)
    Children were often a focal point of the struggle over Utah's path to statehood.

source: Carol, wife and partner, an unending source of inspiration with her encouragement and support. She should be decorated for tolerating two years of my walking through the house, quoting aloud from diaries. So, too, do I thank my dad and mom, Mario and Marge, for encouraging from a young age their son's interest in history.

Finally, while I have seized the opportunity to write these lines as a foreword, it is important to share whatever enjoyment the reader may take from this volume with my collaborator, Richard Firmage. Against long odds in a short period of time, he has helped steer me through this initial authorship experience. His love of Utah history, timely input to the writing, and vision for crafting the presentation of the material have helped form a disparate mass of material into this book. I am grateful for this partnership.

Not long ago I was in Washington interviewing a cabinet officer for another public-television project. During the course of the interview he quoted a simple, eloquent passage from the Bible about the role and relevance of history: "Each day informs the next." It is my deepest hope that your time spent leafing through these pages that illustrate the early years of the Utah experience will remind you that history does indeed shape each day of our lives; that your actions are as important for the future as were the efforts of pioneers who went before; and that, when all is said and done, history is the story of people like you and me, trying to make the best of what we have around us and within us.

—Ken Verdoia

UTAH:
THE STRUGGLE FOR STATEHOOD

Chapter One

BEGINNINGS
1845–1850

As many as one million people die or are dislocated through the Irish Potato Famine....War with Mexico and gold in California transform the American West....Railroads and steamships highlight the Industrial Revolution....The Opium War is waged in China....The first women's rights convention is held in Seneca Falls, New York. The nation's population in 1850 is 23,191,876.

IN 1846 THE WORLD AND THE UNITED STATES were rapidly changing. The nation was at war with Mexico, a conflict many saw as inevitable. The concept known as "manifest destiny"—that it was the nation's destiny, sanctioned by divine will, to control the sprawling continent from the Atlantic to the Pacific—steered national interest westward. At stake were the vast, open lands of North America from the western border of the Louisiana Purchase, roughly the Rocky Mountains, to the Pacific Coast. Success in the war was certain to transform the face, and the future, of the nation.

Society in the United States was at a pivotal point as well. Eastern seaboard cities such as New York, Boston, and Philadelphia had grown from small

Below: Mormon wagon train, Echo Canyon, c. 1860. (USHS)
A Mormon wagon train makes its way through Echo Canyon in Utah Territory during the 1860s. Wagon trains similar to this one formed the backbone of the early Mormon trek westward and, along with the handcart companies in the 1850s, dominated pioneer emigration until completion of the transcontinental railroad in 1869.

urban centers into full metropolitan giants. Famine, social revolution, and disease epidemics in Europe had pushed open the American door to a flood of immigrants. References to a poverty class and to ethnic enclaves within the

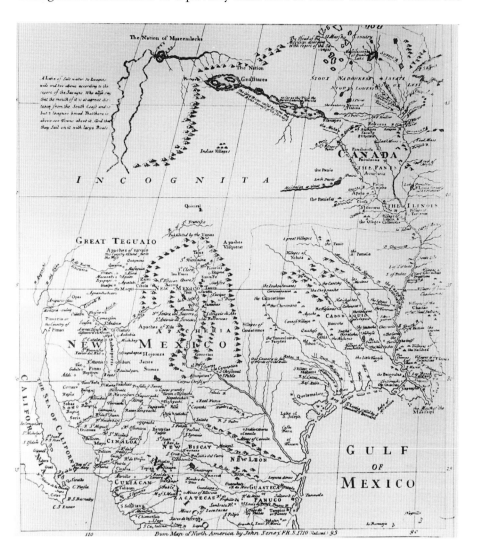

Spanish Map of "New Mexico," 1710. (USHS)

Early maps, drawn from sketches and hearsay reports of the geography by explorers, often reflected wild inaccuracies—especially in charting the vast region encompassing present-day Utah. Many cartographers wisely preferred to label the area *terra incognita*—unknown land.

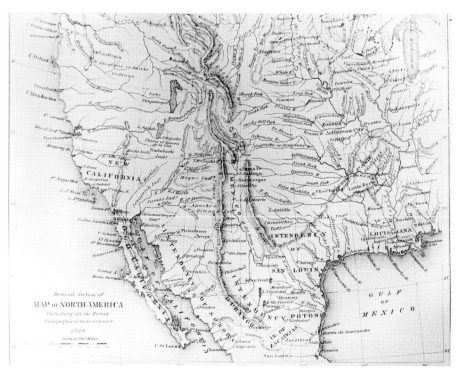

Map of North America, unknown cartographer, 1826. (USHS)

By 1826 trappers were beginning to swarm over the region, and maps started to assume broad accuracy. The existence of a reported enormous salt lake beyond the Rocky Mountain range was confirmed, but this map's efforts to link it to the Pacific Ocean by two rivers would soon be disproved by others.

cities appeared with greater frequency in the nation's press along with startling accounts of the death toll from urban plagues of cholera and typhus.

Yet it was generally a time of national confidence and optimism. Steamships and railroads were the visible sinews as the nation began to flex its industrial and agricultural muscle. Inventions were challenged in the public fancy only by the amazing accounts of discovery and opportunity coming from the unexplored western reaches of the continent. Readers of the popular press marveled at accounts of the discoveries and exploits of explorers John C. Frémont and Kit Carson, some of which took place in a region that was being called the "Great Basin." This was described as a land of barren deserts, fertile valleys, and an enormous inland dead sea beyond imposing ranges of the Rocky Mountains. The accounts echoed earlier tales told in different settings by conquistadors, missionaries, and traders from Spain and by rugged trappers and mountain men working their trap lines along the rivers and streams of the unmapped territory. By 1846 wagon trains in large numbers were heading west on the Oregon Trail to California and the Oregon country. A few followed a route promoted by entrepreneur Lansford Hastings that broke south from the traditional path in what is now western Wyoming and passed through a valley on the shores of a great salt lake.

Captain John C. Frémont, U.S. Army surveyor and explorer, c. 1845. (USHS)

In 1843 John C. Frémont explored the Great Salt Lake and Utah Lake, in part with the aid of an India-rubber boat. He and scout Kit Carson carved a cross on the highest point of what would become Fremont Island in the Great Salt Lake—a landmark that exists to this day. His subsequent book of the exploration had a profound influence on Mormons preparing for their trek westward.

The Great Salt Lake Valley, c. 1850. (LOC)

The first European explorer to see the Great Salt Lake may have been Baron Lahontan in 1703, although most historians are skeptical of the story. More accept the claim of trapper Jim Bridger that he reached the lake in 1824. By that time native cultures had lived near the lake for hundreds, if not thousands, of years. Nineteenth-century artists found the lake a fine subject for romantic treatment—whether or not they actually saw it themselves.

JOSEPH SMITH AND THE EARLY MORMON CHURCH

Joseph Smith, Jr., was the founder and early leader of the Church of Jesus Christ of Latter-day Saints (LDS, or Mormon). Smith began reporting religious visions at the age of fourteen, and in 1830 brought forth *The Book of Mormon*, soon to be regarded as a sacred scripture among those who followed him and the new religious movement. Opposition and persecution dogged Smith and the Latter-day Saints through several relocations in Ohio, Missouri, and Illinois in the 1830s and 1840s.

Two shattering events thrust the members of the Mormon church into motion which would eventually lead them to the western frontier. The savage murder of Joseph Smith and his brother Hyrum by a mob in June 1844 seemed to crystalize his earlier prediction that his people would not be safe until they established their vision of a new religious-based society in a haven beyond the Rocky Mountains. The Mormons were then driven at gunpoint from their settlement in Nauvoo, Illinois, in 1846. These events, along with other examples of what the group perceived as overt persecution and open hostility, convinced church leadership they had to remove themselves from the United States.

While Smith died three years before the Mormon trek to the Great Basin, he had a profound influence on the relocation of his church and the development of life in what would become Utah. His "Plat of the City of Zion" was part of a design for building a unique religious society, and it influenced many of the decisions made by Brigham Young in laying out Great Salt Lake City. Smith also confided to a select group of fellow Mormons a divine revelation on plural marriage, the practice of which would have a profound impact on his church for decades following his death.

Above: Joseph Smith, Mormon church founder, c. 1842. (USHS)

Below: Drawing, "Expulson of the Mormons from Nauvoo, Illinois," in September 1846. (LOC)

from the City of Nauvoo Ill September 1846.

THE HASTINGS CUTOFF, THE DONNER PARTY, AND THE MORMONS

In their temporary settlements near the Missouri River, Mormons eagerly read the exploration journals of John C. Frémont and a new western emigration guide authored by promoter Lansford Hastings. Hastings had helped pioneer the Oregon Trail in 1842, but argued that overland companies to California could save time and find an easier path by taking his proposed cut-off, following a route south of the Great Salt Lake across the desert that includes the area now known as the Bonneville Salt Flats.

While the Mormons studied his *Emigrant's Guide* in preparation for their journey, another party accepted Hastings's urging to try the "Hastings Cutoff"... with tragic results. In 1846 the Donner-Reed party struggled

Right: Lansford Hastings, guide and entrepreneur, c. 1845. (USHS)

THE
EMIGRANTS' GUIDE,
TO
OREGON AND CALIFORNIA,
CONTAINING SCENES AND INCIDENTS OF A PARTY OF
OREGON EMIGRANTS;
A DESCRIPTION OF OREGON;
SCENES AND INCIDENTS OF A PARTY OF CALIFORNIA
EMIGRANTS;
AND
A DESCRIPTION OF CALIFORNIA;
WITH
A DESCRIPTION OF THE DIFFERENT ROUTES TO
THOSE COUNTRIES;
AND
ALL NECESSARY INFORMATION RELATIVE TO THE
EQUIPMENT, SUPPLIES, AND THE METHOD
OF TRAVELING.

BY LANSFORD W. HASTINGS,
Leader of the Oregon and California Emigrants of 1842.

CINCINNATI:
PUBLISHED BY GEORGE CONCLIN,
STEREOTYPED BY SHEPARD & CO.
1845.

through the difficult canyons of the Wasatch Mountains, tiring their animals and taking up precious time. They then became mired in the salt flats, losing more time and many of their possessions. The ill-fated group subsequently entered the Sierra Nevada dangerously late in the season. When early snows trapped the wagon train, dozens died of starvation and exposure; some resorted to cannibalism to survive. Survivors cursed the name of Lansford Hastings, and his cutoff route was thereafter shunned.

One year after the tragedy, the vanguard wagons of the Mormon exodus would follow much of the path laboriously cut through the canyons leading to the Salt Lake Valley by the Donner-Reed party.

Left: Title page, Hastings's *Emigrant's Guide to Oregon and California*, 1845. (LOC)

In 1846 the beleaguered nucleus of what was viewed by some Americans as the most controversial religious group in the seventy-year history of the United States was mending its wounds on the banks of the Missouri River. The group's founder and revered prophet, Joseph Smith, had been murdered two years before. The members of the faith popularly known as the Mormons had just been driven from the beautiful city-state they had built up along the banks of the Mississippi River at Nauvoo, Illinois, and were forced to leave virtually all of their worldly possessions behind. Group members also had struggled among themselves over leadership. They recently had also lost five hundred of their most able men to the United States Army. They were told that, if the Church of Jesus Christ of Latter-day Saints would "volunteer" the 500-man battalion to fight the Mexican Army, the federal government would allow other members of the sect to temporarily stay on the banks of the Missouri River. The battalion would march into the wilderness, draw desperately needed army pay for the cash-poor Latter-day Saints, and eventually be allowed to rejoin their families somewhere in the West. It was a goal that could be realized only if the five hundred untrained volunteers survived what would become the longest march in U.S. Army history.

Brigham Young, c. 1850. (USHS)
The task of leading the Mormon people to a new land of sanctuary fell on forty-five-year-old Brigham Young, who had earned a living in construction and woodworking trades. Young would emerge as one of the nation's most dynamic figures of the nineteenth century, and one of the most important leaders in the development of the American West.

James K. Polk, eleventh president of the United States, c. 1848. (LOC)

President James Polk was suspicious of the Mormon people and their intentions, but he also viewed them as a means of laying national claim to lands that were later seized as a result of the Mexican War. Accepting an offer from Brigham Young to use the Mormon people to claim lands involved in the dispute with Mexico, Polk turned the request for support of a peaceful wagon train into marching orders for a small army of Mormons when he proposed the creation of what became the Mormon Battalion.

Staying in what would become Nebraska Territory was never an option for the group popularly known as Mormons. For years they had been told that their destiny was in the West, and they were deliberately seeking virgin territory removed from other settlements. Even apart and removed from the government of the United States. For years church members had viewed politicians as conspiring partners in an effort to crush their faith. At the same time, the Mormons had produced much resentment in the areas in which they had congregated. Sudden infusions of church members had changed political and economic landscapes overnight. Familiarity bred contempt for Mormon and non-Mormon alike. Brigham Young, emerging as the popular choice for leadership in the church, was determined in 1846 to move his flock as far from settlements and governments as possible. Church leaders were certain that this meant leaving the United States.

Where the Mormons would turn was far from certain. At the time of their negotiated exodus from Nauvoo, Young had indicated that Vancouver Island on the Pacific Coast was the ultimate destination. References were made at the time to other possible homelands in British Oregon territory or in Mexican California territory. But the writings of Frémont and Hastings, coupled with descriptions of the Great Basin and advice given by the friendly, wayfaring Jesuit priest Pierre DeSmet, had convinced Brigham Young of his group's ability to survive in lands beyond the Rocky Mountains that were sparsely populated by Indians and only roughly charted by earlier explorers. Better yet, it was a land buffered on all sides by mountains and deserts. It was isolated. Even better, it was in unadministered Mexican territory.

In revisiting all great events, including pioneering treks, intervening years tend to magnify the features, which can lengthen the subsequent shadows of heroic figures and create larger-than-life turning points that seem to shape

THE MORMON BATTALION

Brigham Young sent Jesse C. Little to Washington to urge President Polk to support a Mormon overland trek to the West as a means of colonizing the vast lands of the Great Basin. Polk's return offer was not for a peaceful citizen's caravan but rather for the creation of an army, achieved by drafting 500 of the fittest Mormon men to serve in a battalion to march against and, if needed, to fight the Mexican army. The group's march through the uncharted American Southwest still represents the longest armed military march in the nation's history.

While the battalion had virtually no contact with

hostile forces, its members suffered heavily from disease and even had to fend off an attack of wild bulls. Eventually they would play an important part in establishing national control over Los Angeles and San Diego during the Mexican War. After mustering out, a number of battalion members made their way to the new Mormon settlement near the Great Salt Lake, stopping near Sacramento long enough to become central figures in the discovery of gold at Sutter's Mill. Membership in the Mormon Battalion subsequently was viewed by Mormons as a unique badge of honor.

Left: Jesse C. Little, Brigham Young's special representative to President Polk, photograph c. 1860. (LDS)

Right: Members of the Mormon Battalion, c. 1850. (USHS)

Kanesville (later Council Bluffs), Iowa, c. 1851. (USHS)

Council Bluffs, Iowa, and Winter Quarters in Nebraska Territory were primary temporary settlements for the Mormon people as they re-grouped for their eventual immigration to the west. Council Bluffs was originally named Kanesville, in honor of Thomas Kane, an army officer who developed a friendship with Brigham Young and became quite fond of the Mormon people. Kane would be an important but somewhat shadowy figure in Mormon political history for the next decade.

Mormon wagon train fording the Platte River, Nebraska, c. 1860. (LOC)

On the overland trek, many wagon trains followed the Platte River as a natural path to the west and a certain source of fresh water. Shown here in a photo from the 1860s, wagon trains were forced to ford the Platte when it was dangerously swollen with late spring runoff.

destiny. The westward migration of the Mormon people to the Great Salt Lake Valley, though it was clearly an achievement of faith and determination, was no exception to the inflationary rule.

As hard and demanding as was the overland journey, the Mormon pioneers did not blaze a trail to the new territory in the summer of 1847. They followed a trail cut by the ill-fated Donner-Reed party the previous year. In fact, the delays endured by the Donner party, as they desperately tried to follow the half-baked advice of Hastings's travel guide while cutting paths through the canyons leading to the Great Salt Lake Valley, contributed significantly to their being trapped by early snows in the Sierra Nevada.

The first Mormons to enter the valley were Orson Pratt and Erastus Snow on July 21, 1847. Catching a first glimpse of the site from Big Mountain, they had worked their way to the broad valley and found it thick with grass and brush that made entry difficult. The next day, seven additional advance settlers arrived in the valley and selected a campsite near one of the creeks that flowed to a large river that split the valley in two. By the 23rd of July many in the advance Mormon company of 148 men, women, children, and three black slaves had arrived and were at work plowing the valley floor to plant potatoes, beans, corn, and wheat. To begin irrigating the fields, a dam had already been built across what would later be named City Creek.

On July 24, 1847, Brigham Young approached the Salt Lake Valley in the back of a wagon driven by fellow church authority Wilford Woodruff. Young had been seriously ill for days, sometimes too sick to travel. Years later, his illness would be retroactively diagnosed as Rocky Mountain Tick Fever or

Fort Laramie, in present-day Wyoming, c. 1860. (USHS)

In 1847 Fort Laramie was an isolated outpost in the wilderness operated by private trappers and traders who had good relationships with surrounding Native American tribes. The fort was an important resupply point for Mormon wagon trains. This photograph shows the fort after it had passed to U.S. military jurisdiction later in the pioneer period.

"Mormons in the Kanyons of the Rocky Mountains," illustration from *Harper's Weekly*, c. 1855. (LOC)

Early travel through the canyons of the nation's mountain ranges was not as easy as represented in this artist's optimistic rendering from the 1850s. While paths had been cut by wagons on the flat stretches of the overland trail, the canyons were a frightening series of water crossings and steep drops throughout the pioneering era.

perhaps even a rare form of high-altitude malaria. Racked with fever, and sometimes slipping into a semiconscious state, Young was in no condition to stand, let alone offer an extended oration, as he entered the valley. A later diary entry by Woodruff depicted Young rising from the back of the wagon to offer a confirmation that the scene before them was the right place.

Regardless of who may have said the words, the confirmation of a right place and right time answered a deep longing in the hearts of the Mormon

Fort Bridger, c. 1850. (LOC)
The Stansbury expedition's artist's rendering of Jim Bridger's private "fort" on Black's Fork as it might have appeared when the vanguard Mormon wagon train passed nearby in early July 1847. Bridger urged Brigham Young to consider the valley near Utah Lake as a better site for a settlement, saying he would pay $1000 for the first ear of corn grown in the Salt Lake Valley.

"Emigration to the Western Country," illustration c. 1850s. (LOC)
Oxen pulled many of the early wagons to the Great Salt Lake settlement. Far more durable and stronger than horses, oxen provided the muscle for the overland journey and early efforts to carve a niche in the Great Basin.

Orson Pratt and Erastus Snow were the first Mormon pioneers to enter the Great Salt Lake Valley—the two men sharing the back of a single horse as they entered the valley on July 21, 1847. They had been selected to serve as scouts when the van-guard company was broken into sections to negotiate the tough mountain passages and deal with sickness among its members. Others followed the two before the arrival of Brigham Young; in fact, some crops had already been planted when the church leader arrived three days later.

Orson Pratt, Mormon pioneer and church leader, c. 1850. (USHS)

Erastus Snow, Mormon pioneer and colonizer, c. 1855. (USHS)

Brigham Young enters the Salt Lake Valley, July 24, 1847. Illustration from Stansbury Expedition report. (LOC)

On July 24, 1847, Brigham Young was racked with fever as he rode in the back of a wagon driven by Wilford Woodruff. Pausing to give his spiritual leader an opportunity to view the Salt Lake Valley from a mountain clearing, Woodruff would later report that Brigham was moved by the sight and declared: *"It is enough. This is the right place. Drive on."*

people. Here was untouched land, seemingly perfect for building up the Kingdom of God they envisioned. In many respects it even called to mind the Holy Land. A large dead sea that seemed straight from biblical description dominated the region. The river running to that sea gained the name "River Jordan." The Mormons had marched through the wilderness following a new Moses to their promised land, and early pioneer diaries reflect a belief that they had been chosen to endure their trials and that they would flourish under their new covenant with the Almighty.

Within days, both life and death visited the new camp. On August 9 a baby girl was born to the Steele family, a few days after her mother had finished the demanding cross-country trek in the advanced stages of pregnancy. That same week, three-year-old Milton Thirlkill wandered too close to a swift portion of City Creek and fell in, drowning. Orson Pratt offered the sermon for the first funeral in the Salt Lake Valley.

While reveling in the sense of being a chosen people in a chosen land, the new settlers soon confronted evidence that they were not the first people to settle the region. The Salt Lake Valley settlement fell between two strong, vibrant Native American cultures that populated the region. To the south, with one important center of life formed around a large, freshwater lake soon dubbed "Utah Lake," were the tribal lands of a people labeled "Utes" by

Ellen Sanders Kimball, Harriet Decker Young, and Clara Decker Young—the first three Mormon women to enter the Salt Lake Valley, 1847. (LOC)

Three women and two children under the age of twelve were in the vanguard company of 148 Mormons that reached the Salt Lake Valley in July 1847. The group also included three African-American slaves, considered the property of church converts from the southern states.

The Salt Lake Valley, looking south from a position consistent with present-day Temple Square, c. 1849. (USHS)
"After issuing from the mountains among which we had been shut up for many days...we could not refrain from a shout of joy which almost involuntarily escaped from our lips the moment this grand and lovely scenery was within our view." —Orson Pratt, July 21, 1847. (USHS)

explorers, after the Spanish "yuta," referring to natives found "higher" on their exploration trails. To the north were the Shoshoni people, with a culture woven tightly around the game and open grasslands of the valleys north and east of the Great Salt Lake. For years the Salt Lake Valley had served as a buffer zone between the Utes and Shoshoni.

In subsequent years Mormon pioneers would find clear evidence of the ancient civilizations of the Anasazi and Fremont cultures that had flourished south and east of the new settlement in the cliffs and canyons throughout the vast geologic landscape known as the Colorado Plateau. As scouting parties

NATIVE AMERICANS IN UTAH TERRITORY BEFORE THE COMING OF ANGLO-AMERICANS

It was soon evident to the Mormon pioneers that they were not the first people to settle in the Great Basin. As they ventured out from the Salt Lake Valley to explore the surrounding region, they came across evidence of vanished cultures. The Mormons often ascribed spiritual explanations to the burial sites and rock art of the ancient Anasazi and Fremont people they discovered, relating them to the Lamanite people—ancient inhabitants of the continent featured in the *Book of Mormon*.

The Great Basin and Colorado Plateau areas of the territory had been occupied for at least 10,000 years by Paleo-Indian hunter-gatherer groups and their successors on the land, who included the Anasazi and Fremont peoples. Both of these later cultures had developed corn horticulture and more settled village life; the Anasazi especially have been celebrated for their architectural, ceramic, and basketmaking accomplishments.

By the 1400s both groups had been succeeded on the land by ancestors of modern Indian groups. The Salt Lake Valley settlement fell in a natural neutral zone between the two dominant Native American cultures of the region at the time. The Shoshoni people were to the north, and many tribal groups lumped under the label "Ute" were to the south. Both peoples had benefited from early trading experiences with white trappers, and Ute representatives especially made welcoming gestures and sought to trade with the new Mormon arrivals in the earliest days of the settlement before increased friction developed.

Excavation of Anasazi burial site near Glen Canyon, c. 1960. (USHS)

Ute Indians, c. 1870. (USHS)

Shoshoni Indian village in the Great Basin, c. 1870. (USHS)

ventured farther from the hub settlement they confronted pictographs and petroglyphs of a lost people. As settlers muscled their way through steep canyons and labyrinths, they would find stone dwellings defying gravity along the cliff walls, silent memorials to those who had lived in the land hundreds, even thousands, of years before.

Mid-nineteenth-century Mormons offered a rather unique approach to Native American cultures encountered in the general Anglo-American westward expansion. Although they were still determined to secure lands they deemed important to their vision of an inland empire, church members believed a doctrinal teaching that acknowledged ancient ties to the Indian cultures. Brigham Young often advised church members that more peace would be enjoyed by feeding the native people rather than fighting them. Subsequent events, however, would demonstrate the willingness of church members to take up the rifle against both the Utes and the Shoshoni people when the reality of Mormon expansion was recognized by the native cultures, which faced dire straits as they were driven from the land and, as a result, began to aggressively fight back against the invaders.

Mormon pioneers in 1847 also had at least one settled Anglo tenant to deal with in their new homeland. While roving trappers had been working and living in the region for almost twenty years, trader Miles Goodyear had established a permanent settlement on the Weber River in 1845. For two years he had offered his "Fort Buenaventura" as a stop for mountain men and westbound wagons. By November 1847 Mormon leadership decided to buy Goodyear out in order to secure their title to the fertile valleys fronting the Wasatch Mountains.

Although they were a people determined to flee the perceived malevolent hand of government, the Mormon settlers soon found themselves buffeted by strong political winds. The year 1848 brought a victorious end to the Mexican War for the United States, and the subsequent Treaty of Guadalupe Hidalgo delivered virtually all Mexican land holdings in North America north of the present-day Mexican border to the jurisdiction of the federal government.

John Young, brother of Brigham Young and early Utah settler who initially despaired over the bleak conditions of the early Salt Lake City settlement and advised his brother to direct the Saints elsewhere, c. 1850. (USHS)

THE "MIRACLE" OF THE SEAGULLS

The settlers' first crop in the spring of 1848 virtually disappeared under an invasion of crickets—a marked increase in the usual numbers of the insect, found by later researchers to occur at irregular intervals when climatic conditions are propitious for the small animals. Attempts by the settlers to combat the insect hordes had little effect, but relief was was found when seagulls from the Great Salt Lake were attracted to the scene and gorged themselves on the hordes of insects. The event itself was not greatly stressed in contemporary journal accounts and did not have quite the dramatic stature it assumed in later retellings as it grew to mythic proportions in some accounts; still, the dramatic loss of food prompted John Young to urge his brother Brigham to direct Mormon wagon trains to a more favorable location lest the people die of starvation.

It has been argued that Native Americans perhaps looked with dismay on the settlers' attempt to destroy the insects, since the periodic invasions of the creatures were looked upon by the Indians as a special blessing, and the seagulls would have been looked upon as competitors for the foodstuffs—they being the unwelcome invaders in an Indian account. Indians gathered and feasted upon the insects at such times, storing the surplus (which was often dried, salted, and ground up) as a food staple for less plenteous times. Although settlers were forced on occasion to eat insects, the small creatures never became part of the general diet of the new immigrants to the region.

"Bird Island," Great Salt Lake, c. 1920. (USHS)

Zachary Taylor, twelfth president of the
United States, c. 1848. (LOC)

Letter from William Smith to President
Taylor, 1850. (NARA)

President Zachary Taylor initially wanted
to lump the Mormons' proposed State of
Deseret together with California to create
one huge "super admission" of new territory
into the Union. The concept fell apart, in
part due to Californians' reluctance to accept
the merger. Taylor soon became an outspoken critic of the Mormons, vowing never to
let them have a state or territory of their
own. A contributing factor to his hostility
may have been a letter he received from a
rival group who accused Brigham Young of
seeking to create a theocracy—the domina-
tion of government by the church. It featured
the signature of William Smith, a brother of
Mormon church founder Joseph Smith.

Also included under this new jurisdiction were the Mormon settlers. To
maintain self-determination, church leaders decided to attempt to secure their
borders by making a direct bid for statehood, bypassing a territorial period,
and thus securing the opportunity to govern themselves with a minimum of
external control.

In 1849 the pioneering settlers held an election, formed a rough legislative
body, and drafted a constitution for what they called the State of Deseret,
drawing the name from a *Book of Mormon* reference to the industrious
honeybee. Church leaders attached a petition for statehood to the constitution
and sent it off with a delegation to Congress. On its face, the constitution was
unremarkable. What created gasps—and some chuckles—was the enormous
scope of the proposed State of Deseret: Brigham Young had laid claim to all
land between the Sierra Nevada and the Rocky Mountains, extending north
past the 42nd parallel along the present northern borders of Nevada and Utah
and south to the Gila River in present-day southern Arizona. It even included
a corridor extending all the way to the Pacific Coast to provide a seaport for
the Mormon empire. The proposed land mass alone was enough to stall the
remarkable attempt to bypass territorial status in favor of the outright
granting of statehood. But Congress also balked at the small population base
for such a large territory. In addition, Congress and the White House were
receiving the opening salvos of mounting attacks against Mormon statehood
on the grounds of the sect's alleged theocratic governance and "peculiar
institutions." Torn by more pressing issues tied to the nation's emerging
sectional rift over slavery, Congress opted to award territorial status to the
Mormon pioneers as part of the Compromise of 1850, after substantially
trimming their land request and dropping the church-inspired name of Deseret
in favor of Utah.

Beyond political issues, life in the territory the first three years had been
filled with numerous trials. The first winter had been relatively mild, but the

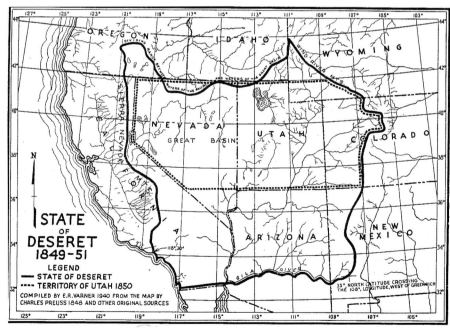

Map of the Provisional State of Deseret, 1849–1851, drawn by E.R. Varner. (USHS)

Brigham Young used the geography of the region to help define the boundaries of
his proposed State of Deseret. The result was an enormous land mass, embracing all or
part of nine future states. It even included a harbor on the coast of southern California.
Others were not sympathetic to the huge land grab the Mormons attempted. In creating
the Territory of Utah, Congress dropped the name of Deseret and began the process of
whittling down the size of the territory—a process that continued for more than two
decades, until the territory eventually reached the dimensions of the future state.

early spring brought a terrible infestation of crickets to the croplands of the Salt Lake Valley. The intervention of seagulls from the Great Salt Lake, while boosting pioneer morale, actually had little impact on the devastating hordes of insects that were thick enough to blacken the sky. Men, women, and children fought the creatures desperately with fire, shovels, and bare hands, yet the pioneers still lost huge amounts of their crops. This tragedy was followed by a cruel winter in 1848–49. Grain supplies were depleted, rations were cut, and a number of pioneer diarists despaired over the group's ability to survive in the Great Basin.

A pivotal, perhaps even saving, event was the discovery of gold in California and the resulting wave of westward immigrants to the gold fields. Because Salt Lake City was strategically located on the overland trail, many immigrants bought supplies from the Mormon settlers or traded trail-weary animals for stock from the relatively well-fed and rested herds in the Salt Lake Valley. Throughout the year 1849, Mormon traders drove hard bargains and made handsome profits while servicing the wagon trains and miners heading west. There is no small irony in the fact that the California gold rush was triggered by a discovery made by members of the Mormon Battalion working in the Sacramento area while making their way to Utah after the battalion's

Early depiction of the gold discovery at Sutter's Mill, near Sacramento, California, 1848. (LOC)

The discovery of gold in California created a frenzy across the nation. Thousands of "Forty-niners" left their homes to travel to California in search of wealth. Salt Lake City became an important resupply and resting point on the Overland Trail. Mormons were able to charge high prices for goods and supplies—a factor that helped the settlement survive.

THE STANSBURY EXPEDITION

The arrival of an army survey team in 1849 created suspicion among the Mormon people, who were still distrustful of the federal government for refusing to intervene on their behalf during the years of persecution in Missouri and Illinois. Captain Howard Stansbury, a fifteen-year veteran of mapping uncharted regions for the U.S. Army, reassured the settlers that he was simply a topographical engineer on a mission to chart the West. Stansbury, however, had a secondary mission: to observe the Mormon settlement, study its people, and assess their colonizing efforts in locations along the front of the Wasatch Mountain range, such as at Fort Utah, the forerunner of Provo.

Doubting Stansbury's motives, Brigham Young made sure the movements of the survey team were closely watched. Stansbury and his assistant, Lieutenant John Gunnison, stayed in Salt Lake City through the winter of 1849. They produced a series of excellent maps of the overland route to the Great Basin, and Stansbury's subsequent report, *Expedition to the Valley of the Great Salt Lake of Utah,* was a critical and commercial success on the east coast. Providing a detailed account of travel to the little-known region of the Rocky Mountains, and a surprisingly accurate report of the unique geologic structures and plant life of the area, Stansbury's book, along with Gunnison's own book, *The Mormons,* provided a balanced description of the recent Mormon settlements that gave every appearance of thriving in the hard lands of the West.

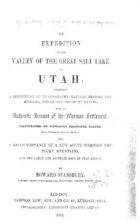

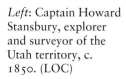

Center, above: Title page of Stansbury's *Expedition to the Valley of the Great Salt Lake,* 1852. (LOC)

Left: Captain Howard Stansbury, explorer and surveyor of the Utah territory, c. 1850. (LOC)

"Fort Utah—Valley of the Great Salt Lake" (actually the early settlement of present-day Provo), from Stansbury report, 1852. (USHS)

Unofficial flag of Deseret (front and back), c. 1855. (UARA)
The State of Deseret never had an official flag, but an ambitious group of Mormon emigrants crafted a banner for their overland company that they subsequently offered as a territorial flag. Produced in the early 1850s, it boldly proclaimed spiritual themes of the settlement, but it never went into use.

Albert Carrington, Brigham Young's private secretary and assistant to the Stansbury Expedition, c. 1860. (USHS)
Albert Carrington was the first Mormon in a position of leadership to graduate from college. He served as Brigham Young's private secretary, helped author the first constitution for the provisional State of Deseret, and served as Brigham's personal "observer" on the Stansbury expedition. Carrington Island in the Great Salt Lake was named after him.

incredible cross-country march during the Mexican War. Pouches of gold dust carried by members of the battalion arriving in Utah helped the church and the settlement weather the difficult first years. Much of the gold dust found its way into the first currency minted in the territory.

By the end of the decade, 1850, the Mormon settlement had survived and was developing an air of permanence. The settlement had taken the name of Great Salt Lake City on new maps of the territory completed by the expedition of Howard Stansbury and John Gunnison for the United States government. The settlers were pursuing an egalitarian, self-sufficient society in which religion was a cornerstone, and they were reveling in an ability to nurture their close-knit community free from interference and persecution.

But, while the sun seemed to shine so brightly after years of trial and doubt, storm clouds were building anew for the Mormon people and for Utah Territory.

Drawing of Great Salt Lake City, 1850. (NARA)
After three years, the primary settlement had adopted a formal name, Great Salt Lake City, and was acknowledged as the capital of the provisional State of Deseret and official Territory of Utah. The city itself was presenting an increasing appearance of permanence to the passing traveler. Communal farming was done in a large open area known as the Big Field, which started about half a mile south of the community's center. Individual homes made of adobe bricks had started to appear, replacing the more temporary cabins and the fortress built for protection in the earliest days of settlement.

Chapter Two

STORM CLOUDS OVER DESERET
1850–1855

Uncle Tom's Cabin fans anti-slavery sentiment in a nation with more than three million slaves....Commodore Matthew Perry opens the door to trade with Japan....Charles Darwin is writing *The Origin of Species*....Sir Richard Burton (who later comes to Utah in 1860) becomes the first European to venture to Mecca and Lake Tanganika....The Republican party is founded.

BY THE SUMMER OF 1850 more than 11,000 members of the Church of Jesus Christ of Latter-day Saints had gathered in the fledgling Utah Territory. The vast majority carried memories of weathering the storms of expulsion from Missouri, the murder of church founder Joseph Smith, and the grim uncertainty they faced as they were forced out of their homes in Nauvoo, Illinois.

Below: Great Salt Lake City, c. 1855. (LOC)
   An artist's view of Great Salt Lake City in its first decade distorts the geography but accurately reflects the vitality of the settlement. Broad streets allowed a wagon team to turn around without backing.

Right: Panoramic view, Salt Lake Valley, c. 1850. (USHS)

"*No elections, no police reports, no murders, no wars in our little world. It is the dream of poets actually fulfilled.*"
—Parley P. Pratt, 1848.

Although all was not quite as blissful as Parley P. Pratt proclaimed, Mormons increasingly looked back fondly on the first years of settlement, before a large number of "gentiles," or non-Mormons, took up residence in the region.

Millard Fillmore, thirteenth president of the United States, photograph c. 1860. (LOC)

President Fillmore signed into law the creation of the Territory of Utah in 1850. Impressed with the Mormon delegates sent to represent the territory in Washington, Fillmore's attitude towards the Mormons was a dramatic departure from that of his predecessor, Zachary Taylor. Appreciating the president's relative good will toward them, Utah Mormons subsequently named both a town and a county after him.

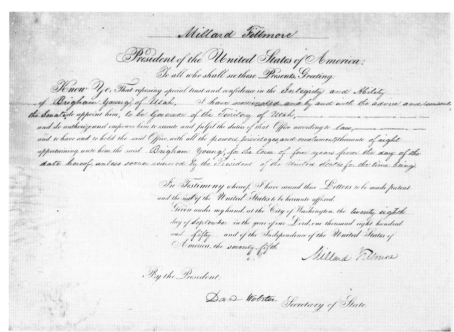

Brigham Young's certificate of appointment as Utah Territorial Governor, 1850. (USHS)

President Fillmore accepted the strong urging of Utah's delegate to Washington, Dr. John Bernhisel, to appoint Brigham Young as Utah's first territorial governor. Bernhisel argued that Young was overwhelmingly viewed as the region's civil as well as spiritual leader, and that it would be best for officials in Washington to realize that fact and attempt to work with the Mormon leader in territorial affairs. Fillmore sought to balance the government of the new territory by appointing half of the necessary officials from the Mormon population and half from political ranks outside the territory.

For a people who believed in a symbolic "gathering of the Saints" this was most difficult—all previous attempts to gather together had ended in violence and expulsion. The westward migration was an act of continued devotion and, in some respects, desperation as the Mormon people affirmed their commitment to upholding their religion and way of life.

In Great Salt Lake City the Mormon emigrants enjoyed what was in some respects a near utopian existence, although in other ways it was tempered by the realities of subsistence living in the wilderness. Church and state were formally separate but functionally one. A communal spirit embraced the new

Brigham Young, c. 1855. (USHS)
   Brigham Young proved to be a masterful colonizer. He deftly made use of the influx of some 3,000 immigrants per year in the founding of outlying settlements throughout the territory. His colonizing influence and vision reached throughout the West, and he remains one of the most powerful and important leaders in the national settlement of the western United States.

The *Deseret News* office, Salt Lake City, c. 1860. (USHS)
   In 1850 the territory took ambitious steps forward with the opening of classes of the University of Deseret, a precursor of the University of Utah, and the publication of the *Deseret News*. Shown here at a later location on South Temple, the *News* served as a news organ for the Mormon church. The paper would print information gathered through letters from the east, and enjoyed nearly a complete monopoly on the news business—and editorial opinion—in Utah for nearly twenty years.

settlers, who were quickly placed to work in a well-ordered society. Political, economic, social, and sectarian differences were virtually nonexistent.

   Life in the territory, which was still largely an agrarian cooperative for the Mormons, started to take on the signs of permanence. Individual houses were under construction, replacing the communal fort system that had provided early security and shelter. A first attempt at advanced education was made when the University of Deseret was established and held a few classes in the city in 1850. A printing press allowed the *Deseret News* to begin publishing that year as a church newsletter.

"FORTING UP"

Many of the early settlements in the territory, including Salt Lake City, started out as forts. The forts offered protection from hostile and uncertain relations with Native American tribes, and also reinforced the communal nature of the settlements and their common purpose.

The forts were often formed by building homes side to side in a square to form an enclosure, with the back walls of each home forming a common wall of defense. The male settlers were generally given some limited military training to help them to defend the site against attack. This led to some unexpected problems (and later smiles): the diaries of early Scandinavian immigrants, for example, recount the frustration of a militia officer barking orders in English to recently armed new arrivals who could not speak the language.

Eventually, some forts were built with thick stone-and-mortar walls surrounding the homes inside the fort. As settlers expanded throughout an area, they would return to the local fort for supplies, or flee to its safety if a violent outbreak occurred with the Indian tribes in their area. Fort Union represented an early effort to expand living room in the Salt Lake Valley at a time when Ute hunting parties were still routinely traversing the valley. Cove Fort represented a later effort to extend settlements in the southern reaches of the territory, an area often plagued with tension between the settlers and nearby tribes.

Fort Union, Salt Lake Valley, c. 1854. (USHS)

Cove Fort, southern Utah, photograph c. 1890. (USHS)

Frederick Auerbach, banker and merchant, c. 1860. (USHS)

Frederick Auerbach joined his brother Samuel among the first non-Mormons to establish permanent residence in Utah Territory. A merchant, Auerbach and his family would make lasting contributions to the commercial life of the area while helping to establish a Jewish community in Utah.

William H. Hooper, merchant and delegate to Congress, c. 1860. (USHS)

William Hooper served for a time as the territory's delegate to Congress. Public records show that Hooper purchased and held slaves in the territory, a practice that was made legal by the territorial legislature in 1852. Brigham Young did not encourage the practice of slavery among the Mormons, but he considered southern converts within their rights to travel to the territory with slaves and then continue to maintain their bondage.

The city had already emerged as a principal stop on the overland journey to the west coast. A view of the city nestled fast against the foothills of the Wasatch Mountains was a welcome sight to members of wagon trains after the tough canyons that dominated the trail from Fort Bridger to the Great Salt Lake. Hundreds of acres of neatly tilled fields spread out from a town that ended nine blocks south of the city center. There was little in its appearance to set the town apart from other mid-nineteenth-century settlements in the West. Few non-Mormons stayed in Utah; however, the 1850s did witness the arrival of the first Jewish merchants interested in servicing the settlements. Mormon church leader and writer Parley Pratt waxed rhapsodic about the "perfect peace" that seemed to embrace the valley and the people.

But the Territory of Utah was not wholly immune from issues tearing at the national fabric in the early 1850s. Three million slaves were held in the United

States at the start of the decade; only fifty slaves were held in Utah, but slavery was condoned by both society and territorial law. Some converts from southern states paid their religious offerings or tithes to the Mormon church in the form of slaves, with Brigham Young releasing the slaves from indentured service to take paying positions in his household or the community. Slaves were bought and sold in Great Salt Lake City, although without the spectacle of the open slave markets of the southern states.

In the 1850s Mormon migration to Utah Territory underwent a transformation. The trek west from the temporary church settlement—Winter Quarters—that had been established on the banks of the Missouri River was deemed complete. Now church leaders turned their attention to fulfilling the vision of an international gathering of followers in the new Zion of the Great

THE PAIUTE PEOPLE OF UTAH TERRITORY

The Paiute people had lived in the southwestern portion of the territory for more than 600 years before Mormon settlers first arrived in the 1850s. The family-oriented tribes concentrated much of their activity around the Virgin and Muddy rivers of present-day Utah. The Paiutes were generally a peaceful people and attempted to maintain good relationships with white pioneers, a fact appreciated by the settlers who were facing increased tensions with the more aggressive Ute and Shoshoni Indians of the region. The Paiutes had adapted superbly to existence in the marginal semiarid lands they frequented, but the Indians were generally misunderstood and looked down upon by explorers and settlers for what they considered to be the Indians' primitive lifeways.

Mormon settlers made concerted efforts to share their lifeways, customs, and religion with neighboring tribes, including the Paiutes. While the efforts could lead to the baptisms of some native people, they could not overshadow the emerging tension in many locales that resulted from steady Mormon inroads into (and appropriation of) traditional tribal lands. By the late 1850s the traditional lifestyle of Paiutes near the Virgin River had been greatly disrupted by Mormon agricultural settlements in the area. Widespread starvation resulted, and the Paiute population of southern Utah was decimated. The Paiutes would eventually sign a treaty with the federal government in 1865, but would not receive their own reservation lands until 1891.

Southern Paiute family camp site, Utah Territory, c. 1870. (USHS)

Mormon baptism of Paiute Indians near St. George, c. 1870. (USHS)

Dedication of the Mormon temple site, Salt Lake City, 1853. (LDS)
In one of the earliest known photographs of the Salt Lake settlement, hundreds gather in the heart of the city for groundbreaking at the site of the projected Mormon temple. This is a rare photographic glimpse of life in the early territory, showing the limited extent of the city and the emergence of its first permanent structures.

Basin. The Perpetual Emigrating Fund was established to loan money to aid thousands of Mormon converts in the journey from their homelands in England, Scandinavia, and continental Europe to the United States. It was a journey not to be taken lightly. In immigration not directly tied to Mormon converts, three passenger steamer ships sank in the North Atlantic in a two-year period of the early 1850s, drowning more than one thousand European emigrants who had dreamed of new lives in America.

Once they were in the United States, a harrowing part of the journey still awaited the new arrivals. While church loans could pay for steerage-class passage on steamers, Brigham Young now stressed the need for greater economy in completing the journey to Utah. Wagons and teams were not generally available to transport all the new arrivals to Zion, so many converts were asked and expected to cover the final 1,000 miles across the plains to Salt Lake City under their own power, which, for the vast majority, meant by foot in companies led by Mormon "captains" experienced in traveling the overland trail, with a few possessions stacked in handcarts that they would pull across the continent. For five years thousands of men, women, and children formed a determined stream of humanity across the plains. The handcart companies were unique in the western migration across America. Often the immigrants

Mormon church leaders, 1850. (USHS)

This collection of photographs shows the First Presidency and the Quorum of the Twelve Apostles of the Church of Jesus Christ of Latter-day Saints as they were constituted in 1850. In addition to Brigham Young, the photograph features two future presidents of the Mormon church who later would be instrumental in the struggle for statehood, John Taylor (third row, far left) and Wilford Woodruff (second row, far right).

Freight wagon train, Emigration Canyon, c. 1860. (NARA)

In the lower reaches of Emigration Canyon a freight wagon train makes its way into the territory. Freight and mail could take four months to reach Great Salt Lake City during the winter months,...if they reached the settlement at all. In 1856 the territory had to wait six months to find out the results of the presidential election in which James Buchanan defeated John C. Frémont, candidate of the newly founded Republican party, with its platform to combat the "twin relics of barbarism"— slavery and polygamy.

would arrive in Salt Lake City in tattered clothing and even barefoot after months of battling the elements. They had crossed a rugged land, were far from their native lands, and, in many cases, were unable to speak English; yet they had pushed on in a determined personal testament of faith and conviction.

IMMIGRATION TO UTAH TERRITORY:

Throughout the 1850s up until the end of the century thousands of European converts to the Mormon church left their homelands to travel to Utah, as church leaders called on the faithful to gather to the new "Zion" in the Great Basin. Often supported by the church's Perpetual Emigrating Fund, they would book passage on sailing or steamer ships plying the North Atlantic. It was risky and dangerous, for ships could capsize and disease could sweep the cramped steerage holds below decks. Some of the greatest challenges came when the emigrants encountered haphazard checkpoints in New York and New Orleans. Health officials could arbitrarily order the emigrants to be quarantined in filthy holding areas where outbreaks of typhus and cholera were common. In later years, New York and the nation would devise a marginally better system of emigrant processing at Castle Garden, a predecessor of Ellis Island. After their struggle to reach the United States, the Mormon emigrants still faced months of footsore and dangerous overland travel to reach Utah Territory.

Left: Mormon missionaries, c. 1890. (USHS)

Right: Unidentified "Fulton Class" steamship, c. 1865. (NARA)

"On board an Emigrant Ship—The Breakfast Bell," illustration from unidentified publication, c. 1860. (LOC)

GATHERING THE FAITHFUL TO THE NEW ZION

Even at the peak of the gathering of the faithful in the Salt Lake Valley, the Mormon church maintained an active missionary program overseas and in much of the nation. The missionaries assisted thousands of European converts in making the epic journey to what they considered the Kingdom of God on Earth—Utah. Several missionaries were killed in the mid-1800s when anti-Mormon fervor reached its peak. Illness and accidents claimed others, many of whom were husbands with dependent young children. Not only were they expected to fend for themselves but also their wives were expected to raise the couple's children without outside aid from the church. Plural wives often mutually assisted each other, fostering close communal bonds, which in turn helped many women accept the principle of plural marriage.

Below left: Deck of a transatlantic steamer, c. 1865. (NARA)

Below right: Wagon train negotiating Echo Canyon, c. 1865. (NARA)

Castle Garden immigration center, New York, c. 1880. (LOC)

Martha Spence Heywood, c. 1854.

She viewed herself as a simple woman of faith who happened to keep a diary. But Martha Spence Heywood would emerge as one of the most important chroniclers of early life in Utah Territory. Heywood, a late-marrying plural wife, documented the human story of the pioneer experience from childbirth in a covered wagon on a frigid winter night to the outbreak of the Walker War.

"I have just had the melancholy intelligence that amongst the many that have died of cholera, Sister Margaret MacDonald and Sister Dana are reckoned among its victims." —July 10, 1850

"My darling boy was born on the 18th of November in the wagon. Suffered much unnecessary pain...from the smallness of the wagon and its openess." —January 1, 1853

"Nine indians coming into our camp looking for protection and bread from us. And without knowing they did the first evil act...were shot down without one minute's notice. It cast considerable gloom over my mind." —January 1, 1854

In 1856 the handcart saga turned tragic. Eager to complete the journey, yet slowed by swelling numbers, the handcart companies of James G. Willie and Edward Martin left their Iowa City gathering point dangerously late in July. They were the two largest companies that would be assembled during the handcart era, and included more than 1,000 men, women, and children. Handcarts that had been hurriedly made of green wood soon failed on the jarring trails across the plains. In Wyoming Territory the companies were trapped by an early blizzard. Temperatures dropped below zero. Food ran out; cattle died. With many of the immigrants coatless and even without shoes, the weather began to claim lives. The worst nights came near South Pass, usually viewed by immigrants as an encouraging midway point as they passed through this low, wide spot on the continental divide and moved west of the Rockies. Here in October 1856 dozens of Mormon faithful died each night, strangers in a strange land, waiting for relief parties from Salt Lake City to break through the snowbanks. By the time relief finally did arrive, more than 200 of the pioneers were dead, and a similar number had been crippled by frostbite. It was the single worst disaster in the history of the overland migration.

Once in the territory, the immigrant was expected to step up and make an immediate contribution with daily work. Although they were allowed some recovery time, new arrivals were quickly processed and identified according to their trades and skills. Some were able to contribute beyond the work regimen. A group of eighty Welsh immigrants with training as a congregational choir arrived in the valley in 1849 and formed the core of a formal church choir linked to meetings in the first tabernacle erected in the heart of the city. The concepts of a "Tabernacle Choir" and a faith celebrated in song would prove to be enduring hallmarks of the Mormon people.

The John Parry family, c. 1860. (USHS)

Photographed with his family shortly after their emigration from Wales, John Parry organized the first formal choir for the Mormon church in 1850—a choir that became the predecessor of the world-renowned Mormon Tabernacle Choir. By the early 1850s the Utah Territory had a distinct international character as a result of the steady stream of Mormons pouring in from European missions, and it was not unusual to hear four or five languages spoken on the streets of Great Salt Lake City.

Almost from the first arrival of the Mormon pioneers in the Salt Lake Valley, Brigham Young had given voice to a strategy for organizing and controlling a broad, productive territory. Mission calls went out to followers, drafting them for service in settling the distant reaches of what church leaders still referred to as "Deseret." Some, such as the Iron Mission in Cedar City and the Cotton Mission in St. George, were designed to enable the Latter-day Saints to establish a self-sufficient economy free from the control of the outside, or "gentile," world. Others, such as missions to Cache Valley and Fort

Left: Council House, Salt Lake City, c. 1860. (USHS)

The Council House was an early church/government meetinghouse in the territory. Housing everything from the territorial legislature to court sessions to classes for the early University of Deseret, the Council House would be destroyed by a fire and explosion in 1883. Reconstructed following the original design, the building was relocated to Capitol Hill in Salt Lake City where it can still be seen.

Original tabernacle and bowery, Temple Square, Salt Lake City, c. 1858. (LDS)

A landmark for the community was the construction of a tabernacle for worship in 1852. The tabernacle replaced the outdoor bowery shaded with tree limbs and brush, seen adjoining the new building in this early photograph of Temple Square. The tabernacle sits on the site of the future Assembly Hall, while the bowery occupies a position later taken by a new, and enduring, tabernacle, erected in the 1860s.

THE ESTATE OF BRIGHAM YOUNG

The huge personal compound of Brigham Young dominated the heart of Salt Lake City for the settlement's first thirty years. Sprawling well into the adjoining foothills and surrounded by a wall constructed by recently arrived immigrants looking for work, Young's compound was anchored by the Beehive and Lion houses. Young was far and away the territory's wealthiest citizen, and he managed or held title to a number of businesses and investments for the Mormon church. In the course of time his holdings and church property became commingled in a financial jumble that would confound the courts and some heirs at the time of his death.

The gabled Lion House piqued the curiosity of travelers passing through the territory anxious for a glimpse of Young's plural wives, a number of whom were housed there. The floor plan reflected a need to balance space and standing among the wives. Contrary to the suggestion of a few wags, the numbers associated with each living space were room numbers, not wife numbers. Young would die in the Lion House in 1877.

As president of the church and governor of the territory, Young maintained an office and primary residence in the Beehive House. Both homes were built to Young's exacting standards, and feature his passion for craftsmanship that he developed as a carpenter in Vermont. The Eagle Gate was originally erected as a formal entrance to Young's compound, but the estate eventually was carved by developing city streets, and the expansive wings of the eagle assumed more public service as an unofficial gateway to the city.

Right:
Brigham Young's compound, c. 1860. (USHS)

PRINCIPAL STORY.

Above: Partial floor plan for the Lion House. (USHS)

Left: The Beehive House and Eagle Gate, c. 1860. (USHS)

Utah (later Provo), were called to expand the living room available for the thousands of new arrivals. Each new settlement or mission served as a hub for further settlement. And each hub was organized under carefully selected local leaders who had unquestioned faith in and loyalty to the leadership of their church.

The theocratic reach of this "church-as-state, state-as-church" relationship stunned the first handful of federal officials sent to Utah in 1851 as part of its new territorial status. They were part of an uneasy attempt by President Millard Fillmore to share power between the federal government and local Mormon leaders. While each American territory can spin long stories from its own history about strained relations between "carpetbagger" federal appointees and local settlers, few reached the outright stages of conflict frequently manifested in Utah Territory. With the first arrival of federal authority in 1851, a pitched struggle unfolded that would endure for forty-five years regardless of which national political party was in power or the changing face of Mormon leadership.

The federal officials, often selected for their political connections rather than their ability, considered Brigham Young's emperor-like role of church president/territorial governor/federal Indian superintendent as an abomination. Utah elections were viewed by the federal officeholders as little more than sustaining votes for church-selected candidates, since there was no political party system. The federal appointees viewed the Mormon church as controlling every aspect of territorial life—from government to the economy to the school system. In return, Young viewed the appointees as mere nuisances and fine examples of the corruption he felt gripped the national government. Rather than apologize or explain, Young offered thunderous sermons extolling the virtues of the church's approach to organizing a society, and blistered the appointees' ears with attacks against "Babylon" and government by bribery. As would continue to be the case throughout the territorial years, each side could find ample evidence to document its complaints, and each side showed little restraint in ascribing wildly sinister motives to bolster that evidence.

Deseret currency three-dollar note, 1858. (USHS)

A currency note offered by a financial arm of the Mormon church in 1858, guaranteed by the signature of Brigham Young. The paper was underwritten with cattle since gold was so scarce. Financially strapped from its first days, the territory had to circulate scrip to pay for goods and services within its borders, saving what little gold it accumulated for purchases "back in the states" and for helping to pay for the passage of church emigrants from Europe.

MORMON MISSIONS—ST. GEORGE AND THE COTTON MISSION

Mission calls within the territory and public works projects were offered to many of the immigrants arriving in the territory in the early 1850s. The missions were actually economic development schemes to help make the territory self-sufficient. Mission "calls" were carefully planned to assemble a workable collection of talents and trades to make the resultant communities balanced and viable from the outset. Cities like St. George and Cedar City trace their roots to early mission work to produce cotton and iron, respectively. In Utah's "Dixie"—the warm southwestern portion of the territory—it was hoped that cotton could be grown,...which it was, to a limited extent. While the missions generally failed to fully realize the vision of producing products in sufficient quantity to wean the territory from dependence on the United States, they still allowed settlers to often establish lasting footholds in the territory, thus helping fulfill Brigham Young's plan to settle and populate the vast landscape.

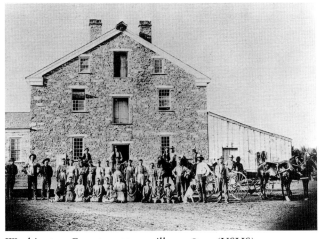

Washington County cotton mill, c. 1870. (USHS)

St. George Social Hall (Opera House), c. 1880. (USHS)

Brigham Young's receipt for federal funds to build a territorial capitol building, 1852. (UARA)

In an effort to honor Millard Fillmore for appointing Brigham Young as territorial governor, the territorial legislature created Millard County and decreed Fillmore City as the new central seat of territorial government. Territorial leaders viewed it as brilliant planning, a master stroke of political accountability, and a rare opportunity to create beauty on the desert's edge. In the end it was one of Brigham Young's rare failures in centralized planning. Congress appropriated twenty thousand dollars for construction of a new capitol building, and Salt Lake Temple architect Truman O. Angell soon produced a design featuring four wings forming a cross with a large dome in the center. Brigham Young reportedly selected the site for the building, and work on the first wing was soon under way.

However, the plan was a colossal failure. Lawmakers complained about traveling to the site in winter and held only one full legislative session in the single completed wing, in 1855. By 1856 the legislature voted to return the capital to Salt Lake City. Still standing as one of Utah's earliest governmental buildings, the statehouse wing is now a museum.

Territorial capitol building, Fillmore, photograph c. 1920. (USHS)

However, the straw that snapped the camel's back was not related to the struggles for economic or political control. Instead, it came from what would soon be known as the most peculiar of the "peculiar institutions" in Utah Territory. In 1851 Brigham Young publicly confirmed a belief in plural marriage as part of the faith of the Church of Jesus Christ of Latter-day Saints, and he acknowledged its practice by many of the faithful within the church.

Plural marriage, forced somewhat inaccurately under the label of polygamy, had been a quiet tenet and aspect of the Mormon faith for more than ten years. Church founder Joseph Smith acknowledged that he had taken multiple wives under divine guidance; however, he had confided the call for plural marriage to a few trusted associates. Rumors and allegations of plural

Right: Quarrying granite for the Salt Lake LDS Temple, Little Cottonwood Canyon, c. 1870. (NARA)

Those immigrants lacking trades or skills often were offered manual-labor positions such as working with the crews quarrying massive slabs of granite in Little Cottonwood Canyon for the construction of the Salt Lake Temple.

LIFE IN UTAH TERRITORY—EARLY FARMING

The economic backbone of Utah Territory was farming. Success meant a thriving community able to feed the thousands of newly arriving immigrants; failure could mean starvation. Recurrent problems with insects would plague farming communities through the 1860s, sometimes threatening their very existence. A very early photo of the William Kendall family and farm reflects the rugged, simple nature of pioneering farm life in the first years of settlement during which large families were expected to labor together for survival.

Farm work, Salt Lake Valley, perhaps 1860s. (USHS)

William Kendall family, Weber County, c. 1860. (USHS)

Heber C. Kimball's compound, Salt Lake City, c. 1860. (LDS)

Heber C. Kimball, c. 1860.

Firm, principled and notoriously blunt, Heber C. Kimball was a powerful Mormon church leader, member of Brigham Young's First Presidency, and a captivating preacher. Reluctant to embrace the principle of plural marriage when it was first introduced to him by church authorities, he eventually married forty-three wives and emerged as one of the most adamant defenders of polygamy. He was reported to have fathered sixty-five children and had more than 300 grandchildren. His compound in Salt Lake City, facing North Temple Street, though relatively dwarfed by that of his neighbor Brigham Young, was still substantial, provided room for his ample family, and reflected his very high standing among the Mormon people.

marriage were among the aspects of the confrontation with non-Mormons that resulted in Smith's murder by a mob in 1844. Under Brigham Young the practice would flourish, though it would never be practiced by a majority of Mormons. Still, it was an easily spotted practice among church leaders and a trademark of early life in the territory, earning notation in a memoir authored by Captain John Gunnison after he had toured the region in 1849–50.

The public confirmation by Brigham Young was delivered quite pointedly to the Utah Territorial Assembly, a virtual guarantee that the message would

The original Salt Lake Tabernacle, c. 1855. (LDS)

Built in 1852, the first permanent building on Temple Square could hold more than 2,000 worshippers. It was the site of the public announcement of the Mormon practice of plural marriage in 1852, and weathered blistering speeches from Brigham Young and other church leaders as the conflict with federal authorities reached the boiling point later in the decade. This early view of the Tabernacle shows the site before Temple Square was enclosed by a stone wall.

land at the feet of federal officials in Utah. "I have more wives than one," said Young; "I have many and I am not ashamed to have it known." With the wraps off, Young sent Jedediah M. Grant to the east to coordinate a spirited, affirmative public-relations campaign on behalf of the Mormon practice. This was followed by a stirring public defense of plural marriage by Orson Pratt in 1852 in the first tabernacle. In a wide-ranging, impassioned speech, Pratt defended polygamy as a sacred opportunity for righteous men and women, intimated that Jesus even may have been involved with polygamy, and concluded that what the Mormons did was nobody else's business.

"I think, if I am not mistaken," said Pratt, "that the Constitution gives the privilege to all the inhabitants of this country of the free exercise of their religious notions, and the freedom of their faith, and the practice of it.... And should there ever be laws enacted by this government to restrict them from the free exercise of this part of their religion, such laws must be unconstitutional."

The first four federal appointees never heard the speech. They had already fled Utah, filing a report in Washington claiming that the Mormon church was exerting complete control over the people of this territory of the United States, undermining the very principles of the American experience.

It would take forty years, dozens of acts by Congress, several Supreme Court rulings, and at least one revelation attributed to divine origin to resolve the dilemma of whose interpretation of religious liberty would carry the day in Utah Territory. But first there would be a "war."

Chapter Three

A PHONY WAR AND REAL BLOOD
1856–1858

The *Dred Scott* decision by the Supreme Court further divides the country on the issue of slavery....Abraham Lincoln and Stephen Douglas engage in a series of debates over the future course of the nation....The Crimean War ends....John Brown raids Harpers Ferry, and the nation drifts closer to sectional war....The population of the United States in 1860 is 31,443,321.

IN THE SUMMER OF 1853 crews began digging the foundation and carving the first granite blocks for the construction of the crowning glory to the Kingdom of God the Mormon people believed they were building in Utah Territory. Based on a sketch by Brigham Young passed along to architect Truman O. Angell, the Salt Lake LDS Temple was viewed as a monument to the faith of the members of the Church of Jesus Christ of Latter-day Saints and a testimony to the enduring nature of the homeland they had created in the Great Basin. The temple would, in some respects, become symbolic of the Mormon struggle for self-determination, starting in dreams of pure faith and taking forty years to reach fruition.

From the first days of the arrival of Mormon settlers in the Salt Lake Valley the concepts of "The Kingdom" and Temple Square had provided a focus for virtually every aspect of daily life. The temple site was the first landmark identified by Brigham Young as he surveyed the valley floor. Streets and land plots were laid out in all directions from its boundaries. Boweries served as early gathering sites before a first simple tabernacle could be raised for

Below: Great Salt Lake City, looking south from Ensign Peak in the early 1850s. (USHS)

The popular success of books by John C. Frémont and Howard Stansbury prompted many roving writers and artists to travel the West, reporting upon and making artistic renderings of the people and scenes. Many, like the artist in this early sketch, would elaborate on or exaggerate features in order to excite or impress east-coast audiences. In 1850 the first semi-official census in the territory counted 11,300 residents.

meetings in 1852. In 1855 an "Endowment House" was opened to function in the capacity of a temple until a monumental structure could be built in the heart of the city. Enclosed by a wall built as a public-work project by newly arrived immigrants, Temple Square and Brigham's adjoining sprawling compound served as the spiritual and temporal focal points for the inhabitants of the territory.

Above: Truman O. Angell, with wife and daughter, c. 1860. (USHS)

Truman Angell took a sketch by Brigham Young and turned it into the architectural design for the Salt Lake Temple. Though not formally educated, Angell was soon recognized as the first architect for the Church of Jesus Christ of Latter-day Saints. A brother-in-law to Brigham Young, Angell also designed the Beehive and Lion houses for Brigham, as well as the territorial statehouse for the failed capital city in Fillmore. He made important contributions in the design of the Tabernacle on Temple Square, and he even designed and printed the first paper currency in the territory.

648   HARPER'S WEEKLY.   [OCTOBER 10, 1857.

SCENES IN AN AMERICAN HAREM.

BRIGHAM YOUNG AND HIS FAMILY ON THEIR WAY TO CHURCH.

Artist's drawing of Brigham Young and his family going to church, 1850s. (LOC)

As the Mormon church and the federal government drifted dangerously close to war in the 1850s, the national media quickly dispatched correspondents to Utah Territory. Most had an overriding fascination with polygamy, and sought to capture "the harems" of leading church figures, such as the artist's fanciful rendering of Brigham Young and his family en route to church published by *Harper's Weekly*. The media's portrayal of the Mormons contributed to the breakdown of relations between the church and the national government in 1857 and would continue to compromise the relationship throughout the struggle for statehood.

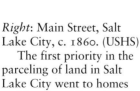

Right: Main Street, Salt Lake City, c. 1860. (USHS)

The first priority in the parceling of land in Salt Lake City went to homes and farming. Thoughts of a downtown or business district played little part in laying out the plat for Utah's primary settlement. In the 1850s farmland began less than a half mile from the construction site of the Temple, and City Creek was diverted through ditches along the wide streets for irrigation of the fields.

The Beehive and Lion houses, Salt Lake City. (USHS)

The Beehive House was built in 1852 and served as Brigham Young's executive mansion while he held the office of territorial governor. The house's name comes from a beehive, Young's symbol for industry, featured prominently on top of the house. The Lion House was built in 1854 and could house as many as twelve of Brigham's wives. The house takes its name from a small sculpted lion that sat on the portico facing South Temple street. Young died in the Lion House in 1877.

The Salt Lake Tithing House, sometimes called the Deseret Store, 1860. (USHS)

The donation by members of the Mormon church of a portion of their income, also known as tithing, was instituted in 1860 and helped support a broad range of church activities, including the transporting and feeding of immigrants. Since there was little money in the territory, virtually all early tithing payments were made in the form of crops, livestock, homemade goods, or labor.

The Deseret Woolen Mill, c. 1870. (USHS)

As the territory struggled for economic self-sufficiency, a woolen mill was established to produce cloth for local clothing and for export to "the states." One of the first territorial industrial endeavors, the mill was located southeast of the small city center, with the Wasatch Range forming a backdrop.

City Hall, First South and State Street, Great
Salt Lake City, c. 1869. (USHS)

A home for city government and public
services in Salt Lake City was lacking in the
earliest years. Construction of a city hall
started early in the 1860s and was completed in 1865. Besides providing offices for
the mayor and a meeting site for the city
council, City Hall served as nominal
headquarters for early police work, which
was inspired by the occupation of the
territory by federal troops. The volunteer
fire department that served the city had little
structure and generally met only when called
to service by the clanging bell of a fire
alarm. The clock tower on top of City Hall
served as an unofficial timekeeper for the
city. The building was superseded in the
1890s by the ornate, much larger, and still-
used City-County Building. It eventually was
demolished to accommodate expansion of
the downtown business district.

The Social Hall, Great Salt Lake City, c.
1858. (USHS)

Built from adobe brick and designed
from the outset as an amusement center for
the people in the territory, the Social Hall
opened in 1852. With the strong backing of
Brigham Young, the Deseret Dramatic
Association staged plays on the small stage
in the hall. An orchestra would provide the
music for dances. The Social Hall ceased its
performances with the arrival of federal
troops in 1858, and was eventually replaced
on a grander scale as a drama venue in 1862
by the Salt Lake Theatre.

But of even greater consequence to daily life in Utah Territory was a deep
commitment by Mormon leadership to "build up the Kingdom of God" in the
new territory, enabling the gathering place to emerge as a contemporary Zion.
As an organizational principle, the building of the Kingdom of God made it
incumbent upon every faithful member to perceive each action as either
contributing to or detracting from a new covenant with the Almighty. Land
decisions, the holding of political offices, and economic transactions all were
viewed as part of the spiritual experience. Mormon church leadership served
as the definitive arbiter of proper conduct. Many conflicts were resolved in
ecclesiastical "Bishop's Courts," or in the lower-level civil government "probate" courts that were staffed by members of the church and exerted broad
authority over civil and criminal affairs. A variance from the established norm
meant a reprimand at the least, exclusion and isolation in extreme instances.
In the early years, while the society was generally homogeneous, theft was
considered among the greatest crimes against the society, and it was dealt with
harshly, with "lashes on the open back" serving as punishment.

Members of the Ferdinand Hayden surveying expedition to the West, c. 1870. (NARA)

Artist's rendering of the Ives Expedition on the Colorado River, c. 1858. (NARA)

GOVERNMENT EXPLORERS AND SURVEYORS IN UTAH TERRITORY

Between 1850 and 1880 nearly a dozen exploration and survey expeditions passed through portions of the Utah territory. In addition to filling in the gaping holes that existed on maps of the territory and the Colorado Plateau region, the expeditions did some of the earliest work in documenting the earlier Anasazi and Fremont cultures in the region. Most of the earliest expeditions, including those of Edward Beckwith, John W. Gunnison, Edward Steptoe, and James Harvey Simpson, were conducted by the U.S. Army through its Corps of Topographical Engineers. Virtually all of these earliest explorations were designed to find routes to link the east and west coasts through the difficult terrain of the Great Basin and eventually establish a route for an anticipated transcontinental railroad.

Among the important early missions to the West was the geographic and geologic expedition of Ferdinand Hayden in the early 1870s. Joined by acclaimed photographer William H. Jackson, Hayden explored the northern Rocky Mountains from a base in Ogden. He also completed some of the earliest documentation of the Yellowstone region.

Certainly the oddest exploration of the region was undertaken by U.S. Army Lieutenant Joseph Ives in 1857. With hostilities between the Mormons and the government deemed imminent, Ives was instructed to explore a possible shipping link to the Utah territory by forcing his way *upstream* on the Colorado River by means of a paddlewheel steamship. Through sheer determination

Government surveyors in Utah Territory, c. 1870. (USHS)

Ives and his party were able to coax their ship, *The Explorer*, as far as Cottonwood Valley in present-day Arizona. From there, Ives pressed forward on foot, and his party provided the first documented white exploration of the floor of the Grand Canyon.

Faithful rank-and-file church members did not feel constrained by the order that grew from the Kingdom of God. They viewed the total integration of church and state as the natural condition of a faithful people, and they were confident that their view of a civil society was in perfect alignment with laws greater than those created by men. There was little effort expended by leaders to restrain settlers who chose to leave the community because they did not share the vision.

UTE INDIANS—THE WALKER WAR

Although his name was mispronounced by the pioneers as "Walker," Wakara was recognized as the strongest and most influential of leaders among the Ute people, although their social system of family and gathering defied the notion of central authority. The Utes, who preferred to call themselves "Nuciu"—the people—actually formed two major bands at the time of the Mormon arrival in the Great Basin. The southern band of the Ute Indians lived primarily in lands that would become Colorado and New Mexico. The northern band was made up of twelve smaller groupings that spread across the Utah Territory to the western slope of the Rocky Mountains. The powerful Utes had experienced good dealings with early trappers and traders in the region, so they initially welcomed the Mormon settlement in 1847, with Wakara even being baptized into the faith. Brigham Young, in return, preached a policy of "feed rather than fight," and urged a peaceful coexistence with the Utes. The relationship deteriorated as the Mormons began to push into traditional Ute lands in central Utah, and further eroded when Young acted to end the Ute practice of slave trading in captured Indian children. The sometimes bloody Walker War of 1853–54 was the result. War would erupt again in 1863, but by then the reservation movement was well under way, and the Utes were eventually forced onto reserved lands of eastern Utah and western Colorado.

Above: Wakara, Ute Indian Chief, 1855. (USHS)

Right: Ute Indian family group with tepee, date unknown. (USHS)

Captain John Gunnison was captivated by many of the aspects of the Mormon Kingdom of God when he traveled through Utah Territory as part of Howard Stansbury's survey expedition, which ended in 1850. His book *The Mormons* was the initial firsthand account of the new settlement near the shores of the Great Salt Lake. While noting a blending of church and state that made "Americans" uncomfortable, Gunnison's portrait of the Saints and their singular society was well received by a church leadership sensitive to their group's portrayal to the general public and the federal government. Gunnison's book, which was published in 1852, even proved prophetic, noting an inevitable conflict between "theo-democracy" and national tradition, yet warning against actions aimed at crushing what some might view as a Mormon insurrection:

> But we must remember that this is no insurrection ... the population is a unit engaged to a man in the sacred cause of their freedom to govern themselves. They must be convinced of error, before they can abandon their position without disgrace.

Above: Captain John W. Gunnison. (UU)

Gunnison's first trip to Utah Territory with the Stansbury expedition produced his balanced and insightful book *The Mormons*. His second expedition, to explore a route in 1853 for the proposed transcontinental railroad, ended in tragedy when he and some of his men were killed by members of the Pahvant band of the Ute tribe. The murder of Gunnison caused a national outcry, including claims that the Mormons had conspired to have his party attacked. An 1854 investigation by Col. Edward Steptoe cleared the Mormons of wrongdoing.

Gunnison returned to the territory in the fall of 1853 to map a potential central route for a much-discussed transcontinental railroad. Working his way west from Manti, Gunnison split his survey team to explore the open land that had continued to remain a question mark on maps of the region. He ventured into the lands of the Pahvant tribe only days after emigrants in a passing wagon train had killed and wounded members of the tribe in a brief and one-sided firefight. At sunrise on October 24, Gunnison and eleven others were surprised on the banks of the Sevier River by a Pahvant raiding party. Eight were killed, with one account detailing fifteen arrow wounds in Gunnison, who died pleading friendship. The bodies were horribly mutilated.

The death of the popular Gunnison caused national outrage. Several newspapers accused Mormon leaders of stalking and killing the army officer because of the truthful nature of his book. Colonel Edward Steptoe, commanding more than 300 soldiers and civilians, was sent to investigate the murder as well as explore a viable military road to California. While in Salt Lake City, Steptoe was informed that President Franklin Pierce intended to dump Brigham Young as territorial governor and appoint him to the post. Steptoe spent the winter in the territory, and he concluded that the Pahvants had acted alone in murdering Gunnison's party. He also came to the conclusion that the solidarity and loyalty of the Mormons to their leaders would make it virtually impossible for him or another non-Mormon to govern after the ouster of Young. He declined the commission to be governor and completed his expedition to California.

The death of Gunnison came at a time of frayed relations between the Mormon settlers and Native American tribes. The expansion of settlements in the territory was swiftly driving Utes, Shoshonis, and Paiutes from their traditional tribal lands. Although they espoused their link to the "Lamanites" (the Mormons' term for the Indians, which reflected scriptural ties to the *Book of Mormon*), the Mormon pattern of settlement and expansion into prime lands in Utah made conflict between settlers and native tribes inevitable.

The Ute chief Wakara, sometimes dubbed "Walker," had befriended the Mormons soon after their arrival, even being baptized into the church in 1850. The relationship soured when the settlers took steps to break up an Indian slave trade that had existed between the Utes and Spanish and (later) Mexican traders for at least a hundred years. Losing the slave trade cut into Wakara's wealth and power, and his anger was fueled by the steady inroads of settlers into tribal lands around and south of Utah Lake. Hostilities erupted in 1853 as the "Walker War." For the next ten months Mormon settlers and militia would battle Ute raiding parties and stage attacks on Ute campsites. Brigham Young ordered his central Utah settlements to "fort up"—that is, to withdraw to the safety of stockades to ward off Ute attacks. Two dozen settlers would die and hundreds of head of stock would be run off during the months of battle;

President Franklin Pierce, 1854. (LOC)
Swayed by eastern critics of the Mormon church, Pierce decided not to reappoint Brigham Young as territorial governor. But when he offered the post to Col. Edward Steptoe, in Utah for the Gunnison investigation, Steptoe told the president that an outside appointee would be powerless in the face of Brigham Young's authority.

An unidentified early fort in the Utah Territory, c. 1850s. (LDS)
Unsteady relations between the Mormon settlers and the Ute people led the pioneers to build small forts for protection as they sought to establish new communities and push deeper into the traditional hunting and gathering lands of the Utes.

Jim Bridger, c. 1860. (USHS)

Bridger may have been the first non-native explorer to reach the shores of the Great Salt Lake in the 1820s. Remaining in the region, he established a small fort on Black's Fork of the Green River to trade with Indians and eventually to resupply

but the Utes suffered far greater losses of life before a summit meeting of Brigham Young and Wakara on the banks of Chicken Creek near present-day Nephi ended the conflict in 1854. The unofficial "treaty" would hold the peace, if not resolve the troubles, until Wakara died in 1855.

The Walker War also crystallized a long-brewing conflict between Brigham Young and legendary trapper Jim Bridger. Young, as territorial governor, had claimed jurisdiction over Bridger's outpost near the Green River in what is now Wyoming. He had sent a team of Mormons to the area to manage local affairs and to aid immigrants on the final stage of their journey to Salt Lake City. There was some resentment of Bridger for profiting from supplying western wagon trains that could be serviced by Mormons. Bridger, for his part, resented Mormon attempts to undermine his business.

At the height of the Walker War, Governor Young, wearing another hat as territorial Indian superintendent, decided to act on questionable charges that Bridger was trading whiskey and weapons to tribes while admonishing them to attack the Mormons. A small Mormon army swept into Fort Bridger in the summer of 1853, bent on arresting Bridger and seizing his "contraband." Bridger fled to the nearby hills, evaded the posse, and made his way back east. His stock was seized, and the supplies of liquor were "destroyed by doses," according to an account by one of the posse members. Mormon settlers quickly moved into the area and established their own way station known as Fort Supply. A financial settlement was made with a partner of Jim Bridger for the purchase of the fort; however, it was far from the end of the story.

overland wagon trains heading to California. Originally friendly to Mormons because of the potential for a boom in his business, Bridger eventually turned unfriendly as he repeatedly clashed with Brigham Young over authority in the region and the right to profit from Mormon overland travelers. Claiming Bridger was selling whiskey and guns to the Indians and goading them to attack the Mormon settlements, Young ordered a large posse to arrest Bridger. The savvy mountain man slipped into the hills and eventually escaped to the east, telling a tale of suffering at the hands of the Mormons. He would return in 1857 as a guide for the army sent to crush the alleged rebellion of the Mormon people against the government.

Fort Supply, near Fort Bridger, 1853. (USHS)

Originally conceived as a means of resupplying Mormon wagon trains entering the last stage of their transcontinental journey, Fort Supply also served to stake a more certain claim by Utah Territory to land in present-day Wyoming. Built only twelve miles away from the fort of Jim Bridger, Fort Supply eventually failed because its elevation of more than 7,000 feet prevented it from growing its own crops; hence, it had to be supplied from Salt Lake City, and in time folded under the expense.

UTAH TERRITORIAL MILITIA (NAUVOO LEGION)

Tracing its roots back to the defense of Mormon homes in Illinois, the territorial militia in Utah was actually a Mormon army under the direct control of Brigham Young. Proudly calling itself the Nauvoo Legion, the militia was sprinkled with veterans of the Illinois struggle at Nauvoo and the Mormon Battalion expedition of the Mexican War. Despite near-mythical claims of its excellence, the Utah militia, like many territorial militias of the era, was poorly trained, poorly equipped, and little match for an organized army. But the territorial militia had several distinct advantages as it prepared for a conflict with United States troops. First, the Legion was made up of loyal and fervent men hardened by the pioneer experience. Second, a brilliant holding and harassing strategy had been developed by Brigham Young and commanding officer Daniel Wells. Finally, the men of the territorial militia were preparing to fight for their homes and families, and were determined to prevent a repetition of the nightmare persecutions they had suffered in Missouri and Illinois. If an armed conflict was to break out between the Legion and the U.S. Army in the fall of 1857, it could be expected that hundreds would die.

Utah Territorial Militia troops (commonly known as the Nauvoo Legion) in formation, c. 1860. (USHS)

Daniel Wells, commander of the Nauvoo Legion, about the time of the Utah War. (USHS)

Bridger's dramatic and often fanciful tale of being driven from his rightful claim and robbed of land and belongings by an armed mob joined a stream of other anti-Mormon tales and sentiment pouring into the east. Contributing to the angry reports were federal officials who whipped through a virtual revolving door, as they would routinely cap their short, confrontational stays in Salt Lake City with reports attacking polygamy and Mormon church control of every facet of territorial life, even claiming that the Utah population was disloyal. An Illinois attorney, W.W. Drummond, raised the hyperbole to a new level when he took office as an associate judge in the federal court system in Utah in the mid-1850s. Drummond and the Mormons were at each other's throats from the outset. After a brief stay, Drummond quit his post and fired a damning resignation letter to Washington, D.C.:

> The federal officers are daily compelled to hear the form of the American government traduced, the chief executives, both living and dead, slandered and abused from the masses, as well as from the leading members of the church, in the most vulgar, loathsome and wicked manner that the evil passions of men can conceive.

Drummond accused the Mormons of destroying court documents, freeing Mormon criminals while arresting innocent non-Mormons, and being directly responsible for the Gunnison massacre as well as the deaths of other federal

John M. Bernhisel, c. 1860. (USHS)
A university-trained doctor, Bernhisel served five terms as Utah Territory's non-voting delegate to Congress. He constantly was putting out political fires during the 1850s as relations between the Mormon church and the government soured.

Brigham Young, c. 1860. (USHS)
By 1860 Brigham Young had adopted the trademark beard he would retain for the rest of his life. Concerned about complacency among the Mormons as the Utah settlement neared its tenth anniversary, Young encouraged a spiritual rededication among his people with fiery orations and a new catechism of personal conduct.

territorial officials. In short, W.W. Drummond pronounced the Mormon people armed, dangerous, and in a state of rebellion against the United States.

Brigham Young, reflecting on a series of visitors and federal appointees who had taken the time to attack Mormon practices, took to the podium in the Tabernacle and fired back:

> I am and will be governor. I do not know what I shall say next winter if such men make their appearance here as some last winter. I know what I think I shall say: if they play the same game again, so help me God, we will slay them.

Onto this incendiary situation was poured the fuel of national politics. The election of 1856 brought forth a new factor in the national partisan political scene. In its initial party platform, the fledgling Republican party pledged a campaign to eradicate the "twin relics of barbarism"—slavery and polygamy.

Polygamy was portrayed as no less cruel servitude than the slavery trade which was ripping the nation apart. Political speakers and newspaper editorials labeled the Mormons as un-American, licentious, and dangerous.

There is little evidence that Democrat James Buchanan spoke out on the notion of a Mormon rebellion as he battled Republican John C. Frémont in the 1856 election. Unimaginative in his previous offices, Buchanan was a loyal party figure who was carried to the White House through the support of southern states which correctly read his sympathy for their region on the pivotal issue of slavery. Mormons also viewed Buchanan's victory as a

Right: James Buchanan, fifteenth president of the United States, 1857. (LOC)
Buchanan's presidential victory in 1856 was viewed by many as the nation's best chance to avoid war over slavery. Instead, his often corrupt and blundering administration almost surely helped push the nation into the Civil War. His hopes for a quick and decisive victory in what he perceived as the Mormon rebellion froze under the weight of a Wyoming winter that stalled the troops he had dispatched.

THE MARCH TO WAR

By the spring of 1857, the nation's capital was abuzz with the searing allegations contained in the resignation letter of former Utah territorial judge W.W. Drummond. Charging the Mormons with everything from the murder of John Gunnison to the destruction of legal records to running religiously biased courts, Drummond fanned the smoldering embers of anti-Mormon sentiment in the east with his stunning, undocumented stories of rebellion.

"Should such a state of thing actually exist as we are led to infer from these reports, the knife must be applied to this pestiferous, disgusting cancer which is gnawing into the very vitals of the body politic."
—Senator Stephen A. Douglas of Illinois

Soon the national media were pressuring the new administration of President James Buchanan to strike a decisive blow against the Mormon church, Brigham Young, and Utah Territory. "The interests of the country," claimed the *New York Times*, "may require much bloodshed." Buchanan, already struggling with a financial panic in the east and the increasing possibility of the disintegration of the nation over slavery, seized the "Mormon crisis" as an opportunity to demonstrate the resolute nature of his leadership.

"This is the first rebellion which has existed in our territories, and humanity requires that we should put it down in such a manner that it shall be the last.... We ought to go there with such an imposing force as to

convince these deluded people that resistance would be in vain." —President James Buchanan

Buchanan ordered 2,500 troops, some not-so-fresh from Indian wars in Florida, to march to Utah Territory under the direction of General William Harney. Harney had a reputation as a ruthless and stern leader, and was quoted by associates as intending to hang the Mormon leaders once he stormed the city. Mormons, notably Brigham Young, viewed Harney's appointment as confirmation that the army was intent on death and destruction in Great Salt Lake City.

It took months to assemble the troops and supplies at the army's westernmost camp, Fort Leavenworth. Soon, sectional strife in Kansas would cause Washington to hold Harney back to deal with another crisis. In effect leaderless, the army units and supply trains were under way by the summer of 1857. In a foolish gesture designed to snub Brigham Young, or an outrageous oversight, Buchanan never attempted to inform Utah territorial officials of his decision to replace Young as governor and send an army of occupation. The uncertainty of the federal intent heightened fear in the territory, and enabled Mormons to assign the worst motives to the army.

Left: The Capitol Building, Washington, D.C., 1857. (LOC)

Right: General William Harney, U.S. Army. (USHS)

John Floyd, Secretary of War, 1858. (LOC)

Floyd, one of many southerners serving in the Buchanan administration, viewed the mission against the Utah Territory as an opportunity to divert national attention from the sectional struggle over slavery. Poorly informed about the West, including its terrain and the great distances to travel, Floyd assumed the army would crush the Mormons before the first snows of 1857.

triumph over the stinging criticism of the Republican platform and an apparent endorsement of a path of self-determination for states and territories.

In practice, from its first day, Buchanan's presidency was one crisis after another. Unable to control the avalanche of issues such as slavery, economic depression, corruption, and a nation on the brink of collapse, Buchanan prepared to act decisively on the one issue he perceived within his grasp—the rebellious Mormons.

If the immediate future of the Utah Territory had not been compromised enough by the swirl of events and national politics, another development now played out which virtually assured a confrontation between the Mormons and "outsiders." Concerned that the overcoming of the early obstacles and reaching a point of stability had made the Saints complacent and comfortable, Brigham Young called for a "reformation" of the faith. In effect, Young demanded a spiritual recommitment on the part of each Mormon. It was an emotional call to repentance coupled with a demand for selfless dedication to building up the Kingdom of God. It produced an atmosphere that bordered on fanaticism, with fire-and-brimstone sermons delivered throughout the territory stressing solidarity among the Saints and a commitment to defend Zion against the sins and actions of the world. The reformation touched every town and settlement in the territory and renewed the determination of Mormons to live, and defend, their faith.

In Washington, President Buchanan had selected a course of action. In an attempt to break the union of church and state in Utah, Buchanan would terminate Brigham Young's service as territorial governor. He would send Alfred Cumming, a courtly southerner lately in service as an Indian superin-

Army supply train, Nebraska Territory, 1857. (USHS)

The army marching against the Mormons in Utah, known by late 1857 as the Utah Expedition, had to carry along enough food and supplies for the troops and their animals for six months. Each wagon carried a specified load—for example, all of the uniforms, all the boots, or all the coffee—for its assigned unit, a packing method that later would create misery when Mormon attackers burned many of the wagons in Wyoming.

THE MORMON REFORMATION

Was life too easy in the Utah Territory in the mid-1850s? For Brigham Young there was a genuine concern that nearly ten years of peaceful isolation beyond the Rocky Mountains had eroded the spiritual unity that had saved the Mormon people during their years of persecution. Young was angered by reports of questionable business dealings and a growing fascination among Utah Mormons with fashions and goods from the east coast. At first on his own from the pulpit of the Salt Lake Tabernacle, then through a network of horseback-riding preachers, Young delivered powerful messages to the Latter-day Saints urging them to reclaim their spiritual roots, build the Kingdom of God on earth, and practice a catechism of personal and public conduct to lead more pure lives. Representatives like George A. Smith of the church's First Presidency would urge constant vigilance and the need to defend the Mormon Zion from infection or invasion by ill-intentioned outsiders.

One of the most controversial aspects of the Mormon Reformation of the 1850s was Brigham Young's repeated references to blood atonement. Stressing that people commiting certain acts could be redeemed only by the spilling of their blood, Young was perhaps only affirming that such acts had no place in the special religious community the Mormons were building. Others took it as a mandate to hunt down offenders and dispatch them without benefit of argument or trial. When the Mountain Meadows Massacre took place in 1857, some observers inside and outside the territory commented on the role of blood atonement in the attack.

Another side effect of the Reformation was the explosive growth of plural marriage. Entered into by many as a demonstration of faith, plural marriage grew at such a rate that Brigham Young would race through the sealing, or marriage, ceremony in slightly more than one minute.

"All are trying to get wives," Wilford Woodruff wrote to George A. Smith in 1857, "until there is hardly a girl fourteen years old in Utah but what is married or just going to be." Two years later, Young would complain about the sea of divorce petitions engulfing his office, many of them the aftermath of the polygamy boom of the mid-1850s. "It is not right for the bretheren to divorce their wives the way they do," wrote Young. "If men don't stop divorcing their wives, I shall stop sealing." Brigham Young would grant more than 1,600 divorces during the thirty years of his church presidency in Utah.

Right: George A. Smith, First Presidency, Church of Jesus Christ of Latter-day Saints, 1857. (USHS)

---

tendent on the Missouri River, to the territory as the new governor. He also would surround Cumming with an array of new federal judges. All of the appointees were non-Mormon, and all would be escorted into office by 2,500 troops of the United States Army assembled under the orders of Secretary of War John Floyd. By July 1857 the "Utah Army" was under way from Fort Leavenworth in Kansas.

The huge military caravan was impossible to hide and, in fact, was never intended to be a secret. But, somewhere in the process, Buchanan had decided not to notify Utah Territory officials, including Brigham Young, of his decisions. Mormon riders on the overland mail routes soon got wind of the military expedition's mission and dashed for Salt Lake City. Ample evidence suggests that Brigham Young actually knew of the expedition before it left Fort Leavenworth, but final confirmation of federal troops marching on Utah came dramatically on July 24, 1857. As thousands of Latter-day Saints gathered in the mountain air of Big Cottonwood Canyon near Salt Lake City to celebrate their tenth anniversary in the region, riders galloped in shouting news of the impending invasion. According to some accounts, Young rose, spoke confidently of the Saints' ultimate triumph in the face of adversity, ordered the celebration to continue, and sat back to enjoy the musical performances.

The settlers of the territory immediately set to work in preparation for war. Young issued a call to Mormons in the thriving settlements of San Bernardino

Right: Colonel Albert Sidney Johnston, U.S. Army, 1857. (USHS)

A decorated veteran of the Mexican War, Johnston assumed command of the Utah Expedition after General William Harney was ordered back to Kansas. A sound leader who had a penchant for settling disputes with duels, Johnston was viewed, nonetheless, as less savage than Harney.

Above: Lot Smith, Nauvoo Legion, 1858. (USHS)

Courageous, intelligent, and daring, Lot Smith led a unit of Mormon guerilla fighters against the advancing army supply trains as they neared Green River in present-day Wyoming. When one army wagonmaster implored him not to burn the wagons "for God's sake," Smith replied, "It's for his sake that I *will* burn them!"

Right: Echo Canyon, Utah Territory, c. 1858. (USHS)

The Utah territorial militia intended to use the sheer cliffs of Echo Canyon as a defensive bottleneck to thwart the advancing federal army. Besides lining the clifftops with sharpshooters, militia leaders formulated plans to flood portions of the canyon to block the passage of army troops.

in California and Carson Valley in what would become Nevada to return to church headquarters at once. Similar calls went to missionaries in Europe and on the East Coast. The Nauvoo Legion, as the territorial militia was known, was called to arms under the command of Daniel Wells.

Wells's defense plan called for guerilla raids against the advancing army's supply trains as well as a scorched-earth policy to slow the military's progress and demonstrate the determination of the Mormons to resist. Even as an emissary from the army was negotiating with Brigham Young, Lot Smith and other raiders from the Nauvoo Legion struck against the army's supply wagons and herds in Wyoming. Dozens of wagons were burned and hundreds of head of cattle run off, dramatically cutting supplies for the advancing army, now under the command of Colonel Albert Sidney Johnston. Fort Bridger was burned to the ground by the Mormons, and fortified defense positions were

PROCLAMATION

BY THE GOVERNOR.

CITIZENS OF UTAH---

WE are invaded by a hostile force who are evidently assailing us to accomplish our overthrow and destruction.

For the last twenty five years we have trusted officials of the Government, from Constables and Justices to Judges, Governors, and Presidents, only to be scorned, held in derision, insulted and betrayed. Our houses have been plundered and then burned, our fields laid waste, our principal men butchered while under the pledged faith of the government for their safety, and our families driven from their homes to find that shelter in the barren wilderness and that protection among hostile savages which were denied them in the boasted abodes of Christianity and civilization.

The Constitution of our common country guarantees unto us all that we do now or have ever claimed.

If the Constitutional rights which pertain unto us as American citizens were extended to Utah, according to the spirit and meaning thereof, and fairly and impartially administered, it is all that we could ask, all that we have ever asked.

Our opponents have availed themselves of prejudice existing against us because of our religious faith, to send out a formidable host to accomplish our destruction. We have had no privilege, no opportunity of defending ourselves from the false, foul, and unjust aspersions against us before the nation. The Government has not condescended to cause an investigating committee or other person to be sent to inquire into and ascertain the truth, as is customary in such cases.

We know those aspersions to be false, but that avails us nothing. We are condemned unheard and forced to an issue with an armed, mercenary mob, which has been sent against us at the instigation of anonymous letter writers ashamed to father the base slanderous falsehoods which they have given to the public; of corrupt officials who have brought false accusation against us to screen themselves in their own infamy; and of hireling priests and howling editors who prostitute the truth for filthy lucre's sake.

The issue which has been thus forced upon us compels us to resort to the great first law of self preservation and stand in our own defence, a right guaranteed unto us by the genius of the institutions of our country, and upon which the Government is based.

Our duty to ourselves, to our families, requires us not to tamely submit to be driven and slain, without an attempt to preserve ourselves. Our duty to our country, our holy religion, our God, to freedom and liberty, requires that we should not quietly stand still and see those fetters forging around, which are calculated to enslave and bring us in subjection to an unlawful military despotism such as can only emanate [in a country of Constitutional law] from usurpation, tyranny, and oppression.

This is, therefore,

1st:—To forbid, in the name of the People of the United States in the Territory of Utah, all armed forces, of every description, from coming into this Territory under any pretence whatever.

2d:—That all the forces in said Territory hold themselves in readiness to march, at a moment's notice, to repel any and all such threatened invasion.

3d:—Martial law is hereby declared to exist in this Territory, from and after the publication of this Proclamation; and no person shall be allowed to pass or repass into, or through, or from this Territory, without a permit from the proper officer.

{ L. S. }

Given under my hand and seal at Great Salt Lake City, Territory of Utah, this fifth day of August, A. D. eighteen hundred and fifty seven and of the Independence of the United States of America the eighty second.

BRIGHAM YOUNG.

Declaration of Martial Law, 1857. (UU)

This is arguably one of the most important documents from the first forty years of the Utah Territory. Citing a history of federal outrages against the Mormon people and the advance of an "armed mercenary mob," Brigham Young here put the territory on full military alert in the early fall of 1857. The document, which had no legal basis since Young had been dismissed as governor and had no authority over the militia, the people, or the territory, ordered a sealing of the borders and preparations to "repel any and all such threatened invasions." The tone of the declaration contributed to the defensive and hysteric atmosphere that fostered the Mountain Meadows Massacre.

set up along the cliffs of Echo Canyon to rake the army with gunfire should it attempt to enter Salt Lake City.

The determination to resist in an armed conflict was voiced by Brigham in a stirring public proclamation issued on August 5, 1857, and reissued one month later. Young labeled the army approaching Utah "an armed mercenary mob" and called on the citizens to prepare to "repel any and all such threatened invasions." In conclusion, he proclaimed:

Martial Law is hereby declared in this Territory . . . and no person shall be allowed to pass or repass into, or through, or from this Territory without a permit from the proper officer.

The proclamation, coupled with the fervor of the reformation, the fear of an impending invasion, and the memory of previous atrocities against the Mormon people, set the stage for the darkest chapter in the history of Utah's territorial years.

On August 10th, five days after the initial proclamation, a California-bound wagon train arrived in Salt Lake City, nominally under the leadership of the John T. Baker and Alexander Fancher families. Like other wagon trains bound for California, it entered Utah without a "permit from the proper

Left: Parley P. Pratt, c. 1856. (USHS)

Poet, philosopher, and preacher, Parley P. Pratt was extremely popular among his fellow Mormons. Pratt led an important early exploration of the southern reaches of Utah Territory, with the surveys contributing to settlements and/or use of lands at Richfield, Beaver, Cedar City, and Mountain Meadows. Often called on by his church to do missionary work, Pratt was assigned to the southern states in 1857. After a highly charged altercation involving a woman and her husband, Pratt was killed by the husband in Arkansas. Utah mourned the loss, and a widespread negative opinion against the people of Arkansas was fostered. The Arkansas roots of the Baker-Fancher party are often cited as contributing to its being attacked at Mountain Meadows.

THE MOUNTAIN MEADOWS MASSACRE

It may be the American West's most tragic example of the wrong people in the wrong place at the wrong time. More than one hundred members of the Baker-Fancher overland wagon party died a brutal death at the hands of Mormon militia members and their Native American co-conspirators. Marching out from their defensive positions after three days of attacks, under a flag of truce, the men of the wagon company were shot by their guards near a slight rise in the the Meadows (#5 in the photo below). The women and older children were gunned down farther along the path (#7). Only the very young children were spared in the attack.

While a verifiable, documented account of the tragedy of the mass murder in the Mountain Meadows of southern Utah remains elusive through nearly fourteen decades of silence, obfuscation, and outright lying, few people disagree with the central conclusion that it was a crime that should have been prevented.

What caused the tragedy? Was it war hysteria produced by the march of the federal army on Utah in 1857? Was it a surly, confrontational attitude by the wagon company? Was it lingering hostility in the Utah territory with the people of Arkansas in the wake of the murder of Parley Pratt in that state, the home of the majority of the Baker-Fancher party? Was it the wagon train's poisoning of Indians through tainted meat? Or poisoned water? Was it the religious fervor of the Mormon Reformation? Or the dark side of blood atonement? Did Brigham Young order the murders, or did he desperately try to assure safe passage for the party through the territory?

Was John D. Lee made a scapegoat for the slaughter? What did Isaac Haight do to form the killing field that September of 1857, or was he lost in the swirl of events, capable only of saying "too late" when a messenger rode in with word to prevent the murders? Unanswered questions still linger more than a century later.

But it is beyond doubt that the wrong people were in the wrong place at the wrong time—and the wrong thing happened. As news of the massacre filtered east, residents throughout the nation were shocked, and the accompanying outrage greatly hindered Utah's attempts to join the Union in the following decades.

Above left: Isaac C. Haight, c. 1860. (USHS)
Above right: John D. Lee, c. 1877. (USHS)

Isaac Haight was considered by many to be the leader of the Mormons involved in the massacre, and was later excommunicated from the church—according to some, in order to help spare him from harsher punishment and unwanted attention. John D. Lee became the only Mormon punished for the crime—executed some twenty years later.

Left: The Mountain Meadows, c. 1920. (USHS)

officer"; but this group also was from Arkansas, where beloved Mormon writer, apostle, and missionary Parley Pratt had been murdered just months before while on church assignment. Mormon merchants refused to resupply the Arkansas company, following Brigham Young's counsel that supplies should be held in reserve in the event of a lengthy struggle with the approaching federal troops. Tension was high as the Arkansas company turned south to follow the warmer but lengthier route to California.

In southern Utah the Baker-Fancher company encountered increasing hostility, and its members did little to ease the tension, reportedly goading and mocking the local Mormons. The communities of Parowan and Cedar City had recently been inspired by the impassioned speeches of church apostle George A. Smith. Knowing they defended the territory's "back door" against a feared army invasion from California, local militia units were armed and ready to fight. The Baker-Fancher company was viewed as belligerent and a threat to encourage a federal army to intervene from California. A local decision was made to eliminate the company, but the decision was put on hold temporarily while final confirmation was sought from Brigham Young.

Low on food, their animals strained and underfed, the company decided to recuperate for a few days in a cool meadow on the Old Spanish Trail to California. Ironically, the area—called Mountain Meadows—was one of Parley Pratt's favorite resting spots in southern Utah. As the company entered the area, the local militia decided to abandon its wait for further orders. On September 7 the wagon train was attacked by Indians and militiamen dressed as Indians. For nearly five days the company defended itself against repeated attacks, its food and water supplies nearly exhausted. Approached by militiamen under a flag of a truce, the company members accepted an offer to surrender their weapons, leave their belongings, and be escorted by the militia away from the "Indian attack."

Loading their wounded and small children into wagons and separating into groups of men and women, the Baker-Fancher party started walking out of their campsite on September 11. In a series of gentle rises a mile beyond their camp the lines of unarmed men and women were attacked by Indians and other militiamen lying in ambush. When the attack was complete, more than 100 company members lay dead, including the wounded men, who were executed as they lay in the wagons. Only seventeen small children were spared.

Sadly, on September 13 a rider returned to Cedar City with word from Brigham Young that the Baker-Fancher company was to be left in peace. A code of secrecy soon enveloped the events at Mountain Meadows, and for nearly twenty years local residents would blame Indians, acting alone, for the violence. Attempts were made by participants and church members to ignore the attack, reduce its true scope, turn attention from it, and even justify it.

Below left: "The March Across the Plains, the Utah Expedition, 1857." (LOC)
Below right: "Soldiers on Bivouac, the Utah Expedition, 1857." (LOC)

Illustrations from *Harper's Weekly* show the dire straits facing the Utah Expedition when it was halted by an early winter near Green River in present-day Wyoming. By this time, roughly November 1857, army morale was plummeting in the face of supply trains burned by Mormon guerilla fighters, hunger, and bitter below-zero temperatures.

"Animals lying along the road every rod, hourly dying as they are driven along the road. Snow is about seven inches deep. Hundreds of animals die every twenty-four hours. When all things are taken into consideration you will come to the conclusion that we are having a pretty hard time. We are."—Captain Jesse Gove, 10th Infantry, in a letter to his wife, November 9, 1857.

AFFAIRS AT SALT LAKE CITY.

Brigadier-General BOMBSHELL, of the Mormon Army, before leaving his home to exterminate the ruthless Invaders from the States, confides the care of his Twenty-seven Wives to his Chief—Brother YOUNG.

Major BAYONET, of the Mormon Irregulars, consents, in a rash moment, to give each of his devoted Wives a Lock of his Hair. The result is very painful to behold.

Above: Political Cartoons, *Harper's Weekly*, May 1, 1858. (LOC)

National news magazines had a field day with what was variously known as the Utah War or the Mormon Rebellion. Ignoring the winter sufferings of the army in Wyoming, or the lingering potential for a bloody armed conflict when the canyons opened with the spring thaw, the *Harper's Weekly* cartoonist here focused his attention on what he imagined were unique challenges of polygamists going to war.

Right: Camp Scott, Utah Territory, 1858. (LDS)

When winter hit, the Utah Expedition was ordered to make camp until the spring thaw. They settled in for a frigid stay at Camp Scott, their makeshift settlement two miles south of Fort Bridger. Many of the territorial officials appointed by President Buchanan to replace ousted Mormons or prior appointees who had fled made their winter quarters in adjoining Ecklesville, named after appointed Chief Justice Delana Eckles, who was there waiting his forceful installation in the Salt Lake Valley.

In the fall of 1857 far more attention in the territory was focused on the east. At first it appeared that advance units of the army would attempt to force their way into Utah before the snows; but nature intervened. Just as another had devastated the Willie and Martin handcart companies the previous year, a Rocky Mountain fall blizzard slammed into the army of Colonel Johnston. Dozens of head of the army's livestock froze to death each night as the temperature plummeted below zero. Bristling to carry out his occupation orders and trigger a fight if necessary, Johnston resigned himself and his poorly supplied army to dig in for the winter months and wait for the spring thaw.

The "cold war" of 1857–58 provided a window of opportunity for a peacemaker from the east. Actually, the man, traveling as one "Dr. Osborne," rode in from California through the back door to the territory after a journey that had led him from his Philadelphia home through the Isthmus of Panama to the west coast and then overland to Utah. In reality, the good "doctor" was an old Mormon acquaintance, Colonel Thomas Kane. Working with the approval, if not the direct commission, of beleaguered President Buchanan, who was increasingly becoming the target of congressional criticism for the Utah expedition, Kane offered his ties to both the Mormons and the army as a means of breaking the stalemate before it led to war. Over the winter months he shuttled between Salt Lake City and the federal camp. A breakthrough was finally achieved.

In the spring, Colonel Johnston marched his army through the canyons unopposed to occupy Utah and install Alfred Cumming as territorial governor. Entering the city, the infantry burst into song, offering a bawdy barroom

Thomas L. Kane, 1850. (USHS)
Shown from his days as a colonel in the U.S. Army, Thomas Kane was an early friend to the Mormon people. He befriended them during the time of isolation after their expulsion from Illinois, and he proved a deciding factor in the 1858 stand-off with the federal government. Traveling through the Isthmus of Panama to California, Kane made his way to Utah Territory and earnestly tried to defuse the crisis. Viewed with great suspicion by Colonel Johnston and other army officers, Kane managed to convince territorial governor-designate Alfred Cumming to meet with Brigham Young. The talks produced the first breakthrough in the crisis, and led to its peaceful resolution.

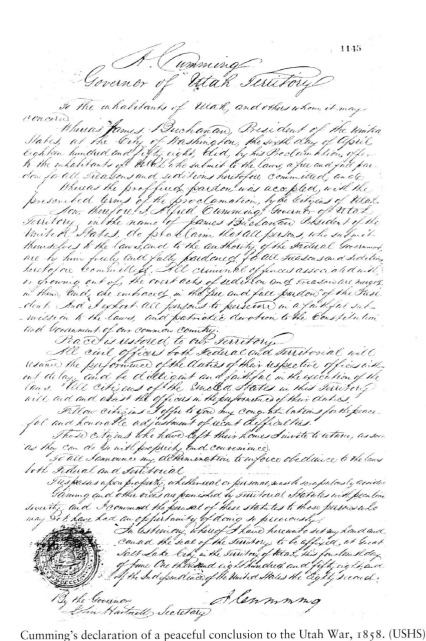

Cumming's declaration of a peaceful conclusion to the Utah War, 1858. (USHS)

Governor Alfred P. Cumming, 1860. (USHS)

Alfred Cumming was a relatively obscure political appointee who had made excellent profits selling goods to army outposts and serving as an Indian superintendent prior to his appointment by James Buchanan as the second territorial governor of Utah in 1857. Joining the army of occupation at its winter quarters in present-day Wyoming, Cumming at first advocated a tough military approach and a complete Mormon surrender. As time passed, however, he was impressed by the resolute nature of the Mormons' defense of their faith and homes, and was amenable to negotiations when approached by Thomas Kane in 1858. Cumming, eventually joined by peace negotiators appointed by Buchanan, met with Brigham Young and negotiated a respectful relationship between the federal government and the Mormon church. He also pardoned any and all offenses relating to the "rebellion."

Above: Captain Philip St. George Cooke, U.S. Army, 1858. (USHS)

One of the leading officers in Johnston's Army, Philip Cooke had led members of the Mormon Battalion on their dramatic march through the Southwest during the Mexican War. Loyal to his commission, Cooke never indicated favor or softness toward the Mormons during the stand-off. However, at least one report indicates that Cooke removed his cap as a gesture of respect to the Mormons as his unit marched through Salt Lake City.

Right: Shanties in Provo City, 1858. (LOC)

As if to deliver final punctuation to the resolution of the conflict, Brigham Young led an exodus of the Mormons from Salt Lake City just prior to the army's march into the territory. Designed as an affirmation of his leadership over the people, the "move south" was brief. Thousands of families made temporary homes in shelters erected in Provo and other nearby areas prior to their return to their permanent homes in Salt Lake City.

Above: Artist's drawing of U.S. Army units marching along South Temple past Brigham Young's residence, 1858. (USHS)

Part of the resolution made between Governor Cumming and Brigham Young allowed the army to make a show of marching through Salt Lake City as it occupied the territory in the summer of 1858. But the army then had to keep moving, as part of the agreement, until it reached an isolated area near Utah Lake forty miles south. Army units sang a bawdy barroom ballad at the top of their lungs as they marched past Brigham Young's compound in the heart of the city.

BRIGHAM'S SHANTIES AT PROVO CITY.—[FROM A PHOTOGRAPH BY BURR & MICO.]

tune aimed at offending the Mormons. However, they found almost no one there to offend. Brigham Young had led an exodus of the Mormons from Salt Lake City to Provo in a short-lived "move south" to demonstrate the on going ability of his people to resist and isolate the occupying force.

But the scene was far from a federal victory by other measures. In the windows of city homes members of the Nauvoo Legion crouched with rifles at the ready and hay stacked in the rooms to serve as fuel for burning the buildings. Under terms of the negotiated settlement, the troops continued to march until they were almost forty miles outside of Salt Lake City. If the federal troops stopped, the legion members were prepared to open fire and burn the city. Cumming followed the troops in and assumed the post of territorial governor; however, President Buchanan had pardoned the Mormons en masse, assuring there would be no penalties or punishment for church leaders.

CAMP FLOYD, UTAH TERRITORY

Brought into being by the Utah War, Camp Floyd had a wild, short life, then died a sudden death that left smiles throughout Utah Territory.

When Alfred Cumming negotiated the arrival of federal troops sent to occupy the territory to assure federal sovereignty, Brigham Young insisted that they come nowhere near the heart of the territory at Salt Lake City. The closest acceptable spot for Young was an isolated location in Cedar Valley near Utah Lake.

The army took possession of the land in the late summer of 1858 and quickly christened the installation Camp Floyd, after Secretary of War John Floyd, who had ordered the army's original march to the territory. The number of soldiers stationed at the fort soon swelled to over 3,000—making Camp Floyd the largest military installation in the United States.

Hundreds of support personnel and hangers-on soon flocked to Camp Floyd and the nearby town of Fairfield. Bars, gambling dens, and houses of prostitution dominated the small town, which picked up the nickname "Frogtown" from the soldiers. On the less blighted side, the army staged dramatic plays and band concerts for the soldiers of the camp.

In 1861, with the Civil War raging in the east, the troops of the camp were recalled from Utah. Commanding officer Albert Sidney Johnston had already resigned his commission to join the army of the Confederate States of America. Federal authorities, now wanting only to be rid of the site, sold the entire camp at auction. Everything from the barracks buildings to the government safe went to Mormon buyers for pennies on the dollar. It was an immense financial windfall for the territory.

Left: Camp Floyd, 1858. (LDS)

Below: Army musicians at Camp Floyd, 1858. (USHS)

Brigham Young remained very much at the head of the Mormon church and its people, and would continue to serve as the primary, albeit de facto, helmsman for the territory for the foreseeable future.

Thus, the "Utah War" ended in a delicate balancing act without a clear victor. While the fate of the Baker-Fancher party served as a powerful argument against the notion that it had been a "bloodless" conflict, both Brigham Young and James Buchanan were relieved that the dogs of war had not been let loose in the Utah Territory. Still, the conflict of 1857–58 served as a crucial turning point for the territory and its relationship with the nation: no longer would its people or their practices be considered beyond the reach of the federal government.

Right: "Going to Church," Salt Lake City, 1858. (USHS)

With the easing of tensions between the Mormon church and the federal government, life in Utah Territory returned to a more normal pace. Alfred Cumming was governor, but nobody, including Cumming, doubted that Brigham Young remained in charge. Still, the occupation of Utah by the federal army represented the symbolic end of an era; no longer would peaceful isolation be the predominant feature of the territory.

Salt Lake City panorama, looking southeast from Arsenal Hill, c. 1860. (USHS)

Chapter Four

"A LOG IN THE FIELD"
1860–1869

The Civil War....The Homestead Act opens government public-domain land for settlement....Lincoln is assassinated...."Seward's Folly" purchases Alaska....A constitutional amendment forever prohibits slavery....The Ku Klux Klan is formed....Garibaldi leads an Italian nationalist movement....Pasteur develops a germ theory; Lister introduces antiseptics....The Suez Canal opens.

THE 1860S WAS A DECADE OF POWERFUL CHANGE in Utah Territory. The calm air of confidence generated by the buffered isolation that had graced the Great Basin for the first fifteen years of Mormon settlement would be swept away by the stormy gales of Manifest Destiny and the hot blasts of advancing technology. The federal government, distracted by the wrenching conflict of the Civil War, would still find time and opportunity to exert greater control over the territory and its people. Of greatest consequence for the future would be the changing face of the population, with a continuing sea of Mormon immigrants now joined by non-Mormons recognizing (and pursuing) opportunities in Utah.

Below: Great Salt Lake City, 1867. (USHS)

An imaginative artist's view of Utah's capital city shortly after the end of the Civil War. The caption calls it the "most beautifully laid and watered city in America," but the picture itself is replete with inaccuracies. The artist, Philip Ritz, depicts the Great Salt Lake as ending very close to Main Street, while the mountains (completely encircling the valley without break) are reported to be up to 150 miles away. Ritz also finished the Salt Lake Temple twenty-five years ahead of its actual completion.

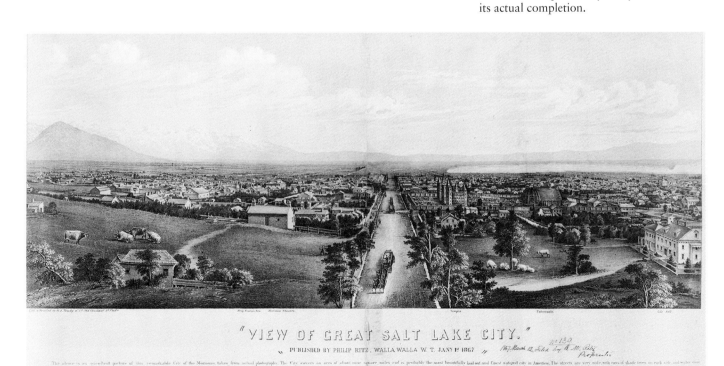

"VIEW OF GREAT SALT LAKE CITY."

PUBLISHED BY PHILIP RITZ, WALLA WALLA W. T. JAN'Y 1ST 1867

The decade dawned with 3,000 federal troops firmly in place at the military camp near Utah Lake named after Secretary of War John B. Floyd. Before the Civil War greatly swelled the ranks, Camp Floyd would hold nearly 25 percent of the army's total force, making it the single largest aggregation of troops in the nation. Both the Mormons and the troops themselves considered the soldiers of Camp Floyd an army of occupation. But camp officers made a concerted effort to avoid confrontation with the local residents, and troops managed to serve important auxiliary missions of exploration and of protection of the overland mail and wagon routes. The camp also brought into

Camp Floyd, 1860. (USHS)

Shown here in its last days, the army's camp of occupation in Utah Territory was about to undergo a name change. Secretary of War John B. Floyd, the camp's namesake, had fled to the southern states when they seceded from the Union. Rechristened Camp Crittenden, the base was formally closed in 1861.

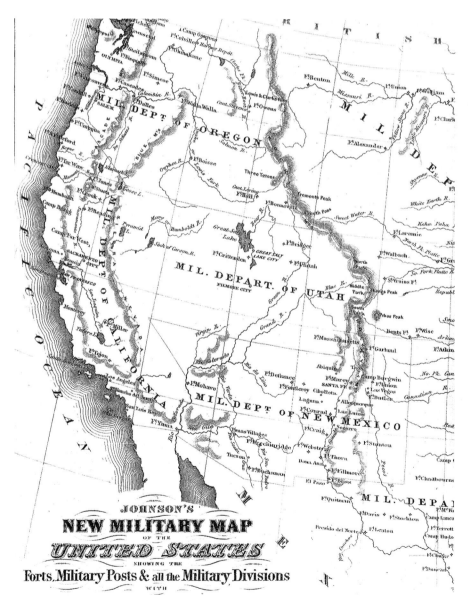

Johnson's Military Map of the West, 1862. (USHS)

When the Civil War broke out, military districts in the West were more exactingly drawn to allow for easier administration, if not actual protection of inhabitants. While the Department of New Mexico would experience actual Civil War hostilities, the Department of Utah was more concerned with fighting increasing Indian attacks against the overland stage and mail services, as well as attacks against settlements in the region. With troops desperately needed in the east, protection of the territory was eventually assigned to a force of volunteers from California under the command of Colonel Patrick Edward Connor, a figure destined to play a significant role in Utah's history.

The U.S. Capitol Building, 1860. (LOC)

With Lincoln's election and the subsequent secession from the Union of the southern, largely Democratic, states, Republicans enjoyed large majorities in both houses of Congress. The nation's capitol building was under construction, and Lincoln had ordered that work on the dome continue as a symbolic gesture of the enduring nature of the nation in the face of war. While Lincoln would claim that he was too busy to worry about a number of domestic issues, Congress would find the time and energy to take up the matter of the Mormon church and its practice of polygamy.

President Abraham Lincoln, c. 1862. (LOC)

Familiar with the Mormons from their days in Illinois, where he served as an attorney and state legislator, Lincoln nonetheless accepted his party's position linking polygamy with slavery as evils worthy of eradication. But he made it clear that all other items on the political agenda paled next to preservation of the Union. Asked by Utah writer T.B.H. Stenhouse what he intended to do about the Mormons, Lincoln told of plowing fields during his childhood. Occasionally, he said, a log in the field would prove too tough, so he would merely plow around it. That, he offered, was what he would do with the Mormons.

THE CIVIL WAR AND UTAH TERRITORY

While the Civil War raged in the east, the Mormon people remained distant and even aloof from the conflict. Several historians have noted that residents of the Utah Territory actually seemed to desire both sides to self-destruct, despite the fact that Brigham Young offered several public statements in support of the Constitution and the survival of a single nation.

Many of the Mormon church's leaders delivered public addresses exhorting faithful members to prepare for leadership, for the Civil War was to be the last great conflict—one that would destroy the nation. The reports of carnage on the battlefields and the total destruction of southern cities seemed to provide compelling evidence to support this vision. When the nation fell, said the leaders, the Mormon people would pick up the standard and give laws to the nation and, eventually, to the world.

"The corruption of the nation has sealed its doom. The people, whom the very great majority have striven to obliterate, will step forward and sustain the falling banner and continue to honor the heaven-inspired Constitution bequeathed to us as so rich a legacy by our forefathers."
—Brigham Young, 1860.

While a very few individuals from the territory may have joined Union units during the conflict, no organized unit represented Utah Territory on the field of battle during the Civil War. For a time, a small armed unit was commissioned to provide protection for overland wagon routes; but after a few months the unit was replaced by formally commissioned volunteers from California. Eventually, however, Utah's overland guard units were recognized by the national Civil War veterans association as having served honorably in the forces of the United States.

President Lincoln and officers, Army of the Potomac. (NARA)

The destruction of Richmond, Virginia, 1865. (USHS)

Andrew Johnson, seventeenth president of the United States, 1865–68. (LOC)

The only American president ever to be impeached, Johnson dodged by one vote in the Senate the attempt of Congress to remove him from office. Busy with the effort to remove him from office and the first awkward steps of Reconstruction, Johnson paid little attention to the West, Utah Territory, or the Mormon people.

Horace Greeley, 1859. (LOC)

Greeley is shown as he looked when he traveled the West as a roving and influential correspondent for the newspaper he edited and owned, the *New York Tribune*. His two-hour interview with Brigham Young on July 13, 1859, captured national attention as the two discussed slavery, theology, and intricacies and details of the practice of polygamy.

AFRICAN-AMERICANS IN UTAH TERRITORY

Donald Freeman, Utah Territory, c. 1880. (UU)

Unidentified woman, Utah Territory, c. 1880. (UU)

For years a debate has raged over the status of African-Americans in Utah during the territorial years. The record is a mixed message about opportunity and enslavement.

In 1852, at the request of then-Governor Brigham Young, the territorial legislature legalized the holding of slaves in Utah. This simply codified an ongoing and widely accepted practice. Slaves had existed in Utah since the arrival of the first pioneers in 1847. Three of the first immigrants were African-American slaves who were sent ahead by southern converts to the Mormon church to prepare the way for the slaveholders' arrival. Slaves were bought and sold in the territory, although on a very limited scale, and never in a marketplace setting such as characterized the horrifying indifference of the plantations of the south. On several occasions Mormons from the southern states arriving in the Utah Territory would offer to pay their church tithing in slaves, although there is no record of the church ever holding slaves. Brigham Young is reported to have released the slaves into the workforce, where they would assume extremely low-paying jobs.

In his 1859 interview with Horace Greeley, Brigham Young would both acknowledge the existence of slaveholding in Utah and offer the opinion that not only was it a bad practice but also that Utah would insist on being admitted to the Union as a "free state." Young also said that slavery was "of divine institution," however, and would remain because African-Americans were consigned to live their lives under "the curse of Ham."

The holding of slaves never flourished in Utah. At the outbreak of the Civil War only about 100 African-Americans lived in the territory, and their numbers were roughly split equally between free men and women and slaves. In 1862 Congress formally acted to outlaw slavery in all United States territories, ending the slave era in Utah. The role and standing of African-Americans in the Mormon church, however, would continue to spark controversy for another hundred years.

existence "Frogtown," a derogatory name for nearby Fairfield, which became overrun by liquor merchants, gamblers, and prostitutes serving the isolated soldiers. Similar to such camps at every nineteenth-century military post, "Frogtown" was viewed by Mormons as a fitting example of "Babylon" and a corrupt, immoral government.

The secession crisis spelled the end for Camp Floyd. The three prime figures charged with addressing the "Mormon Rebellion" of 1857—John Floyd,

Salt Lake Tabernacle under construction, 1865. (USHS)

Construction on a new, magnificent meeting hall for the Mormon people started in July 1863 on Temple Square in the heart of Great Salt Lake City. As many as 250 workers were employed on the project at a time. The large, domed interior was a marvel of mid-nineteenth-century architecture, and contributed to the amazingly pure acoustics that would enable a speaker to address more than eight thousand listeners in those days before the development of public address systems.

Northeastern quadrant, Great Salt Lake City, 1869. (USHS)

From the dome of the recently completed tabernacle on Temple Square, a photographer looks due east to the foothills of the Wasatch Mountains. In the extreme foreground is the foundation of the Salt Lake LDS Temple, still in its earliest stages of construction. Beyond the foundation are the walled sides of Main Street, followed by the tithing yards where Mormons contributed crops and livestock to their church. Next is the compound of Brigham Young, highlighted at this angle by the Lion House and Young's private schoolhouse with its bell tower. Stretching east and north is the stone wall that encircled Young's compound during his lifetime.

Governor Alfred Cumming, and Colonel Albert Sidney Johnston—all resigned their commissions to return to their native South and wage war against the government of the United States. Camp Floyd was renamed, then unceremoniously closed, as the troops were reassigned to the war in the east. The camp's supplies and fixtures were sold to the Mormons for pennies on the dollar, providing a huge economic lift to territorial businessmen, with Brigham Young actively taking part in buying lumber, supplies, and even the camp's safe as the army went out of business in Utah.

As the conflict raged between North and South, the Mormons largely went about their business, offering (and having) little if any direct participation in the war. Some Mormons viewed the Civil War as an anticipated "Armageddon," destined to leave a corrupt nation broken and leaderless while the Kingdom of God in Utah would emerge transcendent. Busy trying to ensure that such would not be the case, Abraham Lincoln sent clear signals to Brigham Young that he had his hands full with the war and was completely comfortable with leaving the Mormons alone in their inland empire—at least for the duration of the conflict.

In 1862 there were more than 60,000 permanent residents in Utah Territory. By the standards of the day they were relatively free from poverty and sickness. The infant mortality ran at 26 percent, but a report of the time proudly reported only one documented suicide in the first fifteen years of settlement. Basic laborers earned two dollars per day on construction projects

Agricultural land, Salt Lake Valley, c. 1870. (USHS)

This may be a portion of the "Big Field" that served as the early community's common agricultural land in the Salt Lake Valley. During the 1860s the Big Field and other farming sites in Utah would be visited by the return of devastating cricket infestations. While less ballyhooed than the cricket attack of 1848, the later infestations affected many more people, produced serious food shortages, and created severe economic hardship in the territory.

The State House (Council House), Great Salt Lake City, c. 1865. (LDS)

At first used by the Mormon church's council of leaders to govern the territory, the Council, or State, House served as the primary meeting site for the territorial legislature in the years prior to statehood. Situated next door was one of the territory's oldest businesses, the Globe Bakery. Next door to the Globe was the post office which, in 1865, was becoming more reliable in the receipt and shipping of mail overland.

Telegraph Office, Great Salt Lake City, 1862. (USHS)

The completion of the transcontinental telegraph line in Utah in October 1861 represented a major step in connecting the isolated territory with the nation. Brigham Young sent the first telegram from the territory: "Utah has not seceded, but is firm for the Constitution and laws of our once happy country...." Young played a major role in contracting local laborers to erect poles and string telegraph line to the territory. This office was located near the northeast corner of Main Street and First South.

like the great Tabernacle that was slowly rising in Temple Square. Domestic servants, often immigrants arriving in the valley without trade skills, earned about thirty dollars per month. Many people were paid with goods through barter systems. A small business district lined the dirt streets of central Salt Lake City, with shops carrying limited lines of goods imported at great expense from the east and west coasts. Irrigation canals still flowed through the heart of the city, which ended at the ninth block south of Temple Square. A huge agricultural plot known as the "Big Field" spread south from the edge of the city, with individual farming sections growing in acreage as one traveled south, the size reflecting a family's full- or part-time involvement with farming. The church's tithing herd of cattle grazed on Antelope Island in the Great Salt Lake, the animals being herded to the island while the lake was at a low level.

The territory had long been an information wilderness where news and mail could be delayed months in transit; but the decade witnessed dramatic connections between Utah and the rest of the world. First the Pony Express (1860) and then the transcontinental telegraph (1861) transformed the way the territory was informed, providing first rapid and then almost direct communication links with other locations throughout the country.

CONNECTING UTAH TERRITORY TO THE WORLD

"No mail has been received from the east since last November, and a part of that is still cached in the mountains. As yet we have no certain information who was elected President of the United States."
—Brigham Young, April 13, 1853

In the early days of the territory a six-month delay in receiving mail was considered the norm. In fact, if the mail got through at all during the winter months it bordered on the miraculous. The territory's only link to the nation was through the grueling and slow process of wagon trains heading east and west. At times mail contractors would dump their loads to escape snow-choked canyons when an early winter storm would hit.

The coming of the Pony Express in 1860 was viewed as a communication revolution among the people of the territory. Soon Pony Express stations lined the east-west corridor across the Utah territory, providing fresh mounts and provisions to the legendary riders of the nation's first express delivery service. By means of the Pony Express, a letter could reach Washington in about a week, which was no small consideration for the territory as it struggled with its relationship with the federal government. But the service did not come cheap—it cost $5.00 per half ounce to send letters.

No sooner had the Pony Express established itself than its replacement appeared on the horizon. The transcontinental telegraph offered almost immediate communication, usually at a lower cost. Brigham Young soon augmented the transcontinental east-west telegraph connection with the Deseret Telegraph Company, which provided north-south service from Mormon settlements in Idaho to St. George in southern Utah.

And while messages were moving more quickly, progress also was being made in freighting manufactured goods and supplies to the Utah territory by means of more dependable and regular wagon shipments. The reliability of merchandise deliveries allowed a number of new stores to open in Salt Lake City, several operated by newly arrived non-Mormon businessmen.

The communication and transportation changes brought new faces, new goods, and new ideas to the once-isolated Utah Territory, heralding and then becoming an integral part of an era of change.

Pony Express station, Echo Canyon, 1860. (LDS)

Overland stage station, Great Salt Lake City, 1862. (LDS)

THE SALT LAKE THEATRE

From the earliest days of settlement, Salt Lake City residents have managed to produce dramatic entertainment. At first, pioneers staged open-air dramas to provide a break from the rigors of frontier life. The Social Hall came next as a venue, opening in 1852 to provide a more formal (although small) theatre and dance hall. In 1862 the community made a great theatrical leap forward with the construction of the Salt Lake Theatre.

Located on the corner of State Street and First South, the Salt Lake Theatre was championed by Brigham Young, an avid fan of live entertainment. Young viewed a grand hall as being essential to the cultural advancement of the territory and a means of extending a civilizing, uplifting influence to its people. His belief in the project and its priority is reflected in its early completion during the era of great building that produced the Salt Lake Tabernacle and a string of Mormon temples in the territory.

"I was greatly astonished to find in the desert heart of the continent a place for public amusement which for capacity, beauty and comfort has no superior in America, save the opera houses of New York, Boston and Philadelphia," offered the writer Fitz Hugh Ludlow, an early visitor to the Theatre.

While the Salt Lake Theatre would in time book as many national-caliber acting figures as possible as they rode a circuit around the country, much of the early talent for the Theatre's productions was drawn from the general population. The local dramas perhaps also had an influence on politics in the territory, as both congressional delegate John T. Caine and future Utah governor Heber M. Wells had stints with the Theatre early in their careers.

Reasonable ticket prices kept the programs within reach of most people in the territory, and a visit to the Theatre was usually on the agenda when families traveled to Great Salt Lake City for business or religious reasons. For first-time visitors, the Theatre, which seated 1,500, was an impressive site with its rich decorations and curtains, elegant boxes (including Brigham Young's personal family box), and a first-rate orchestra providing musical accompaniment as well as an occasional concert.

Rules of proper decorum were insisted upon and closely monitored, including oversight of the plays to be staged. When visiting soldiers offered pointed comments about certain female performers, army personnel were banned from admission for a time. Brigham Young also served as an arbiter of a performance's fate; if Utah's leading citizen laughed at a comedy, it was certain that others would soon thunder their applause. Likewise, disinterest from Young could spell an early closing. The Salt Lake Theatre served the community until 1928, when it was razed for downtown development.

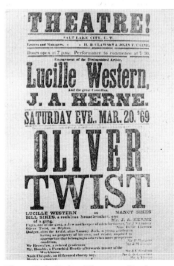

Top: Salt Lake Theatre Orchestra, 1868; *Left*: Portion of theatre bill, 1869; *Right*: The Salt Lake Theatre, 1862. (all USHS)

The Social Hall served on a regular basis as the center for gala dances for a community that enjoyed music and dance as a diversion from its hard labors. Similarly, the community placed a high priority on completing the imposing Salt Lake Theatre in 1861, advancing its construction ahead of ecclesiastical projects such as the new Tabernacle in order that residents might enjoy both local and national touring group performances and entertainment.

With a sense of destiny, tangible evidence of progress, and a reprieve from the military occupation, the people of the territory began the 1860s with a sense of purpose and self-determination. So heady were the optimistic feelings that Brigham Young inserted himself as chief executive during a break in federally appointed governors and called the territorial legislature into session for the purpose of renewing Utah's request for statehood. But the reading of national sentiment by the Mormons was far from accurate.

Utah delegates not only were dispatched from Washington without statehood but also were sent on their way with the first national law targeted against their religious practices. In 1862 Representative Justin Morrill of Vermont pushed through Congress a bill outlawing the practice of polygamy in the territories, disincorporating the Church of Jesus Christ of Latter-day Saints, and requiring the forfeiture of church property holdings valued at more

Above right: Representative Justin Morrill, 1862. (LOC) With the nation in the grip of the Civil War, Republicans in Congress still found the time to attack the "second relic of barbarism" championed in their party platform—polygamy. Representative Justin Morrill of Vermont, who considered himself a "second Lincoln" in style and appearance, led the charge. The Morrill Act of 1862 outlawed plural marriages in U.S. territories, sought to disincorporate the Mormon church, and attempted to seize church assets above $50,000. The bill was clearly designed to attack polygamy and also to shatter the controlling influence of the Mormon church in Utah.

Main Street, Salt Lake City, c. 1865. (USHS)

Each day the dirt streets of Salt Lake City would fill with wagons and foot traffic as the city emerged as a hub of trading and transport in the region. By the 1860s businesses were growing beyond wooden-frame, single-story storefronts to two and occasionally three stories of brick. The Oasis Saloon, near foreground, was one of dozens of establishments offering a strong drink for those so inclined.

Early prospectors, Alta, Little Cottonwood Canyon, 1867. (LDS)

Main Street, Alta, 1873. (USHS)

MINING IN UTAH TERRITORY

"The General commanding the district has the strongest evidence that the mountains and canyons in the Territory of Utah abound in rich veins of gold, silver, copper..."
—Camp Douglas proclamation, November 14, 1863

The general in question, Patrick Edward Connor, had experienced the boom of the California gold rush and was convinced that Utah could have a mining boom of its own. He sent his troops on extended leaves to explore the canyons. When they made their first discoveries of precious metals Connor trumpeted the news throughout the nation, hoping to fuel a rush of non-Mormons to the territory to break Mormon political control.

Placer mining, unknown location, Utah Territory, c. 1870. (LDS)

Church Street, Eureka, Utah Territory, c. 1890. (USHS)

Top left: Bingham Canyon, 1890. (USHS)
Top right: A game of faro, Bingham Canyon saloon, 1890. (USHS)
Above: Woodhull Brothers' silver bullion on display in Salt Lake City, c. 1872. (USHS)
Right: Hard-rock miners, Mercur, Utah Territory, 1890. (USHS)

Land office, Myton, Utah Territory, 1880. (USHS)

Stagecoach on Main Street in Salt Lake City, c. 1865. (USHS)

By the mid-1860s stagecoach lines were offering the quickest form of transportation for those heading east or west in the territory. While several lines operated in the region, the Wells-Fargo Company provided one of the most dependable schedules for travelers to the west coast. While often theatrically depicted as a ripe target for attack by marauding Native Americans, stagecoaches were generally ignored by tribes, who saw greater value in the goods and food carried by wagons. The overland stage was not without problems, however, as it was robbed on numerous occasions in Utah by outlaws. Local enforcer Orrin Porter Rockwell added to his reputation by demonstrating an uncanny ability at tracking bandits, relieving them of the loot and, occasionally, their lives.

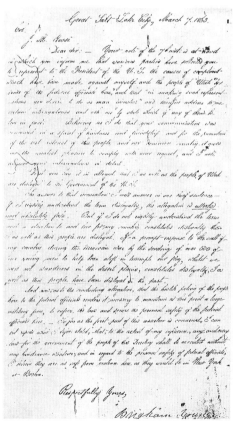

Letter to Colonel J.M. Rosse from Brigham Young, 1863. (LOC)

Learning that federally appointed judges in Utah Territory were writing President Lincoln claiming that the Mormon population was disloyal and that an army should be sent to crush yet another rebellion, Brigham Young dashed his own letter off to Colonel J. M. Rosse defending the loyalty of the Mormon people to the nation. While Rosse is not a major historical figure, he must have had connections, for this letter turned up in the personal correspondence held and read by President Lincoln.

than $50,000. Stunned at the rebuke, most Mormon leaders viewed the law as an unconstitutional infringement of their right to practice their religion.

Ironically, it also served to further inspire the dream of statehood, since Congress could regulate territories with a greater degree of certainty than it could regulate states. Mormon leaders believed that statehood would mean self-determination, greater liberty, and an end to federally appointed officers from outside filing lurid reports about life in Utah.

The Morrill Act served as a powerful assertion of eastern-based federal jurisdiction over the Mormon people, yet it was reinforced coincidentally by a force from the west. After briefly accepting Mormon offers to safeguard the overland mail routes, national military leaders opted for more direct federal control. A contingent of California Volunteers marched east in late 1862 to address an increasing number of Indian attacks against the mail and stage traffic, as well as to protect the influx of miners heading for the new gold fields of Montana.

The California Volunteers were led by Colonel Patrick Edward Connor. A veteran of the Mexican War and the California gold rush, Connor was a tough leader, solid military commander, and a harsh critic of the Mormons. Brushing aside the "gentlemen's agreement" that had placed Johnston's Army outside of the Salt Lake Valley, Connor marched his troops to a foothill directly overlooking Salt Lake City and proclaimed it Camp Douglas after Senator Stephen A. Douglas of Illinois. Brigham Young posted armed guards outside his home and office, convinced that the combative Connor was more interested in arresting church leaders than in protecting federal mail service.

But Connor's first priority was the "Indian problem." Expanding settlements in Cache Valley had eroded the traditional game and food sources for local members of the Northwestern Shoshoni tribe. Militant members of the tribe rallied under "war chiefs" to strike back against advancing settlements in an attempt to feed a tribal population that was literally starving to death in the area that would eventually become the Utah-Idaho border. Connor's orders from his west coast command were broad but direct: Protect the mail, the overland route, and the settlements. Use your discretion. Kill all Indian combatants.

The opportunity for Connor to exercise discretion in carrying out his mission presented itself on January 29, 1863. On the banks of the Bear River, 200 soldiers under Connor confronted a band of Shoshoni believed to have been involved in a recent series of raids against wagon trains and settlements.

Above: Camp Douglas, c. 1870. (NARA)

Above right: Brigadier General Patrick Edward Connor, 1864. (NARA)

Tough, bold, intensely loyal to his country, and touched with a streak of savagery, P.E. Connor rode into Salt Lake City at the head of a detachment of California Volunteers in 1862 on a mission to protect the overland stage route from Indian attacks. From his first day in town he crafted a second mission of directly challenging the Mormon church for leadership in the territory, as he sought to open Utah to the non-Mormon world.

CAMP DOUGLAS AND THE CALIFORNIA VOLUNTEERS

The gentlemen's agreement that ended the Utah War in 1858 had set the ground rules for the subsequent military occupation of Utah Territory. Troops would not be stationed in Great Salt Lake City, would preferably not even *visit* the city, and would make their permanent post forty miles south at Camp Floyd in Cedar Valley. P.E. Connor changed all that in the blink of an eye in 1862.

Labeling the Mormon people "a community of traitors, whores and fanatics" even before he reached the territory, Connor decided to march his California Volunteers, with weapons loaded and bayonets fixed, through the city streets to the first gentle rise immediately east of the community. There he planted the U.S. flag and proclaimed the founding of Camp Douglas—named in honor of recently deceased Senator Stephen A. Douglas who, not quite incidentally, had turned into a bombastic critic of Mormon control of the territory.

Camp Douglas, through Connor, soon became a rallying point and center for the disaffected non-Mormon community. While serving a mission to fight and kill Indians, Connor offered military support to any and all activities that embarassed or angered Brigham Young. Through the 1860s Connor and Young would rattle sabres at each other, launch blistering attacks in their controlled newspapers, and continually accuse the other of pushing the territory to the brink of internal war. Despite the fact that they would influence and infuriate each other for fifteen years, the two would never meet face to face.

Despite all of their outside activities, such as mining exploration and development, the California Volunteers still committed a good deal of energy to building a sustainable military camp. After Connor had been mustered out of the service, the U.S. Army decided that the location and improvements were worth keeping and poured construction dollars into the camp to create a permanent military installation, Fort Douglas.

California Volunteers at Camp Douglas, 1865. (NARA)

Post Chapel, Camp Douglas, c.1870. (NARA)

THE SHOSHONI INDIANS

By the winter of 1862–63 the tension between the dislocated and starving Northwestern Shoshonis and the ever-expanding white settlements reached a critical stage. With tribe members reduced to begging for food and even sifting barn hay for spilled animal feed, young members of the Northwestern Shoshoni decided to make a stand. They began demanding food payments from Mormon settlements in Cache Valley. Emigrant wagon trains, some bound for the newly discovered gold fields of Montana, were attacked and the violence was attributed to the Shoshoni.

Mormon law officers swore out a warrant for the arrest of Shoshoni "war chief" Bear Hunter. When asked if he would aid in serving the warrant, then-Colonel Patrick Connor told the law officers he was set to take his own action under his own orders, and that he intended to take no prisoners. Connor reportedly told a newspaper reporter prior to departure that his orders were to kill all combatants.

The army refers to the subsequent conflict as the Battle of Bear River; some historians call it the Bear River Massacre. To the Northwestern Shoshoni it is the Massacre at Boa Ogoi, their tribal name for the river. Over two hundred Shoshoni men, women, and children died in the four-hour firefight, which was virtually one-sided for its final two hours, with soldiers randomly shooting the natives as they sought to escape to the river. Bear Hunter died a tortured death during the course of the battle.

The Northwestern Shoshoni were shattered by the force and ferocity of the attack. Following tribal chief Washakie, they eventually signed a reservation treaty and withdrew to lands in present-day Wyoming.

Left: Chief Washakie of the Northwestern Shoshoni, c. 1875. (USHS)

Right: Young Shoshoni men, c. 1875. (USHS)

A Shoshoni village, perhaps in present-day Wyoming, c. 1870. (USHS)

The Shoshoni people, and particularly the Northwestern band that was centered around the Cache Valley and the area near the current Utah-Idaho border, were somewhat nomadic in that they followed the seasons to different hunting and gathering locations. This pattern of life was dramatically disrupted by the northern expansion of Mormon settlements in the 1850s and 1860s. With the best lands rapidly occupied by white farmers, the Northwestern Shoshoni were soon struggling against starvation.

The Salt Lake Tabernacle, 1868. (USHS)

Dwarfing the early foundation and slowly rising walls of the Salt Lake Temple, the Tabernacle emerged as the city's dominant landmark upon its completion in 1867. Considered an engineering and acoustic marvel, the massive hall that could seat at least 8,000 people was a spiritual and secular focal point during the territorial years. The Mormon people would use the structure for everything from church conference meetings to the celebration of Utah women's suffrage in 1870.

An initial head-on assault stalled in the face of intense rifle fire from the Indian camp, leaving more than a dozen California Volunteers dead on the field. Splitting his forces in a classic envelopment manuever, Connor surrounded the Shoshoni camp in a second assault and began closing in. The Indians ran out of ammunition, and the fighting soon degenerated into fierce hand-to-hand combat in the thickets along the riverbank. Equipped with rapid-fire pistols, the Volunteers soon swept through the village, killing any Indian they saw. On the banks of the nearly frozen Bear River soldiers carefully took aim and shot those Shoshoni who tried to escape in the icy waters.

After four hours the shooting stopped. Twenty California Volunteers were dead in the snowy field surrounding the camp. But for the Shoshoni it was a nightmare. Two hundred and fifty tribe members had been killed, ninety of them women and children. It was and remained the single greatest loss of Native American life in a military engagement west of the Mississippi River. Broken physically and in spirit, the remnants of the tribe would eventually withdraw to reservation lands. Connor returned to Salt Lake City to a hero's welcome and later received a promotion to brigadier general for his actions on the banks of the Bear River.

But the cheering would not last long among the Mormons. Connor immediately let it be known that he intended to "Americanize" Utah Territory by any means at his disposal. He granted leaves to his troops, encouraging them to prospect the surrounding mountains for mineral wealth, confident that a mining boom would bring enough non-Mormons to the territory to bury Mormon political power. He also founded the *Union Vedette* newspaper to provide a stream of national news and anti-Mormon editorials to a community solely served by the church newsletter, the *Deseret News*. Although they would live within blocks of each other for fifteen years, and stand as clearly recognized symbols of their respective institutions, Patrick Edward Connor and Brigham Young never met, choosing to talk over, around, and through each other.

Orrin Porter Rockwell, c. 1870. (USHS)

It was often reported that visitors to Salt Lake City in the 1860s would want to meet two people—Brigham Young and Porter Rockwell. Rockwell was (and remains) a legendary and shadowy figure in the history of the Mormon people and Utah Territory. Deeply religious and fiercely loyal to church leadership, Rockwell earned a reputation for taking care of difficult and dangerous tasks and assignments. His trademark long hair was the result of a prophecy by church founder Joseph Smith, who promised Rockwell that he would never be injured in service to the Mormon church if he refrained from cutting his hair. As his hair grew, so did his reputation. That he killed a large number of men is beyond dispute, although he viewed most of the incidents as either defending himself or his church. But the circumstances were generally so mysterious and such guarded secrets that it remains difficult to separate myth from reality about the man some called the "Avenging Angel." (USHS)

CITY LIFE IN UTAH TERRITORY—1860s

To live in Salt Lake City in the 1860s was to live in a rapidly changing community rushing headlong to a dynamic but uncertain future. Walking along the wooden boardwalks of Main Street you could still here the gurgle of irrigation water rushing by in the open ditches that ran to the farming plots that began only four blocks south of the Temple Square. In the square itself, the walls of the much-planned temple were only about eight feet high and the large half-built Tabernacle towered over the scene. You could stand by the stone perimeter wall and watch the double-rigged wagons haul in freshly quarried stone from relatively far off Big Cottonwood Canyon. You might even hear talk of the new paper mill that was planned for a gully just below the mouth of that canyon.

There were few restaurants in the city, but if you walked down Main Street to First South you could pick up the distinct smell of fresh loaves coming out of the Globe Bakery ovens. You might hope that was the only smell you would notice, as sewage and waste-disposal systems had not been developed. Also, if you picked up the scent of smoke there could be trouble. The volunteer fire department would have to scramble to assemble together after hearing the bell toll an alarm. They then needed to fire up the boiler on their pump wagon and rush to pull the rig by hand through the heart of the city, hoping the fire would be close enough to an irrigation ditch that their hoses would reach a water source.

Follow the wall around Brigham Young's compound back to the heart of the city. If the weather was nice and

Ogden, Utah Territory, c. 1868. (USHS)

In the late 1860s Ogden was a relatively quiet town with simple storefronts and the irritation of muddy streets after a rainstorm. But just over the horizon was a force ready to transform the city into one of the most diverse and dynamic centers of the territory. Ogden, and the entire Utah territory, would never be the same after the railroad came to town.

his schedule permitted, the president of the Mormon church might step out of his office in the Beehive House, carefully press a top hat in place, pull on gloves, and saunter off with his walking stick. A softly pronounced "a" would work its way from his Vermont roots into his "Good Mahrnin'" greeting as he passed by.

That wouldn't be the most unusual greeting you would hear. If you walked four blocks south to a public square, you could see one of the bi-monthly wagon trains of immigrants arrive after a three-month overland journey to Utah. Mormon translators would be scurrying about trying to round-up the Danish, Swedish, or German emigrants. Or you might hear hundreds of voices sharing the same distinctively accented English of Liverpool. Every arriving wagon train shared its own unique stories of the members lost on the trip to the new homeland.

Turning back to look at the city it took you less than five minutes to walk across, you would see the Salt Lake Theatre dominating the skyline, dust filling the air from wagons in summer, or woodsmoke forming a blanket of haze in winter. Looking south, you would see the entire length of the Salt Lake Valley before you, one solitary dirt roadway stretching out to the distance and the two-day journey to Provo.

Top: Volunteer fire fighters, Salt Lake City, c. 1870. (USHS)

Above: Big Cottonwood paper mill, date unknown. (USHS)

Above: Warm Springs Bath House, 1860. (USHS)

The end of the Civil War was viewed by the Mormons as an opportunity to check the anti-Mormon sentiment that had been reflected in the Morrill Act passed at the height of the conflict. The admission of Nevada as a state and the recognition of Colorado as a territory had dramatically trimmed the Utah Territory land mass, leaving the remaining territory both more populated and better organized than any other potential state. Church leaders decided to challenge Congress to repeal the Morrill Act and pave the way for statehood for Utah.

But again the political climate was grossly miscalculated. After being approached by the Mormon delegation, instead of repealing the Morrill Act, a number of members of Congress demanded an investigation into why the law was not being vigorously enforced. Anti-Mormon bills were soon introduced in Congress, including one ambitious law proposing to cut Utah into three pieces to be distributed to other states. These bills, however, were turned aside or stalled in the legislative process, just as Utah's bid for statehood stalled without a champion.

But not all of the perceived challenges to the Kingdom of God were external in nature. The 1860s also produced a string of internal movements challenging the established authority in the Mormon church.

Below far left: John Dawson, Territorial Governor of Utah, 1861. (USHS)

A native of Indiana, Dawson was appointed by President Abraham Lincoln to serve as governor after Alfred Cumming completed his term and left the territory. In less than a month, the former Indiana newspaperman managed to do everything wrong. He delivered a lengthy speech to the legislature which the all-Mormon body viewed as offensive to their religion and dangerously supportive of high taxes. Dawson then attempted to seduce a young widow and offered a bribe to a reporter to hush up his indiscretion. He finally bolted from the territory, but he encountered a relative of the widow's at a stage stop while he was still in Utah. He was severely beaten, and hobbled out of the territory a disgraced and injured man.

Left: Stephen Harding, Territorial Governor of Utah, 1862. (USHS)

Many of the inhabitants of the territory were certain that anybody would be an improvement over John Dawson as territorial governor. They soon changed that opinion with the appointment by Lincoln in 1862 of Stephen Harding. Starting slowly, Harding soon developed into a caustic critic of the Mormon practice of polygamy and the interrelationship of church and state in the Utah territory. While the small non-Mormon population cheered him on, Harding became the target of numerous, angry mass meetings of Mormons demanding his removal. Anxious to avoid another internecine conflict while the Civil War raged in the east, Lincoln packed Harding off to Colorado, where he served as territorial chief justice until he was removed from office for alleged acts of immorality.

Brigham Young (seated, middle, with top hat) in southern Utah, 1870. (USHS)

By the end of the Civil War Brigham Young had been removed as territorial governor, been targeted by Congress with the Morrill Anti-Bigamy Act, and been faced with ongoing confrontations with the army under General Connor. Yet he was clearly in control of Utah Territory and remained capable of shaping the will of the people. His visits to settlements throughout the territory were significant events for the local townsfolk. Often welcomed with banners, Young was viewed as the embodiment of the Mormons' determination to defend the faith and resist any and all efforts to loosen their control of the territory they had settled.

House of Representatives, Utah Territorial Legislature, 1866. (USHS)

As with all previous sessions of the legislature, the first session after the end of the Civil War was entirely Mormon—an unsurprising profile, since the voting population in the territory remained over ninety-five percent Mormon. Two future presidents of the LDS church served in the House that year: John Taylor as speaker (top) and a young Joseph F. Smith as a representative from Salt Lake (middle row, far left). This group, like several other legislative sessions, would reconvene as the shadow government of Deseret immediately after their adjournment as the territorial legislature. Recognizing Brigham Young as governor, the shadow government would repass all laws created in their legislative session as a means of sanctioning the legislative efforts and removing from them the taint of connection with the federally appointed governor, thus providing the authority to build the Kingdom of God on Earth under the guiding hand of Young. The practice was abandoned by the 1870s.

The so-called "Josephite" movement was actually evangelical proselytizing work done in the name of sons of Joseph Smith who had broken with Brigham Young in a leadership struggle in the wake of Smith's murder in 1844. The movement emerged as the Reorganized Church of Jesus Christ of Latter Day Saints, and in 1864 more than 300 Salt Lake Valley Mormons converted their allegiance to the leadership of their murdered prophet's son Joseph Smith III. Threats and persecution in the valley forced the group to emigrate eastward, leaving Utah under the protection of an armed guard provided by General Connor. Much to the chagrin of Utah Mormon leaders, the missionaries from the "Josephites" would return to the valley in the future and secure additional converts.

The sons of Joseph Smith—David, Frederick, Alexander, and Joseph III—with Lewis Bidamon (far left), second husband of Emma Smith, c. 1860.

Following the death of Mormon church founder Joseph Smith in 1844, a number of his sons refused to follow the leadership of Brigham Young and forged their own gathering, which they considered the true embodiment of the teachings of their father. By the 1860s the group, headquartered in Missouri and known as the Reorganized Church of Jesus Christ of Latter Day Saints, was under the leadership of Joseph Smith III. Smith sent missionaries to Utah, which irritated the local Mormon leaders. More than three hundred converts were secured in a matter of months. However, the tension between the groups made coexistence impossible, and the converts soon left for Missouri to join the other followers of Joseph Smith III.

Above: Robert Taylor Burton, date unknown. (USHS)

Left: The Niels Anderson family, Idaho, c. 1890. (USHS)

Shown in his territorial militia uniform late in life, Burton was at the head of the posse sent to arrest Joseph Morris, a charismatic Mormon who claimed in 1862 to have divine inspiration to lead the people in Utah. The subsequent bloody showdown left Morris and a few followers dead and a number of others wounded, including the young wife of Niels Anderson, Mary, who had her lower jaw blown off by an errant cannonball fired by the posse. Burton was reported to have shot an unarmed woman who attempted to intervene. Seventy so-called Morrisites were arrested on a variety of charges stemming from the stand-off with the posse, but anti-Mormon Governor Stephen Harding pardoned the group and had them escorted peacefully from the territory. Many settled in Idaho. An aggressive federal prosecutor would eventually charge Burton with murder as a result of the incident, but a conviction was never secured.

While the dissent produced by the "Josephites" was uncomfortable, the "Morrisite" movement of 1862 actually erupted into violence in the territory. Joseph Morris began reporting prophetic visions in 1857, identifying Brigham Young as a fallen prophet and declaring an imminent end to the world. By

William Godbe, c. 1865. (USHS)

One of the ten wealthiest men in Utah Territory in the 1860s, William Godbe was constantly pressing the Mormon church to abandon the vision for a communitarian-based society and embrace instead open economic competition and allow free enterprise to drive the economic future of the territory. In the process, Godbe and a group of like-thinking businessmen, soon derisively labeled "Godbeites" by church authorities, became open advocates of social and cultural diversity and championed local integration with the national political and economic systems. Godbe's business building on Main Street soon became a gathering spot for like-minded businessmen. Even after the Mormon church excommunicated Godbe and a handful of others, the group continued its economic and political activism, often establishing connections with the rapidly expanding non-Mormon population of the territory.

Main Street, Salt Lake City, 1870, with the Godbe Building on the left. (USHS)

NEWSPAPERS IN EARLY UTAH TERRITORY

For fifteen years following its initial publication in 1850 the *Deseret News* had been virtually the only source of news in Utah Territory. A distinctly alternative view of events appeared in the early 1860s when General Connor created the *Union Vedette* at Camp Douglas under the early editorship of Charles Hempstead. The *Vedette* unashamedly promoted mining in the territory and unabashedly challenged Mormon political control. In January 1870 the *Mormon Tribune* emerged, succeeding an earlier magazine effort and bolstered by the financial backing of William Godbe. While clearly offering a differing view of events from that of the church-owned *Deseret News*, the *Tribune* did not adopt a strident tone until Godbe sold his interest in the 1870s and the new owners launched a vigorous anti-Mormon crusade.

Charles Hempstead, editor, the *Union Vedette*, 1865. (USHS)

The *Mormon Tribune* office, Salt Lake City, 1870. (USHS)

1862 more than 500 followers had gathered with Morris north of Salt Lake City in Weber County. Believing that Morris was actually holding his followers against their will, a 500-man posse set out to serve a writ on Morris. "Warning shots" were fired by artillery brought along by the posse, which now looked more like an organized army. The warning shots killed two women and wounded others. A few days later, while negotiating surrender, Morris himself was shot and killed by the posse. His followers surrendered and were eventually escorted out of Utah Territory, again by an accommodating General Patrick Connor.

LDS Temple construction site, Salt Lake City, 1868. (USHS)

Fifteen years after groundbreaking the Salt Lake LDS Temple was beginning to take recognizable shape. The marked granite blocks in the foreground were slated for disposal due to imperfections, reflecting the exacting design of Truman O. Angell and the masons' dedication to detail. Oxcarts were used to move the quarried granite around the construction site, and hanging wooden racks could be lowered and then raised on pulleys to lift the blocks into position.

Mormon church leaders, 1868. (USHS)

Perhaps the earliest existing group photograph showing the First Presidency and Quorum of the Twelve leadership councils of the Church of Jesus Christ of Latter-day Saints. Brigham Young is seated in the center, flanked (on the left) by his counselors George A. Smith and (on the right) Daniel H. Wells, who was also mayor of Salt Lake City. The photo was taken outdoors against a canvas backdrop raised in the backyard of the Beehive House.

THE DESERET ALPHABET

Deseret First Reader, 1868.
(USHS)

The Deseret Alphabet was an effort by Brigham Young to reform the English language and make its mastery easier for non-English-speaking converts to Mormonism. Despite pursuing his dream of a simpler way of writing and reading for more than thirty years, Young never saw the system embraced, and it essentially passed away with him in the 1870s.

Built around the work done by British linguist Isaac Pitman, the alphabet's prime aim was to get around the multiple sounds a vowel could express in written English. Advocated by Young as early as 1850, the Board of Regents of the University of Deseret was given the job of creating the alphabet in 1852. The next year the group came forward with a system of thirty-eight characters that made up the alphabet. The first printing in the new alphabet was not issued until 1868, when the *Deseret First Reader* appeared as an effort to introduce supple young minds to the concept. In 1869 the *Book of Mormon* was published in the alphabet.

In practice the Deseret Alphabet was confusing, complex, and a failure—a fate met by dozens of other attempts to reform the English writing system. The failure of the Deseret Alphabet also meant that Mormons would not have a unique writing system of their own and that they would continue to use the language of the national majority—a fact which helped them later in the accommodation process of achieving statehood.

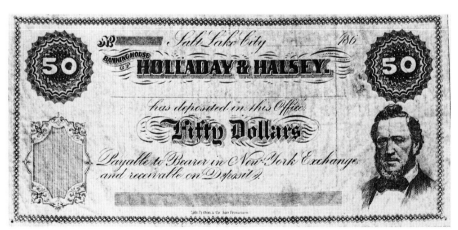

Deseret Alphabet, 1868.
(USHS)

Samuel Clemens (Mark Twain), 1871.
(NARA)

In 1861, twenty-six-year-old Samuel Clemens tagged along when his brother Orion was appointed secretary for the new Territory of Nevada. They stopped in Salt Lake City for a few days, much to the delight of the writer of future classics such as *The Adventures of Huckleberry Finn*. When he finally wrote about the experience ten years later in *Roughing It*, Twain embroidered his brief stay into a fanciful

Negotiable certificate of deposit, Holladay and Halsey Bank, 1860s. (USHS)

Gold coins minted in 1849 from gold dust brought from California by members of the Mormon Battalion were the first currency produced in Utah Territory—a time when the populace still considered it the State of Deseret. By the 1860s, federal officials were increasingly uneasy with Mormon attempts to fashion a workable, internal currency system for the territory, and finally took steps to outlaw the practice. This created difficulty for the cash-poor Mormon church, which had used its previous currency issues as scrip to keep the local economy moving. It also complicated matters outside of the territory, where businesses were reluctant to extend credit to church representatives. One of the answers to the problem was the negotiable certificate of deposit, which a bank could issue affirming that a certain amount of hard money was on deposit and that the certificate could be redeemed at face value from a reputable banking house. Similar to the contemporary traveler's cheque, the Holladay & Halsey certificate's design left little doubt as to who stood symbolically behind the transaction.

profile of life among the Mormons. *"There was fascination in surreptitiously staring at every creature we took to be a Mormon. This was a fairyland to us...a land of enchantment, and goblins, and awful mystery. We felt a fascination to ask every child how many mothers it had, and if it could tell them apart; and we experienced a great thrill every time a dwelling house door opened...for we so longed to have a good satisfying look at a Mormon family in all its comprehensive ampleness..."* —Mark Twain, *Roughing It*, 1871

The third movement of dissent was less spiritual in nature, and it was a decided foreshadowing of major changes that would take place in the social, political, and economic future of Utah as it progressed toward statehood. A convert to Mormonism, William Godbe had been viewed by many in the territory as bright, industrious, and a protégé of Brigham Young. However, by the late 1860s, Godbe and other like-minded thinkers ("Godbeites") started to break with Brigham's tight control of the economic and political power in Utah. At first gently, then with a bluntness seldom seen in church members, they challenged the communitarian and commonwealth themes of Mormonism. They formed their own periodical, the *Utah Magazine*, to express their

Above: Advertisment for the Walker Brothers Store, c. 1868. (USHS)

The four Walker brothers (Samuel S., Joseph R., David F., and Matthew H.) were traveling salesmen in the Utah territory upon their arrival as Mormon immigrants in 1852. They opened their first store in 1859 in Fairfield to serve the troops at Camp Floyd. A sidelight of the business was the store safe that was used to secure valuables for customers and proved to be the start of a banking enterprise. By the 1860s the brothers had prospered and opened a large general merchandise store in the heart of Salt Lake City. They soon disagreed with Mormon leadership over the newly instituted practice of paying ten percent of their earnings as a contribution, or tithe, to the church. The brothers asked to be removed from church membership and Brigham Young complied, raising the stakes by telling church members to boycott the Walker brothers' store. The brothers eventually joined with William Godbe in a number of projects aimed as challenging church control of the territory, including the founding of the Liberal political party in the 1870s.

Main Street, Salt Lake City, 1869. (USHS)

While horses have received much of the wagon-pulling credit, it was not unusual to see ox teams pulling wagons into Salt Lake City in the 1860s. Hearty longhorn breeds fared best on such duty, and could provide interesting road hazards if they decided to lie down for a rest in the middle of Main Street. Among the businesses shown in the photograph is the store of merchant Nicholas Ransohoff. Soon to emerge as one of the West's most successful merchants, Ransohoff was a Jew who developed a cordial working relationship with the Mormons. He even invested in the Mormon cooperative mercantile venture that would become known by its initials, ZCMI.

Left: Salt Lake City, looking south, 1869. (USHS)

From a vantage point on Arsenal Hill, in the Avenues area in present-day Salt Lake City, the view south in 1869 reveals the recently completed Tabernacle and the early work on the Temple. Main Street runs through the near foreground, and the vast agricultural landscape, beginning just four or five blocks south of the city center, reaches out to the Oquirrh Mountains in the distance.

JOHN WESLEY POWELL IN UTAH TERRITORY

John Wesley Powell, scientist and explorer, completed two epic journeys down the Green and Colorado rivers that provided initial work in mapping the rivers and in understanding the geology of the Colorado Plateau.

After losing his right arm as a Union officer at the Civil War battle of Shiloh, Powell returned to military service and earned promotion to the rank of major. He returned to his career interest in the natural sciences at the end of the war and worked with the faculties of Midwestern universities. Powell first came to the West in 1867 and did preliminary research on the Rocky Mountains and the river systems of the region. In 1869 he undertook the adventure of a lifetime that would secure his place in the annals of western exploration. Leading largely untrained men in wooden boats, Powell embarked from the town of Green River in Wyoming Territory in May 1869. Traveling through the often turbulent canyons of the Green River, his boats and men eventually entered the Colorado

River at the confluence in present-day San Juan County, Utah. They undertook the first documented navigation of the rapids through the river's canyons, including the Grand Canyon. Three men who left the expedition were killed by Indians, and two of the party's wooden boats were destroyed by the river.

Returning in 1871–72, Powell found the Colorado River at a much higher level due to a deep snowpack the previous winter. As with his first expedition, he carefully charted the territory and named landmarks along the way. His observations resulted in three influential books. He used his popularity as an explorer and later head of the U.S. Geological Survey to impress upon decision-makers the need for wise management of the natural resources of the semiarid West, emphasizing the need for standards different from those employed in the east. His only child was born in Salt Lake City in 1871, as his wife accompanied him to the Territory of Utah.

Second Powell Expedition, Green River, 1872. (NARA)

Powell Expedition boats and supply wagons, 1872. (NARA)

Right: Southeast Salt Lake City, 1869. (USHS)

views, and then converted it to a newspaper format as the *Mormon Tribune*. After the refusal of Godbe and his followers to heed repeated warnings to temper their criticism and activities, Mormon church leaders excommunicated the Godbeite leaders on October 25, 1869.

At first viewed as a "counter-religion" to Mormonism, the Godbeite movement soon lost many of the trappings of a religious organization. Instead, it actively promoted political, social, and economic diversity, free enterprise,

Brigham Young's Schoolhouse, 1867. (USHS)

Twenty years after the pioneers entered the Salt Lake Valley education in Utah Territory remained wildly inconsistent. There was no uniform school system for children, and teaching was left to the most willing, if the not the most qualified, person in each community or neighborhood. Often the teachers would hold classes in local Mormon church buildings and use religious texts to teach reading to the children—a not uncommon practice in mid-nineteenth-century America. The teachers often would set their own tuition rates per child, since the schools were not supported by public taxes. It was not unusual for a child to leave school for extended periods of time in the face of farming responsibilities or financial difficulties that prevented parents from paying tuition. Teachers were often paid in crops, produce, or livestock.

Brigham Young, the wealthiest man in the territory, placed a high priority on education for his children, and constructed his own schoolhouse in his compound. Sometimes employing a paid teacher, sometimes utilizing one of Young's plural wives, the school could accommodate as many as twenty children. Young occasionally would invite other people's children to attend the school if other facilities were not available.

John R. Park, President, University of Deseret, 1869. (USHS)

Although the pioneers valued education enough to attempt to create a university in 1850, by 1865 the University of Deseret existed in little more than name only. Virtually without public financial support, the school took a significant step forward when the energetic and well-educated John R. Park took over leadership of the university in 1869. For the next fifteen years the school would hold classes in a series of temporary homes, but it would not have a formal graduation until 1886.

Left: Morgan College, Salt Lake City, 1868. (USHS)

Private attempts at "higher education" came and went in the territory. For a brief time a storefront advertised itself as a medical school in northern Utah, but it soon closed its doors in the face of failing confidence from students and patients. Morgan College in Salt Lake City offered business-training courses. Although a far cry from present-day expectations of college-level coursework, the school did provide clerical and accounting classes to help serve the needs of area merchants.

and a more full and complete social and economic integration with the rest of the country. Often portrayed as soured dissenters from the mainstream of Mormonism, William Godbe and his followers would eventually be viewed as the first voices in a new movement that dawned with the driving of the final spike of the transcontinental railroad at Utah's Promontory Point in 1869.

As the decade closed, change was in the air. Unity and cohesion, hallmarks during the early years of life in the Utah Territory, were about to give way to sharpened debate conducted by new voices.

A Mormon family, illustration in a German publication, 1860s. (USHS)

The Mormon settlement in the American West captured the fascinated attention of much of the world. Correspondents for newspapers throughout Europe filed dispatches from this unique community that seemed to both defy and perplex its national government as it followed the dictates of its religion. This engraving, from an unidentified periodical of the late 1860s, shows how a German audience might come to view the Mormons. The frontier domestic scene is highlighted by the tranquil presence of a pipe-smoking Mormon patriarch, his wives, and numerous children. Another family in the distance is moving to stake its claim on nearby lands in the shadow of the mountains.

Collaborative farming, Utah Territory, date unknown. (USHS)

Farmer helping neighboring farmer at times of planting and harvesting has been an American tradition. Utah, with its emphasis on shared effort for the common good, elevated collaborative farming to a high level. By the 1860s most suitable land throughout the state had been divided from common community plots into individual parcels, with some notable exceptions (to be considered next chapter). But, even with the rise of individual farming, there was a sharing of equipment and a pooling of labor to successfully complete the tasks of planting and harvesting, thus reducing the challenge of farming in one of the nation's most arid territories.

Main Street, looking northwest, Salt Lake City, 1869. (USHS)

Chapter Five

AN ERA OF CHANGE
1869–1879

The great Chicago fire levels that city....Susan B. Anthony is arrested for attempting to vote....The first national park is opened at Yellowstone....A.G. Bell invents the telephone; Edison invents electrical lighting....Custer dies at the Battle of the Little Big Horn....Tolstoy writes *War and Peace*....Stanley finds Livingstone in Africa....The population of the United States is 39,818,449.

ON MAY 10, 1869, THE FINAL SPIKE WAS HAMMERED into place on the transcontinental railroad on the isolated flats near Promontory Point in Utah Territory. Anticipated for years, and considered the engineering feat of the century, the dramatic linking of East and West in the nation's most isolated

Below: First South Street, Salt Lake City, 1872. (USHS)
    The Salt Lake Theatre dominated the scene from its location on State Street as one looked east along First South in the 1870s.

Linking of the transcontinental railroad, Promontory, Utah, May 10, 1869. (USHS)
"The days of isolation are now forever past. We thank God for it."
—The Deseret News

The Union Pacific and Central Pacific railroad crews raced into Utah Territory, and actually went past each other before Congress intervened to instruct the ambitious and greedy lines to link near Promontory Point. There was much symbolism, and some irony, in the nation's railroad reaching its completion in isolated Utah Territory.

Anti-immigration cartoon, California, c. 1870. (LOC)

A morbid distrust of foreigners gripped the nation in the 1870s, frequently aimed at the Chinese in California and Irish Catholic emigrants in the east. The fear that was played upon so effectively by the media, including this White & Bauer illustration from the era, was often extended to European Mormons emigrating to Utah Territory.

inland territory served as a tangible sign of Utah's integration with the rest of the nation. No other single development would have a more enduring effect on the people, lifestyles, and future of Utah during the nineteenth century.

Lives were made better overnight. The cost of clothes and other goods, previously imported by overland freight wagons, dropped by half. Immigra-

THE RAILROAD COMES TO UTAH TERRITORY

Other than the original Mormon trek westward, no single event transformed the region and its inhabitants as did the coming of the railroad. Suddenly, goods from the east and west were cheaper, immigrants could travel to Utah in a fraction of the time that it took on the overland route, and Utah's economy would surge because of the new opportunity to ship ore out of the territory. The local social structure also soon underwent dramatic changes— thousands of new faces arriving in the territory added a diversity largely lacking in the years prior to 1869.

The town of Promontory, Utah Territory, 1869. (USHS)

Union Pacific track crews, Utah-Wyoming border, 1868. (UU)

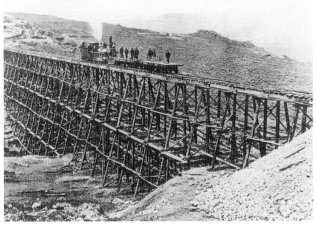

Union Pacific track crews at bridge and trestlework in northern Utah, 1868. (USHS)

Grading Weber Canyon, Union Pacific R.R., 1868. (USHS)

Union Pacific Locomotive #117, Ogden Depot, 1869. (USHS)

tion entered a new and streamlined era, with converts to the Mormon church being able to finish a trip from the eastern seaboard in a matter of days instead of the months required just ten years before. News and mail provided a closer link to events of the world, allowing residents of the territory to read with interest of the completion of the Suez Canal, or with concern that the national debt had reached the daunting amount of two dollars per person in the wake of the Civil War.

The Merchants Exchange, Salt Lake City, 1871. (USHS)

A saloon in the heart of Salt Lake City, the Merchants Exchange was at the center of a pivotal event in the territory. Ordered by the city's Mormon leaders to teach the club a lesson for its refusal to pay a license fee, Police Chief Andrew Burt led a raid against the Exchange in 1871, cracking open kegs of beer and cases of hard liquor. The club's owner, Paul Englebrecht, challenged the legality of the raid, and a federal court jury packed with non-Mormons ruled in his favor. The case was appealed all the way to the U.S. Supreme Court, with the Court issuing new guidelines for the fair administration of justice in the territory. Congress later would attempt to tamper with that decision through the Poland Act.

CORINNE, UTAH TERRITORY

The town of Corinne could be considered a dedicated effort on the part of non-Mormon businessmen to swing economic and political power away from the Mormon church in the territory. Brought to life by the coming of the railroad in 1869, the town was originally briefly called Connor, after outspoken Mormon critic General Patrick Edward Connor at Camp Douglas. Developed as a freight transfer point to unload rail cars and shift the goods to southbound wagons for the seventy-mile trip to Salt Lake City or northward to the expanding markets of Montana, Corinne soon boasted a population of 1,000. Townsfolk also boasted that not one of the residents belonged to the Mormon church. Among its amenities, besides a newspaper, the town had fifteen saloons and as many liquor stores, and soon developed a reputation as a wild railroad town despite the efforts of the permanent residents to maintain order.

Anti-Mormon elements tried to use Corinne as a lever to increase their political power. They petitioned Washington to formally move the capital from Salt Lake City to their new town, and they convinced a member of Congress to introduce a bill that would divide Utah and assign the northern portion to Idaho. While both measures failed, they represented the new, combative era of politics that had dawned in the territory.

Brigham Young's astute building of railroads to serve the north-south needs of the region soon spelled the demise of Corinne as a power center. Merchants from the town gradually moved to Ogden, but they continued their efforts to raise an independent political voice.

Corinne, Utah Territory, 1870. (USHS)

The *Daily Reporter* newspaper office, Corinne, 1870. (USHS)

OTHER RELIGIOUS DENOMINATIONS COME TO UTAH TERRITORY

"In a conversation with President Young he has assured me no minister, nor anyone else, who would come here and mind their own business need have the slightest fear of being disturbed by Mormons..." —Warren Hussey, letter to the Rt. Rev. Daniel S. Tuttle, March 13, 1867

At first they came as tentative clerics to serve small gatherings of their faithful. Within a few years a dozen religious denominations were flourishing in the Utah territory and increasingly turning their attention to missionary and salvation work among the Mormon people.

While a Catholic presence in the region could legitimately be traced in history to the exploration caravan of Francisco de Coronado in 1540, religious worship in Utah apart from the Mormon faith was informal and private prior to the 1860s. The coming of the California Volunteers, the mining boom, and the completion of the railroad provided the area with a dramatic infusion of people from different religious backgrounds.

Missionary Bishop Daniel Tuttle is credited with creating the first regular non-Mormon church services when he sent two young ministers to Salt Lake City just ahead of his arrival in 1867.

Within three

Reverend Daniel Tuttle, Episcopal church, Utah Territory, 1870. (USHS)

years the Episcopal faith had established an active presence in the community and opened its first denominational school, St. Mark's, while beginning construction on a cathedral to bear the same name.

The first Roman Catholic parish in Salt Lake City was formed in 1866 by Reverend Edward Kelly. Territory Catholics rallied in 1873 to the tireless efforts of Reverend Lawrence Scanlon, who rode a circuit through the mining and rail camps of Utah in an effort to serve his religion. Scanlon would also encourage the opening of Catholic parochial schools and would work to provide medical care to the injured. Scanlon would become the first bishop of the Utah archdiocese in 1886.

A broad range of denominations soon established themselves in the territory, often under the banner of missionaries to the Mormons. Methodist and Presbyterian services started in 1869, and the first Jewish rabbi arrived in town in 1873. Many of the clerics earnestly proclaimed their desire to redeem the Mormon people from ways that embraced polygamy. These denominations would become powerful voices in the national dialogue over the future of Utah Territory that would dominate the next two decades.

Rev. Lawrence Scanlon, Roman Catholic church, Utah Territory, 1873. (USHS)

Looking north from First South, Salt Lake City, 1871. (USHS)

St. Mary Magdalene Catholic church dominates this view of the sparsely inhabited blocks east of State Street. Directly across the street from the church are the stables of the Wells-Fargo Company, serving the territory as a stage and freight line. In the 1870s much of the land near the heart of the city was used for residences, but their large yards permitted the raising of ample quantities of garden produce.

The steel rail link to the world also changed the political, social, and economic life of the territory. Efficient transportation lit the fuse on a mining boom in Utah by allowing for the mining and transportation of lower grade ores and minerals. Small-scale claims first staked under Colonel Connor's encouragement gave way to a massive infusion of national and foreign investment to build bigger, more productive mines in the Wasatch and Oquirrh mountains. The mining districts of Park City, Big Cottonwood, and Tintic soon were producing millions of dollars worth of silver and gold ore each year.

Thousands of new faces poured into Utah to cash in on the mining boom. Miners, merchants, land speculators, financiers, lawyers, and roustabouts created new boomtowns and changed the face of existing cities. With increasing frequency voices were raised to counter and challenge Mormon political control. The *Mormon Tribune* changed hands, was renamed the *Salt Lake Tribune*, and became a fierce critic of the ways and means of life in Utah Territory under an alleged theocracy. Both economic and social life in the territory often divided along religious lines.

THE MORMON COOPERATIVE AND UNITED ORDER MOVEMENTS IN UTAH TERRITORY

The cooperative movement in Utah was a concerted effort by Brigham Young and other Mormon church leaders to maintain economic control over the territory for what Young perceived as the best interests of the members of the Mormon church. He feared the inflation that had gripped other western cities, and he wanted stores and businesses to agree to keep prices down and to band together for increased buying power. A number of observers claimed he was also making a bid to crush non-Mormon businesses. By 1876 the various approved businesses were gathering under one roof, soon to emerge as the nation's first department store under the banner of ZCMI. In smaller towns, the cooperative store would remain a vital trading point for the local populace.

A dramatic offshoot of the drive for economic control was the emergence of the United Order movement in numerous locations in the territory in the 1870s. In its most extreme form the United Order was essentially communistic, but its variants assumed many forms throughout the territory. The cooperative movement was modified and the United Order concept abandoned after the death of Brigham Young.

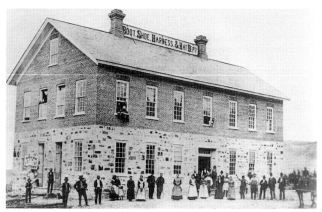

Shoe factory, Brigham City, c. 1870. (USHS)

Brigham City, a United Order town, c. 1870. (USHS)

Lorenzo Snow, civic and spiritual leader of Brigham City, 1870. (USHS)

Cooperative stores, Main Street, Salt Lake City, 1868. (USHS)

J.K. Trumbo Auction House, 1869. (LDS)

By the late 1860s businesses in the heart of Salt Lake City were clearly divided between church-approved cooperative stores and gentile-run independent businesses. The Mormon church stamped a "seal of approval" on the front of stores consenting to join the Zion's Cooperative Mercantile Institution (ZCMI). Non-Mormon stores soon witnessed a dramatic drop in business as church members refused to patronize shops not bearing the all-seeing eye of the ZCMI placard. One non-Mormon businessman, auctioneer J.K. Trumbo, countered by placing his own religious seal over his storefront.

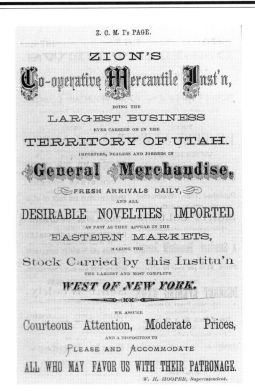

Left: Zion's Cooperative Mercantile Institution advertisement, c. 1880. (USHS)
Bottom left: Cooperative store, Cedar City, c. 1880. (USHS)
Above right: Cooperative store, Orderville, 1880. (USHS)
Below right: Cooperative store, Spanish Fork, 1880. (USHS)

NEWSPAPERS IN UTAH TERRITORY

From its inception, the *Tribune* viewed itself as a necessary voice of balance in Utah. However, that "balance" produced some of the most heated moments of argument and outright battle in the years prior to the admission of the territory to statehood.

Brought to life in January 1870 as a resurrection of the recently deceased *Utah Magazine*, which the *Deseret News* had counseled Mormons to boycott, the *Mormon Tribune* featured the writing talents of Edward Tullidge and was supported by the money and philosophy of William Godbe. Immediately perceived as the voice of the "Godbeite" movement challenging church control of economic and social life, the *Tribune* became the champion of Utah's first political party, the Liberal party, in 1870.

Strained from the outset, the relationship between the *Tribune* and the Mormon church ruptured in 1873 when the Godbe group sold the paper to a Kansas partnership. The *Tribune* and the church-owned *Deseret News* soon were engaged in an on-going slugfest, with *Tribune* editor Frederic Lockley seeing little need for restraint in his attacks against Brigham Young, polygamy, and the Mormons in general. In 1878 Lockley was beaten senseless with brass knuckles by a gang of "unknown assailants."

The relationship between Mormons and the *Tribune* fared only slightly better when the paper passed to the editorial stewardship of C.C. Goodwin in 1880. Goodwin bought out the Kansas partnership in 1883, managed to slightly cool the conflict with the *Deseret News*, and put his full effort behind pushing for equal political opportunity for non-Mormons in the territory. Reluctant to back statehood because of fear that the loss of congressional oversight would allow Mormons to crush their gentile political opponents, the *Tribune* eventually joined the *Deseret News* in supporting admission.

Frederic Lockley, *Tribune* editor, c. 1880. (USHS)

Salt Lake Tribune office, Salt Lake City, c. 1900. (USHS)

C.C. Goodwin, politician and *Tribune* editor, 1880. (USHS)

While quick to perceive the benefits of the transcontinental railroad, Brigham Young was also wary of the tidal wave of transformation that was engulfing the Kingdom of God. Committed to maintaining the economic integrity of his people, Young encouraged a boycott of non-Mormon merchants, supported the creation of large cooperative stores such as Zion's Cooperative Mercantile Institution, and backed dramatic social experiments in anti-capitalism, communalism, and self-sufficiency under the banner of the United Order.

A relatively benign form of Christian socialism, the United Order took on different trappings in various locations. All, however, shared the principles of economic self-sufficiency, responsibility to the community, and a deep religious commitment. In Brigham City this produced a "corporate approach" that was built around community-owned-and-operated businesses. In Orderville personal property was consecrated to the local church organization and then was redistributed according to need. This type of committed communitarianism included the construction of similar styles of homes and the communal sharing of meals in a single town dining hall. Although it was destined to lose favor in a different political climate during the 1880s, the United Order movement nonetheless served as an important religious and economic experiment in the rapidly changing Utah Territory of the 1870s.

But of even greater consequence to the territory's future and its dream of statehood was a dramatic shift in the political wind created by an increasingly diverse population. In 1870 Mormons constituted nearly ninety-five percent of the population in the territory, producing a cohesive and unified social environment effectively controlled at every stage by church leadership. But a rapid infusion of non-Mormon residents of Utah now joined the cast of federal territorial appointees in complaining about the church's political monopoly

Right: Ulysses S. Grant, eighteenth president of the United States, 1870. (LOC)
Plagued with Reconstruction problems and allegations of rampant corruption in his administration, Grant—like other presidents—viewed a crackdown on Mormon polygamy as an issue that transcended politics. While never offering a firm plan of action, Grant repeatedly demanded that something be done about the "Mormon problem."

U.S. GRANT AND THE MORMON PROBLEM

"In Utah there still remains a remnant of barbarism repugnant to civilization, decency and to the laws of the United States....Neither polygamy nor any violation of existing statutes will be permitted within a territory of the United States." —Ulysses S. Grant, message to Congress, December 1871

Shortly after his election, Ulysses S. Grant returned the issue of polygamy to a lofty position in a presidential agenda it had not enjoyed since the early days of the Buchanan administration. With the end of the Civil War, Grant's Republican party was struggling with its past as well as its future. Having championed the abolition of slavery under Abraham Lincoln, the party recognized that polygamy, the "second relic of barbarism" from its party platform of 1856, was still in operation. The Republicans renewed their demand for an end to polygamy in their platform statement, committing Grant in the process to the eradication of plural marriage as a legitimate priority in the national agenda.

Congress added to the pressure on Grant to speak out. With the Civil War won, Congress was ready to aggressively attack plural marriage. When he railed against polygamy, Grant was basically "preaching to the choir,"

since numerous Republican members were ready to champion a broad range of laws targeting Utah and the Mormons. In effect, Grant was doing his best to rush in front of a body politic already on the move.

Public pressure created the hammer that pounded out a call for action against the Mormon church. The national media were publishing outrageous and often fabricated stories about the scandalous conditions in Utah Territory under a "savage polygamic theocracy." Respected religious figures were calling for armies to march on Utah for a bloody final solution. Grant could not ignore the public voice, nor could he ignore his own need for political capital. A hero in the Civil War, Grant was ridiculed and berated as president for inconsistencies, corruption in his administration, and a severe national economic crisis that hit in 1873. Harried on virtually every other issue, Grant knew he could draw applause whenever he lashed out at the image of polygamy's bondage in the American West.

Right: Political cartoon, Brigham Young and Grant, 1871.
The Mormon Problem Solved.
Brigham: "I must submit to your laws—but what shall I do with all these?"
U.S.G.: "Do as I do—give them offices." (LOC)

Ulysses Grant in Laramie, Wyoming, as he visits the West during his campaign for president, 1868. (USHS)

Vice-president Schuyler Colfax, 1870. (LOC)

Vice-president Schuyler Colfax and party, undisclosed location in Utah, 1869. (USHS)

Colfax visited Salt Lake City twice. On his first visit, in the 1860s, while he was still sitting as Speaker of the House, Colfax was marginally accommodating to the unique society he found in Utah. However, he did warn the population on several occasions that the territory could not ignore national laws on polygamy and expect to reap the benefits of statehood. On his second visit, in October 1869, Colfax was U.S. vice-president and made no effort to hide his scorn for the Mormon majority and its refusal to abandon plural marriage. Spending virtually every minute with the growing anti-Mormon population in the territory, Colfax's comments led a number of observers to wonder if the territory was on the brink of war with the national government.

Judge Obed F. Strickland, 1870. (USHS)

An appointee of Governor Shaffer, Judge Obed Strickland was openly hostile to the Mormon church and its members. A Mason, Strickland helped encourage membership in early Utah masonic organizations, yet he would adamantly refuse to consider Mormons for membership.

and control of government. The appointed territorial governors, passing through revolving doors with every partisan change in the White House, viewed themselves as largely powerless in their position aside from offering scathing reports on the practices of one-party politics and polygamy.

The political friction was certain to produce sparks. Vice-president Schuyler Colfax, using the new railroad to tour the West on a fact-finding mission, wondered out loud during a stop in Salt Lake City if war was inevitable between the United States and the Mormons. President Ulysses S. Grant condemned the Mormon church in his state of the nation addresses and in other public speeches. To carry out a promise to save the Mormon people from their leaders, Grant appointed a series of controversial and determined administrators to control the territory.

In one of his first acts, Governor J. Wilson Shaffer sought to disarm the Mormon church by banning drills or assemblies of the territorial militia, still affectionately known as the Nauvoo Legion. The ban stirred suspicions of an armed federal intervention and struck a deep chord in the Mormons, who had vowed to protect themselves in the wake of earlier persecutions in Missouri and Illinois. Ill when he took office, Shaffer died suddenly in October 1870, an event that was greeted with public celebrations and jeering "tributes" in local papers. To emphasize their determination to maintain local control, the Legion sent hundreds of members to the streets in "casual walks" that looked suspiciously like military formations, with many carrying canes over their shoulders in what became known as the "wooden rifle rebellion." Non-Mormons fumed at what they viewed as a direct affront to the United States and the power of the governor's office.

Mormon concerns with the military were sharpened when a riot broke out in Provo involving soldiers from newly established Camp Rawlins on the city's edge. Soldiers armed with their weapons and a good supply of pay-day liquor roared into town on an anti-Mormon spree. They trashed the local cooperative store and briefly seized a city official who, apparently wisely, had denied the soldiers use of a hall for a party. When cooler, or more sober, heads prevailed, the army quickly closed the camp and returned the soldiers to Camp Douglas in Salt Lake City.

Above: J. Wilson Shaffer, Utah Territorial Governor, 1870. (USHS)

Appointed by Grant as part of the president's intent to crush the rebellion he perceived in Utah, John Wilson Shaffer took office as governor in 1870 and within days was locked in a confrontation with the Mormon church. Shaffer viewed the territorial militia, still affectionately known in many circles as the Nauvoo Legion, as an illegal paramilitary organization loyal only to Brigham Young. His efforts to bar gatherings of the militia produced cries of protest from Mormons, many of whom viewed it as an attempt to disarm the territory prior to renewed federal intervention. When Shaffer died after only a few months in office, local newspapers offered mocking obituaries and cheered his passing.

Left: Governor Shaffer's anti-militia proclamation, 1870. (USAR)

On September 15, only days after arriving in Utah, Governor Shaffer dictated this proclamation banning gatherings of the Nauvoo Legion, ordering its members to relinquish their weapons, and barring them from serving in any law-enforcement capacity. Legion members virtually ignored the proclamation, especially the provision requiring them to take orders from noted anti-Mormon General P.E. Connor at Camp Douglas.

VIEWS OF TERRITORIAL LIFE

Much as in contemporary Utah, most of the political and economic news of the 1870s was centered in Salt Lake City. And, just like their modern counterparts, residents of the settlements outside of the capital city felt that their views and concerns too often were overlooked. Nearly 300 communities and settlements had been created in the first twenty-five years of settling Utah. Under the colonizing vision of Brigham Young, and sped along by the mining and railroad booms, the population of the territory had swelled to 86,000, more than doubling the 1860 census figures. Towns outside the Salt Lake Valley, frontier outposts just a few years before, now boasted general stores, banks, and an increasingly diverse population.

General store, Morgan, Utah Territory, c. 1870 (USHS)

Ogden, 1876. (USHS)

The Saddle Rock Restaurant, Ogden, c. 1880. (USHS)

Main Street, Richfield, 1876. (USHS)

C.R. Huntsman general store, Fillmore, c. 1890. (USHS)

Bank, Milford, c. 1880. (USHS)

The military tension was an outgrowth of a time in which political deliverance—the achievement of statehood—seemed to be moving further from Utah's grasp. With 90,000 residents and an extensive settlement and governing structure, Utah in 1870 was far ahead of many territories then being considered for admission to the Union. However, another constitution and petition for statehood were greeted with icy silence by President Grant and by Congress. Instead of admission, the news from Washington, D.C., was dominated by accounts of a new anti-polygamy law being pushed by Senator Shelby Cullom of Illinois as a means of attacking Mormonism. Mass rallies were staged in Utah and memorials were sent to Congress protesting the Cullom bill, many of them orchestrated by cadres of politically sophisticated Mormon women determined to block new attempts to persecute church members for their beliefs.

Above: Susan B. Anthony (left) and Elizabeth Cady Stanton, 1871. (LOC)

Susan B. Anthony and Elizabeth Cady Stanton, advocates for women's rights, visited Utah shortly after the legislature voted to give territorial women the opportunity to vote. During the course of their stay they held a five-hour meeting in the Tabernacle, urging women to use their new opportunity wisely and actively as an example to the nation. The two political leaders found themselves walking a fine line in Utah, since many principal suffragettes in the east were also outspoken critics of polygamy.

Left: Representative Women of Deseret, c. 1879. (USHS)

"*Greatness is usefulness...there is no limit to what we can accomplish.*" —Eliza Roxcy Snow

Eliza Roxcy Snow (center, top, under the crown) was author, poet, public-health advocate, and tireless civic worker. She reorganized the Mormon church's principal women's group, the Relief Society, at the request of Brigham Young in 1867. A plural wife of Mormon founder Joseph Smith, she married Brigham Young after Smith's death. This poster, dedicated to Snow, was printed in Utah and features many women active in the suffrage movement who were also strong public advocates of polygamy. Utah women secured the vote in 1870.

WOMEN'S SUFFRAGE IN UTAH TERRITORY

When the territorial legislature voted to give Utah women the right to vote in 1870, both sides of the divisive polygamy issue cheered the decision. Mormons had long afforded women participation rights in church votes, and were keenly aware that suffrage would double, perhaps triple, the Mormon vote in Utah Territory during this time of a great influx of non-Mormons. Anti-polygamist groups believed that the right to vote would be the key that would unlock the bondage of plural marriage for women in Utah.

Seraph Young, a niece of Brigham's, wasted little time in casting the first ballot by a Utah woman, voting in the Salt Lake City municipal elections of 1870.

The right to vote, which had been won without any organized public demonstration or petitioning of the legislature, would last for only fifteen years. National polygamy crackdowns, coupled with efforts to break perceived Mormon control of the Utah government, led to a series of proposals which began with efforts to ban plural wives from voting and culminated in an 1887 act that, in effect, rescinded the right of women to vote.

The rescission triggered Utah women into full activism on behalf of suffrage in the territory and throughout the nation. They actively participated in national suffrage meetings throughout the 1880s; by 1895 they had built an effective local network to advocate women's voting rights in the constitution being drafted for statehood. They succeeded:

> "...the rights of citizens of the State of Utah to vote or hold office shall not be denied or abridged on account of sex. Both male and female citizens of this state shall enjoy equally all civil, political and religious rights and privileges." —Article IV, Section 1, Utah State Constitution

Left: Susan B. Anthony with Utah suffrage leaders, 1870. (LDS)

Right: Seraph Young, Utah's first woman voter, c. 1880. (USHS)

At the peak of the clamor, the Utah Territorial Legislature passed a law that sent shock waves throughout the nation. Claiming the highest of democratic purposes, the legislature granted women of the territory the vote, joining Wyoming Territory as the nation's only political entities recognizing women as independent and legitimate political beings. Non-Mormons viewed the measure as a church trick but were split in their readings. One group, largely centered in Washington, saw the move as a welcome opportunity for women to use their newfound political power to loosen the enslaving shackles of plural marriage. But many non-Mormon Utah residents saw it as a thinly veiled move to double the Mormon vote, ensuring an enduring Mormon political hegemony in the territory. Regardless of the assigned motives, the granting of the vote to women won the approbation of national suffrage leaders Susan B. Anthony and Elizabeth Cady Stanton, who traveled to Utah to applaud the move.

George Woods, Utah Territorial Governor, 1871–75. (USHS)

Woods served a controversial four-year term, taking office upon the death of J. Wilson Shaffer. Conducting an aggressive campaign against polygamy, he also adopted Shaffer's stance prohibiting gatherings by the Nauvoo Legion. Members of the Legion flaunted the order barring them from drilling by gathering in formation and walking the streets with canes or brooms in their hands. The event soon became known as the "wooden rifle rebellion," and featured the local Mormon population snickering at the indignant response of Woods. Despite a cable from Woods to Washington proclaiming an insurrection in the works, cooler heads prevailed. Woods left the territory when Grant refused to reappoint him to a second term.

The Palace, Salt Lake City, 1872. (USHS)

J.B. Newman's Palace in the heart of Salt Lake City was a recognized stop for traveling miners and rail workers in Utah. Offering rooms, baths, a barbershop, and a saloon that seldom closed, the establishment at 18 Commercial Street flew a flag each day to stress the proprietor's loyalty to the national government.

Samuel Axtell, Utah Territorial Governor, 1875. (USHS)

A mild-mannered attorney from Ohio, Axtell served in Congress as a Democrat, then changed parties and was elected as a Republican. It was that affiliation that earned him an appointment by President Grant to serve as territorial governor of Utah. Axtell was targeted by anti-Mormon voices from his first week in the territory, after he thought it would be appropriate to pay a courtesy call on Mormon church leaders. The *Salt Lake Tribune* raised the roof, soon calling him "Bishop Axtell" and daily criticizing him for being a puppet of church leadership. Complaints from the non-Mormon community convinced Grant to reassess his appointment, and Axtell was apparently quite happy to be appointed territorial governor of New Mexico.

City Hall, Salt Lake City, 1873. (USHS)

This view of City Hall shows the latest addition to local street life—gas lamps. Limited to just a few blocks in the center of the city, the lamps were a first attempt at municipal lighting. Prior to this, individual businesses provided the only illumination of the streets, a situation that was often hazardous to those walking the wooden board-walks. Note the telegraph pole bending under the strain of at least twenty-two beams supporting dozens of lines into the downtown area.

George Emery, Utah Territorial Governor, 1875–80. (USHS)

Emery, a Reconstruction-era federal tax collector in the south prior to his appointment, used his experience working among a hostile population to win modest praise from Mormons and non-Mormons alike. Emery was able to advance some mild election reforms in the territory and increase government services to the expanding population. When his term ended in 1880 the territorial legislature named a newly created county in his honor.

Federal Judge James B. McKean, 1871. (USHS)

McKean served a short and stormy term as chief justice of the federal court for Utah Territory. Appointed as part of the early Grant campaign against the Mormons, McKean took to his task with an enthusiasm that delighted the local anti-Mormon element. Claiming it was his intent to crush "polygamic theocracy," McKean announced that he would accomplish the task by targeting Brigham Young. Using stacked anti-Mormon juries, outrageously questionable witnesses, and a determination bordering on religious fervor, McKean had Young brought up on charges of lewd and lascivious conduct; he also dusted off a twenty-year-old unsolved murder for additional charges against Young and other leading figures. McKean even sat as the initial judge in the divorce case filed by Ann Eliza Webb Young against Brigham, taking apparent delight in ordering the church leader to pay a heavy interim alimony. When Young refused to pay, McKean had the seventy-year-old church leader carted off to the territorial penitentiary for a night. Eventually the charges against Young and 130 others unfortunate enough to enter McKean's court were thrown out by the U.S. Supreme Court. President Grant then pulled McKean off the bench, citing his heavy-handed approach to the law.

The territory flirted with an outbreak of open warfare on Independence Day in 1871. Again seeking to establish local control over the militia, commanding officer Daniel H. Wells ordered the Nauvoo Legion to formation on July 4. Governor George Woods declared the gathering an act of rebellion and ordered troops from Camp Douglas to drive the Legion from their gathering place in Salt Lake City. With artillery reportedly trained on the site, the federal troops advanced with bayonets drawn. The Legion dispersed, never to be called back to active formation again. Church leaders and others, however, for some years would continue to lower flags to half-staff on national holidays as a gesture of protest and self-professed mourning for the loss of their rights.

Governor Woods promised that his use of the troops was only a prelude to a greater struggle for control of the territory, and he believed that the major battles would be fought in the federal courts. In pursuing this strategy he had a willing ally in territorial chief justice James B. McKean, who had been born in Missouri—a source of grave misgivings for many Mormons who harbored deep resentment over being driven from settlements in that state thirty years before. McKean also had spent considerable time as a businessman and local official in Oregon Territory. He was a self-avowed enemy of the Mormon people and immediately set to work using his court as a tool for effecting change. He encouraged an indictment of Brigham Young on charges of "lascivious cohabitation," and decided he need not shield his intent. "While the case at the bar is called The People versus Brigham Young, its other and real title is Federal Authority versus Polygamic Theocracy."

Church president Young, a number of other high-ranking church officials, and the much-storied Orrin Porter Rockwell and Bill Hickman were also indicted for murder in McKean's court for deaths that had occurred years before under murky circumstances. Although Brigham Young was forced into house arrest for a period of time, the indictments would eventually be thrown out under a U.S. Supreme Court ruling criticizing McKean's practice of empaneling stacked juries.

Thomas Hawkins trial, illustration from *Frank Leslie's Illustrated Newspaper*, 1871. (USHS)

In October 1871 Thomas Hawkins was indicted on a charge of adultery and brought to trial before Judge McKean. McKean encouraged, some say compelled, Hawkins's first wife, who was unhappy in polygamy, to testify against Hawkins and his subsequent marriage to another woman. The trial attracted national attention, as evidenced by the lengthy article offered by *Leslie's Illustrated*, a leading national periodical of the day. Many viewed the Hawkins case as a warm-up for McKean's proceeding against Brigham Young. Hawkins was found guilty and sent to prison for three years.

Crowd outside courtroom during Brigham Young's arraignment, 1871. (USHS)

Judge McKean's court was held in a small room above the Faust & Houtz Livery Stable, and on hot summer days the courtroom would fill with the smells of the stables. Many historians believe that this photograph was taken when Brigham Young was in court facing arraignment on the charge of lewd and lascivious conduct with sixteen women as a result of his plural marriages. Young also was indicted in McKean's court along with other prominent community figures for a murder committed during the Utah War of 1857–58. All of the charges were later thrown out by a Supreme Court ruling decrying McKean's tactics in forming hostile juries.

Freight wagons preparing to leave Salt Lake City, c. 1875. (USHS)

Despite the progress in railroad transportation, the vast majority of goods in the territory still found their way to wagons for shipment to outlying settlements. Laden with merchandise from the east, the wagon trains were highly anticipated in the smaller towns of the territory as they made their deliveries. The wagons would often carry return loads to Salt Lake City, ferrying produce or a few manufactured goods to the larger markets along roads that were still very rough in many areas.

John D. Lee execution, Mountain Meadows, March 23, 1877. (USHS)

"I feel resigned to my fate. I have done nothing intentionally wrong. My conscience is clear before God and man. I have been sacrificed in a cowardly, dastardly manner. The evidence against me is as false as the hinges of hell." —John D. Lee

On March 23, 1877, a small group of wagons rolled in to the Mountains Meadows in southern Utah, the scene of the bloody massacre of more than 120 men, women, and children twenty years before. From a wagon stepped John D. Lee. A former ranking leader, Lee had been excommunicated from the Mormon church as he faced murder charges for his alleged role in leading the Mormons who killed the emigrant company in the meadow. It took two trials to convict the industrious pioneer and operator of a vital ferry across the Colorado River. Wearing a broad-brimmed hat and a scarf around his neck against the chill spring air, Lee calmly sat on a coffin for one final picture while prosecuters, marshals, and witnesses gathered around. A few minutes later, a firing squad let loose a volley from another of the wagons, and Lee was dead. The case was closed in the eyes of the law, but questions about the events at Mountain Meadows remain to this day.

Above: Petition for clemency, the case of John D. Lee, March 1877. (USAR)

Hundreds of residents of southern Utah stood by Lee when he was convicted of murder. This petition, with many attached pages of signatures, was sent to Governor George Emery, seeking his intervention to prevent Lee's execution. Despite the fact that the petition carried names of people who knew the circumstances of events during the massacre, Emery declined to intervene.

Left: George Reynolds, at the time of his lawsuit regarding polygamy, 1879. (USHS)

George Reynolds was a quiet, pious man who had served as secretary to Brigham Young. In the late 1870s he was requested, some say unwillingly drafted, to serve as a test case on whether the practice of polygamy was covered by the Constitution's assurances of religious liberty. From the first days of publicly acknowledging their plural marriages, Mormon leaders had proclaimed it a protected expression of religious faith. They subsequently claimed that all efforts by Congress to outlaw polygamy were unconstitutional. For several months the territory waited for a response to appeals made before the United States Supreme Court, which finally came in October 1878.

In another federal court, at roughly the same time, a final chapter was played out in the Mountain Meadows Massacre of 1857. With virtually all criminal cases now being tried before non-Mormon judges under a new congressional act, former Mormon bishop John D. Lee was tried as the central figure in the murder of the Baker-Fancher party in southern Utah. After one trial resulted in a hung jury, a second convicted Lee of murder and the court sentenced him to death. Despite pleas that he was a scapegoat being used to shield other responsible parties, Lee was executed by a firing squad in the fields of Mountain Meadows in 1877.

If Judge McKean viewed the courts as a tool to break the Mormon church, the leadership of the church still had faith that the courts would ultimately vindicate the Mormons by sustaining their unique system of beliefs as protected under the Constitution's guarantee of the free exercise of religion. Brigham Young and other church leaders repeatedly had urged their followers to have faith in the Constitution, citing it as more durable and noble than the personal vendettas of politicians seeking to harm the Saints.

The United States Supreme Court (Chief Justice Morrison Waite, center), 1878. (LOC)

"To permit this would be to make the professed doctrines of religious belief superior to the law of the land, and, in effect, to permit every citizen to become a law unto himself. Government could only exist in name under such circumstances." —Morrison Waite, Chief Justice, U.S. Supreme Court

The Supreme Court told George Reynolds, and each Mormon practicing plural marriage, that they were perfectly entitled to *believe* any religious concept they wanted; however, said the Court, they could not *act* on that belief if the action ran counter to laws developed for a sound and orderly society. The Supreme Court ruled unanimously that the law aimed at crushing polygamy—the Morrill Act of 1862—was, indeed, constitutional and in the best interests of society in general. George Reynolds and about 1,000 other Mormons would eventually go to prison as a result of the ruling.

In 1874 church leaders negotiated with the territorial U.S. Attorney to call a halt to polygamy prosecutions while a test case could make its way to the United States Supreme Court. George Reynolds, a pious practitioner of plural marriage who was private secretary to Brigham Young, was selected for the purpose. For four years the case of *Reynolds v. United States* worked its way through the court system, at its core challenging the constitutionality of the 1862 Morrill Act outlawing polygamy. Early in the October term of 1878, U.S. Supreme Court Chief Justice Morrison R. Waite handed down the unanimous decision against the Mormon church, a decision built on the notion that the laws of the land were based on "Christian" monogamous principles. Chief Justice Waite wrote:

> *Can a man excuse his practices to the contrary because of his religious beliefs? To permit this would be to make the professed doctrines of religious belief superior to the law of the land, and in effect permit every citizen to become a law unto himself.*

The Supreme Court drew a curious line around polygamy in the American religious experience. You could *believe* anything you wanted to, according to the Court, but you could not necessarily *act* on your beliefs. The 1878 decision placed polygamy, and the Mormon church, firmly outside the protection of

Franklin S. Richards, attorney, c. 1880. (USHS)

A talented and capable constitutional attorney, Franklin Richards helped argue the Reynolds case and was often viewed as *the* Mormon attorney during the late nineteenth century. Much of his reputation was made in handling the complex case of Brigham Young's estate, which became mired in controversy when substantial church holdings were found intermingled with personal assets. He gained great favor with church leaders for fending off the lawsuits of disaffected heirs to Young's estate, and also earned a lasting reputation for his spirited defense of Mormon men on polygamy charges during the 1880s.

MORMON WOMEN, POLYGAMY, AND THE REYNOLDS CASE

Eliza R. Snow reflected the shock and sadness of most Mormons when they learned of the Supreme Court decision placing their religious practice of polygamy outside the law of the land. Their last hope for governmental vindication now erased, many feared that they were lambs facing the wolf of an uncaring federal government. Angered by events, Snow picked up her pen and crafted a scathing political essay against the Supreme Court decision.

News of the Supreme Court decision in the Reynolds case had a chilling effect on the Mormon men and women who were practicing polygamy, and none more so than Emmeline B. Wells, an eloquent spokesperson for Mormon women and a frequently quoted defender of the principle of plural marriage. Using broadsides, letters to national newspapers, and the pages of the territorial women's newspaper *The Women's Exponent*, Wells offered impassioned pleas to President Hayes to resist the temptation to target a peaceful and loyal people over an aspect of their religion. In private, however, Wells would confide to her journal moments of personal doubt and anguish regarding her own plural marriage.

Some of the sharpest, angriest debate over plural marriage was generated by the women of the Utah territory, who had no reluctance to share their views with the nation and the world. Gentile women in the territory, now in larger numbers and often well-funded by successful family businesses, staged a large mass meeting in the wake of the Supreme Court decision in the Reynolds case to demand full prosecution of the Mormon people for polygamy. Mormon women, considerably greater in number, responded with a series of mass meetings throughout the territory to tell the non-Mormon women to mind their own business. Throughout the 1880s the women's dialogue on polygamy would be characterized by inflammatory rhetoric.

Above left: Eliza Roxcy Snow, poet and women's leader, c. 1879. (USHS)

Above right: Emmeline B. Wells, writer and political leader, 1879. (USHS)

Left: Political broadside in defense of plural marriage, 1879. (NARA)

Right: Eliza R. Snow's essay on the Supreme Court decision in the Reynolds case, 1879. (NARA)

DECISION

OF THE SUPREME COURT OF THE UNITED STATES IN THE
REYNOLDS CASE.

"Let our eye look upon Zion—let her be defiled."—MICAH.

Let us enter the private sanctuary of domestic life, where, to the honor of this great Republic, the divinity of the marriage tie is acknowledged and held sacred, and where virtue, the crowning glory of the social circle, is bravely and successfully protected.

Let us there, with wanton cruelty, defy the Constitution of our country, and by trampling on the rights of conscience, sever the holy ties of wedlock, separate husbands and wives, parents and children, and ignore the finest affections of the human heart.

Yea, let us cause thousands of honorable, loving wives to be stigmatized as prostitutes, and their offspring as bastards.

Let us cause multitudes of innocent children, that now are being tenderly cherished and educated, to be branded with infamy and deprived of heirship.

Let us desecrate their homes and exterminate the only people of whom our nation can truly boast as protectors of purity and innocence, lest their virtuous and honorable example shall, in the present reign of corruption, rise up before us as a burning reproof.

Let us immure in loathsome prisons those brave men, who, for the sake of worshiping God according to the dictates of their conscience, left their homes and the graves of their noble ancestors, and sought refuge in the sterile American Desert.

Where, nerved by the power of faith in the arm of Jehovah, for a while they battled with the elements for life, and at length, with indomitable energy, overcame the barrenness of the soil, and made the "desert blossom as the rose."

These are the men, who, with their stalwart sons, the offspring of plural, celestial marriage, with stern, unyielding perseverance, established a connecting link between the commercial cities of the East and the rich mining districts of the West, and made practicable for the nation the continental transit of the "iron horse."

Let us erase from the book of remembrance the countless deeds of hospitality and generosity bestowed by those early settlers of the wilderness on our perishing emigrants, when their supplies were exhausted, as they were wending their way through to California.

Let us plant the seeds of devastation in a thriving, peaceful, industrious community—a Territory brought into existence and made to flourish without aid, encouragement, or protection from the government under which it exists.

Yea, let us abrogate the rights of its founders, insomuch that henceforth it shall be controlled by gamblers and speculators, who have no interest in common with the people.

Instead of the Territory of Utah as it now is—a theme of boast as a nucleus of peace, good order and happiness, let us, through our crushing policy, exhibit it to the nations abroad, as a spectacle of confusion, desolation and woe.

Let us tear asunder that mighty shield of the rights of conscience, our glorious Constitution—let us place our veto on the commands of the Almighty, and presume to measure arms with the Great Ruler of the Universe.

THUS SAITH THE SUPREME COURT OF THE UNITED STATES OF AMERICA—THE COURT OF FINAL DECISION—THE HIGHEST TRIBUNAL OF A GREAT AND POWERFUL NATION—THE LAST EARTHLY RESORT TO WHICH AN OPPRESSED AMERICAN CITIZEN CAN APPEAL FOR PROTECTION, AND SUFFERING INNOCENCE FOR REDRESS.

ELIZA R. SNOW.

SALT LAKE CITY, JAN. 21, 1879.

—*From the Deseret News.*

DEFENSE OF PLURAL MARRIAGE,

BY THE

WOMEN OF UTAH COUNTY.

——o——

OVER 2,000 "MORMON" LADIES UNITE WITH THEIR SISTERS OF SALT LAKE CITY, IN PROTESTING AGAINST THE MISREPRESENTATIONS OF THE LADIES ENGAGED IN THE ANTI-POLYGAMY CRUSADE, AND EXPRESS THEIR FIRM AND UNALTERABLE FAITH IN PLURAL MARRIAGE AS A DIVINE ORDINANCE.

——o——

Mass Meetings in Provo, Springville, Spanish Fork, Salem, Payson, Santaquin, Goshen, Cedar Valley, Lehi, Alpine, Benjamin, American Fork and Pleasant Grove.

PROVO.

Upwards of five hundred ladies of Provo and vicinity met in the Meeting House on Saturday morning, December 11th, 1878, "to express their true sentiments with regard to the principles of their religious and political rights as American citizens."

On motion of Mrs. M. John, Mrs. Margaret T. Smoot was called to take the chair; Mrs. Caroline Daniels was elected secretary, and Mrs. L. W. Kimball, assistant secretary.

The choir, under the leadership of Prof. Daniels, sang, "O, God, our help in ages past," etc. Mrs. Mary Duke offered up prayer, and the choir again sang.

Mrs. Smoot, chairman, then arose and said, Ladies and sisters of the Church of Jesus Christ of Latter-day Saints, we meet together this morning for the purpose of declaring to the world and each other our sentiments in regard to our most holy religion,—to enter our protest against that—I was about to say unhallowed—anti-polygamy petition that has re-

meeting and sent to Mrs. Hayes, wife of the President of these United States, for the purpose of influencing hostile legislation against the people and true women of Utah. We will hear it read; then let us weigh every word, take it for what it is worth, and act according to our best judgment.

Mrs. Lucy W. Kimball then read in a clear and intelligent manner, the address of the anti-polygamy ladies of Salt Lake to Mrs. Hayes; also a circular from the same source addressed to the clergymen of the various denominations throughout the United States; both of which documents our readers are familiar with, they having already been published in nearly all the newspapers of the Territory.

MRS. KIMBALL

then said, We understand that a certain Miss Lossee had been invited to run a biblical plowshare under polygamy. We think she will find such an undertaking a somewhat difficult one. The late President Lincoln, referring

Left: Rutherford B. Hayes, nineteenth president of the United States, 1877. (LOC)

In the wake of the Supreme Court's ruling in the case of *Reynolds v. United States,* President Rutherford Hayes called for a swift and immediate crackdown against the Mormon religion. He called on Congress to pass new laws stripping polygamists of the right to vote, hold office, or sit on juries. His recommendations would eventually be passed by Congress in the early 1880s.

Portion of an American anti-Mormon resolution, 1879. (NARA)

The Supreme Court's determination that polygamy was beyond the religious protection provided by the Constitution prompted a number of religious organizations to urge open campaigns against the Mormons. This letter, hastily approved by the American Baptist Home Mission Society during its annual convention in upstate New York, called on President Hayes to aggressively enforce the anti-polygamy laws in Utah.

the Constitution. The Morrill Act, with its promises of prosecuting polygamists and seizing church property, had passed muster with the highest court in the land.

The decision was viewed with shock and sadness by Mormons at a time when they were already faced with a dramatic change in leadership. In 1877, after leading his brethren through thirty years of settlement and progress in the territory, Brigham Young died. His organizing vision had contributed to the establishing of more than 300 settlements in the broad region he viewed as "Deseret." More than 80,000 followers of the Church of Jesus Christ of Latter-day Saints had migrated to the territory at his behest and under his guidance. He had held fast to his principles, yet he had proven to be a shrewd negotiator and a deft wielder of political power. In his final years he was forced to endure the determined attacks of Judge McKean and an embarassing highly publicized divorce petition from Ann Eliza Webb Young, the so-called "twenty-seventh wife." But he had also seen the first grand temple of his church opened in the new homeland. Depending on the observer, he was loved, feared, despised, or idolized. With very rare exception he was viewed as the most important voice among the Mormon people and in Utah Territory.

Although his people had flourished and the community had prospered, statehood for the territory was still beyond Brigham Young's grasp when he died. If he was spared further trials, his people were not: the next years would bring renewed hardship for those who had followed his vision through the wilderness.

Ann Eliza Webb Young, c. 1877. (USHS)
Ann Eliza Webb—known to posterity as the "Twenty-seventh Wife"—was unhappy with her marriage to Brigham Young and successfully sued for divorce, generating great publicity in the process from a national press corps eager to find and report any scandal relating to Brigham Young, polygamy, and the Mormons of Utah.

BRIGHAM YOUNG

Brigham Young never lived to see the decision of the Supreme Court placing his practice of plural marriage, his people, and his faith outside of the law of the land. By the spring of 1877 the president of the Church of Jesus Christ of Latter-day Saints was in increasingly poor health. In his seventy-seventh year, it was more difficult for him to venture out of his compound, and he largely relegated himself to administering the church from his office.

Young had made one final trip to the southern reaches of the territory for what, in some respects, was the culminating event of his life. A new Mormon temple had been completed in St. George, and Young presided over the dedication. He also took the time to symbolically dictate the Temple ordinances, since they did not exist in printed form and their execution for the faithful depended entirely on Young.

On his return trip, Young experienced some hard feelings in southern settlements over the execution of John D. Lee for complicity in the Mountain Meadows Massacre. Arriving back in Salt Lake City, he tried to attend to church business, and even renewed his call for a user-friendly phonetic alphabet to aid immigrants in more rapidly mastering the English language. But, suddenly, he fell very ill in late August.

Brigham Young, 1877. (USHS)
Generally believed to be the last photograph of the great church leader.

"THE LION OF THE LORD"

At the time, doctors diagnosed Young as suffering from "cholera morbus," and confessed that there was nothing they could do for him. They gave him morphine for what was clearly excruciating pain. Years later, medical researchers would reconsider Young's case and offer a diagnosis of acute appendicitis. Other interpretations also exist; it is hypothesized that Young was actually suffering from advanced prostate cancer.

Family, friends, and other church associates clustered around him during his final days in the Lion House. One plural wife would later report that, in a lucid moment breaking the coma into which he had lapsed, Young opened his eyes and called "Joseph, Joseph, Joseph"—an apparent reference, or even vision, of church founder Joseph Smith.

On August 29, 1877, Brigham Young, spiritual leader, power broker, and the most successful colonizer of the American West, died. His funeral was held in the Salt Lake Tabernacle on September 2, with the spillover crowds filling much of Temple Square. Those who loved him championed him in death. Those who fought him seized a final opportunity to berate the man. But all would acknowledge that no other had shaped the Utah territory with the vision, force, and ability of Brigham Young.

Above: Brigham Young and wife Amelia Folsom Young, c. 1868. (USHS)

Poster, 1901. (USHS)

Long after his death, fascination with Brigham Young and his wives would continue.

Right: The program for the funeral of Brigham Young, September 2, 1877. (USHS)

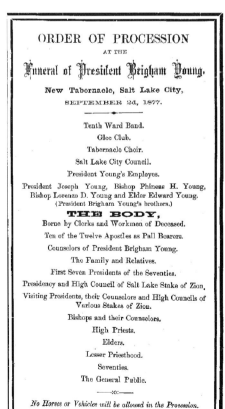

ORDER OF PROCESSION

AT THE

Funeral of President Brigham Young,

New Tabernacle, Salt Lake City,

SEPTEMBER 2d, 1877.

Tenth Ward Band.

Glee Club.

Tabernacle Choir.

Salt Lake City Council.

President Young's Employes.

President Joseph Young, Bishop Phineas H. Young, Bishop Lorenzo D. Young and Elder Edward Young.
(President Brigham Young's brothers.)

THE BODY,

Borne by Clerks and Workmen of Deceased.

Ten of the Twelve Apostles as Pall Bearers.

Counselors of President Brigham Young.

The Family and Relatives.

First Seven Presidents of the Seventies.

Presidency and High Council of Salt Lake Stake of Zion.

Visiting Presidents, their Counselors and High Councils of Various Stakes of Zion.

Bishops and their Counselors.

High Priests.

Elders.

Lesser Priesthood.

Seventies.

The General Public.

——:o:——

No Horses or Vehicles will be allowed in the Procession.

Salt Lake City, looking northwest from the top of the Tabernacle at the dawn of the 1880s. (USHS)

Chapter Six

THE CRACKDOWN
1880–1889

President Garfield is assassinated....Sitting Bull and Geronimo surrender, closing a chapter in the Indian wars....Two thousand die in the Johnstown Flood....Football debuts....John L. Sullivan knocks out an opponent in the 75th round to win the last bare-knuckles boxing title....The Brooklyn Bridge opens....Daimler invents the first automobile.

THE DEATH OF BRIGHAM YOUNG was a pivotal event in Utah's territorial experience. Leadership of the Mormons, once so clearly and firmly held, now passed into a period of collective management headed by John Taylor. While chaos and the collapse of the church predicted by some eastern newspapers did not occur, a decided shift of momentum was discernible. In the 1880s elected officials of the federal government would go on the offensive in an effort to establish the rule of law over what they viewed as a wayward territory.

Below: The Utah Territorial Penitentiary, Salt Lake City, c. 1885. (USHS)

A fortress-like structure, the territorial penitentiary was known for its filthy conditions, horrible food, and hard labor. Men serving time for unlawful cohabitation would often occupy the same large cell with other felons serving time for violent crimes.

President James Garfield delivering his inaugural address, March 1881. (LOC)

"The Mormon Church not only offends the moral sense of mankind by sanctioning polygamy, but it prevents the administration of justice through the ordinary instrumentality of the law." —President James A. Garfield, Inaugural Address, March 4, 1881

Garfield was assassinated after only 200 days in office, but the strident tone of his inaugural address captured the fervor and determination that was to characterize the efforts of the federal government throughout the 1880s to end the practice of polygamy and destroy what many observers felt was the religious control by the Mormon church of Utah Territory.

Chester A. Arthur, twenty-first president of the United States, 1882. (LOC)

Viewed as little more than a career politician from New York who was nominated for vice-president in an effort to balance the James Garfield ticket, Arthur surprised many as a competent chief executive when he took office upon Garfield's assassination. While less concerned with polygamy than was his predecessor, Arthur did become notably agitated with the Mormon church's refusal to abandon polygamy despite the pressure of the 1882 Edmunds Act. Out of frustration, one of his last speeches as president urged Congress to repeal the act which had created Utah Territory.

Early in 1881 newly elected President James Garfield stepped to a podium in front of the Capitol Building in Washington, D.C., and took the oath of office as the nation's twentieth chief executive. In his first address as president, Garfield returned to his roots as a minister in the Disciples of Christ church and offered a stirring tribute to what he viewed as the American principles of home, hearth, country, and patriotism. His most impassioned words, however, were aimed at the Territory of Utah, promising to join Congress in renewed efforts to crush the practice of plural marriage and what he perceived as sectarian control of the political and governmental processes.

In the eyes of disappointed observers in the territory, Garfield was promising a crusade against the Mormon church and offering a virtual guarantee that statehood would not be considered until plural marriage was crushed. The *Deseret News* attacked the president for duplicity when it commented on Garfield's targeting of polygamy:

> If it is the duty of Congress to correct public morals, there is a field for their labors in other directions ... the gross evils that abound in social life, with their disgusting, brutalizing and destructive tendencies, against which no presidential anathema is hurled and no congressional statutes are enacted.

Garfield would serve only two hundred days in office before being shot by an assassin, dying on July 2. His successor, Chester Arthur, picked up the flag (and his predecessor's agenda) and immediately called on Congress to enact new laws against plural marriage, as well as methods for easing prosecution of accused offenders. The fervor of these first presidents of the new decade set the tone for the conflict that would dominate the fortunes of Utah Territory throughout the 1880s.

These presidents, in the tradition of most political figures, were responding to public clamor. An anti-Mormon frenzy was being fed by the national press of the day. Many magazines and newspapers, including the influential *Frank Leslie's Illustrated Newspaper*, sent correspondents to Utah. Their accounts of the evils of polygamy and of church control of politics were lurid, shocking, and almost routinely told from an anti-Mormon perspective. Attempts by the Mormon church and the territorial legislature to offer a countervailing view

POLYGAMY AND THE NATIONAL MEDIA

Throughout the decade of the 1880s the national media corps focused public and governmental attention on what they routinely identified as the "scourge of polygamy" in Utah. Rejecting polygamy as a religious principle, most editors were content to portray the Mormon church as a cruel exploiter of women run by a sinister group harboring violent animosity toward the United States. *Frank Leslie's Illustrated Newspaper* offered a steady stream of articles throughout the decade, many of them shaped, if not dictated, by anti-Mormon elements in Utah.

Right: An "old" wife pummels her husband's "new" wives in the Salt Lake Theatre, c. 1882. (USHS)

Mormon men importing new wives to Utah, c. 1882. (USHS)

Mormon women entering into a life of polygamy in Utah, *Frank Leslie's Illustrated Newspaper*, 1882. (USHS)

"The Jealous Wives" and "Wives as Slaves." In two panels, an unknown artist attempts to capture the public view of plural marriage: domestic storminess and helpless servitude; date unknown. (USHS)

"The Cave of Despair," *Frank Leslie's Illustrated Newspaper*, February 4, 1882. (USHS)

"Woman's Bondage in Utah," *Frank Leslie's Illustrated Newspaper*, March 11, 1882. (USHS)

were virtually ignored by the press and by Congress, with a string of memorials from Utahns to Washington being cast aside with little note. Harriet Beecher Stowe, still revered for her powerful anti-slavery book *Uncle Tom's Cabin*, attacked plural marriage with abandon, offering an open letter to the nation's women decrying the "degrading bondage" of polygamy. Some periodicals and political cartoons even went so far as to advocate a military march on Utah to crush the Mormon church.

The first strike from Congress came in 1882. Senator George F. Edmunds of Vermont, who was viewed as a constitutional scholar in the Senate chamber, powered through a bill renewing each aspect of the Morrill Act of 1862 and creating new restrictions barring polygamists from serving on juries, voting, or holding public office. The Edmunds Act declared all territorial offices in Utah vacant, and it also created a new "Utah Commission" to oversee elections to ensure that polygamists did not vote and were not elected to office.

Left: Harriet Beecher Stowe, c. 1880. (LOC)

Her book *Uncle Tom's Cabin* swayed the national mood against slavery with its heartwrenching, if melodramatic, portrayal of lives in slavery. In the 1880s Harriet Beecher Stowe brought her fame to bear against polygamy, writing several national letters condemning the practice as a continuing form of slavery for women. She even contributed a welcoming letter to early editions of the *Anti-Polygamy Standard*, a short-lived publication whose mission was to assault plural marriage.

Far left: Reverend DeWitt Talmage, New York, c. 1882. (LOC)
Left: Reverend Henry Ward Beecher, 1884. (LOC)
   Among the multitude of public figures attacking the Mormon church in the 1880s, none was more passionate, scathing, and self-promoting than DeWitt Talmage. A popular, pulpit-pounding preacher to his influential congregation in Brooklyn, Talmage urged presidents and Congress to call an army to attack Utah in a holy crusade. Conversely, Henry Ward Beecher, at one time one of the nation's most influential religious leaders, urged the nation simply to ignore Utah, claiming that repeated attacks merely served to create religious martyrs in Utah Territory. Beecher, his own career sullied by allegations of sexual impropriety, was opposed in his own family by his sister Harriet Beecher Stowe and by a majority of the nation's citizens.

The first real consequence of the bill's passage was the unseating of George Q. Cannon, Utah Territory's delegate to Congress. An apostle and member of the Mormon church's First Presidency council, and the openly acknowledged husband of several wives, Cannon had eloquently fought for political equality for his territory and for constitutional rights for his coreligionists. Voted out of his delegate's seat in Congress by nearly a two-to-one margin on the basis of his practice of plural marriage, Cannon offered one parting comment, directed at Congress in defense of minorities:

> It is now said that a law of Congress has been enacted which prevents me from taking my seat.... I pity any gentleman, who, with nothing to sustain him but popular sentiment, is willing to trample upon the Constitution and the law to strike down a people against whom popular sentiment is strong.

Communities in Utah Territory staged funerals for the Constitution, killed, as they saw it, by the twin daggers of the Supreme Court decision in the Reynolds case and the new Edmunds Act. The loss of rights and the renewed threat of prosecution for plural marriage convinced a number of leading voices in the territory to call for a new constitutional convention in Utah and another

Below far left: Senator George F. Edmunds, Vermont, c. 1882. (LOC)
   "The object of the bill is to take the political power in the territory out of the hands of this body of tyrants." —Senator George F. Edmunds, advocating passage of the Edmunds Act, 1882.
   Edmunds, a staunch Republican and one-time chairman of the Senate Judiciary Committee, considered himself a legal scholar and the Senate's most stalwart defender of the Constitution. While adamantly opposed to the practice of polygamy, Edmunds maintained that his energies were dedicated to breaking what he considered to be a religious monopoly of government in Utah Territory, which, he claimed, destroyed his cherished view of representative government.

Left: George L. Miller, newspaperman and politician, Nebraska, c. 1885. (NHS)
   Little noted beyond the borders of Nebraska, Miller served a secretive but important role for the Mormon church and Utah Territory throughout the 1880s. As a Democratic party national committeeman, Miller quietly supported Utah's statehood bids and coaxed national Democratic leaders to go easy in their prosecution of polygamy to further his dream of an American West dominated by the Democrats. But Miller also adamantly argued with Mormon representatives that they would have no chance for statehood as long as they attempted to defy national authority on the subject of plural marriage.

NATIVE AMERICANS: FORTS, RESERVATIONS, AND OTHER GOVERNMENT ACTIONS

For fifteen years following the end of the Black Hawk War in 1868, the relationship between the expanding white settlements in the Utah territory and the Ute Indians had been quietly controlled by the benign neglect of the native population now relegated to reservation lands in eastern Utah.

In the early 1880s relationships among the Utes and between the Utes and the government took a decided downward turn as the federal government sought to resolve its "Indian problem" in the West. In 1881, at the urging of land developers and politicians, the army forcefully removed the White River Utes from their lands in Colorado and sent them to the Uintah Reservation in eastern Utah. In 1882 the federal government forced another Ute group, the Uncompahgre band, onto the adjoining Ouray reservation lands. The government, lumping the distinctly different Ute bands into one uncomfortable heap of humanity, soon created tension among the native people that would flare into tribal violence, with hard feelings enduring for decades. With determined Indian agents urging the Indians to become farmers, the Ute people essentially lost their hunting-and-gathering mode of existence.

The government's response to the increasing violence was to create military outposts in close proximity to the reservations to protect white settlements and discourage the tribal violence from spreading. Fort Duchesne, established in 1886 near the confluence of the Uintah and Duchesne rivers, served as a primary army outpost covering a broad region including eastern Utah, southwestern Wyoming, and western Colorado. Fort Cameron, located in Beaver in southern Utah, was created in 1872 with the dual purpose of Indian *and* Mormon control; but it was disbanded in the early 1880s and its troops reassigned to Fort Douglas in Salt Lake City.

Throughout the late 1800s the federal government would continue attempts to relocate vestiges of the Ute culture to the lands of eastern Utah. Violence would sporadically flare as the Ute people were pushed from place to place as miners and white settlers steadily encroached upon and then demanded some of the ever-shrinking reservation lands.

An Indian agent with Ute Indians, Uintah Reservation, c. 1885. (USHS)

Ute delegation to Washington, c. 1897. (NARA)

Ute Chief Ouray and sub-chiefs, date unknown. (USHS)

Fort Duchesne, during its military heyday, c. 1890. (NARA)

Troops in formation, Fort Cameron, near Beaver, Utah, c. 1880. (USHS)
    Fort Cameron, located near the settlement of Beaver in southwestern Utah, was created in 1872 to control both Indians and Mormons; but it was disbanded a few years after this photograph was taken.

[FORM OF OATH FOR A WOMAN.]

TERRITORY OF UTAH,   }
COUNTY OF_____ } SS.

I,_____ _____ being first duly sworn (or affirmed),
depose and say that I am over twenty-one years of age, and have resided in the Territory of Utah for six months, and in the precinct of
_____one month immediately preceding the date hereof, [and am a native born or naturalized, or the
wife, widow or daughter (as the case may be) of a native born or naturalized citizen of the United States.] I do further solemnly swear (or
affirm) that I am not a bigamist nor a polygamist; that I have not violated the laws of the United States prohibiting bigamy or polygamy;
and I am not the wife of a polygamist, nor have I entered into any relation with any man in violation of the laws of the United States concerning bigamy and polygamy.

Subscribed and sworn to before me this_____day of_____
188___

                         Registration Officer for_____Precinct.
    NOTE.—The Registration Officer, or his Deputy, will erase from the clause between [brackets] such parts as are not applicable to the
case. In every case the female must swear that she is over twenty-one years of age, otherwise she must not be registered.

Left: The Utah Commission, Salt Lake City, 1883. (LDS)
Below left: Women's voter loyalty oath, 1882. (NARA)
    Created under the Edmunds Act to be a "neutral" body of political observers, one of whose tasks was to ensure fair elections in the territory, the Utah Commission soon exerted a profound influence on every city and town. Using voter loyalty oaths as a means of weeding out practitioners of plural marriage, who were then barred from political participation, the commission removed more than 12,000 Mormons from the voting rolls in its first year in service. Despised by the local Mormon population for their arrogance and virulent anti-Mormon sentiments, the commission members were cheered by the local non-Mormon community for whittling down the political power of the Mormon church in Utah. Although it came to temper its efforts during the course of its fourteen-year existence, the Utah Commission placed a heavy hand on the scales of political balance in its first years in operation.

bid for statehood as a means of asserting self-determination. But, as with each previous petition, Utah's bid for admission fell on unsympathetic ears and naively flew in the face of both public and congressional opinion. An accommodating senator from Nebraska introduced a statehood bill in Utah's behalf, but it was promptly assigned to a committee, where it died of neglect.

George Q. Cannon and sons, c. 1880.
(USHS)

Although his influence often has been underestimated since he did not serve as president of the Church of Jesus Christ of Latter-day Saints, George Q. Cannon is arguably one of the three or four most influential figures in Mormon church history prior to Utah's statehood. Publisher, congressional delegate, and member of the First Presidency of the Mormon church, Cannon was pivotal in church negotiations with Washington during the 1880s and led a politically adroit strategy that drew Mormons closer to the Republican party. Two of his sons, Abraham (seated, second from right) and Angus (seated, third from left), would follow their father in high positions of Mormon church leadership.

SONS OF BRIGHAM YOUNG

While denying an interest in creating a type of "royal family" for the LDS church, Brigham Young did actively promote the involvement and leadership of a number of his sons within the church and in church-influenced business affairs. Two of his sons, Brigham, Jr., and John W., were called as apostles by Brigham at tender ages in the 1860s. They also were selected by their father to serve as subcontractors for the grading of roadbeds for the transcontinental railroad—a very profitable undertaking.

After their shared railroad experience, Brigham, Jr., and John W. drifted apart and traveled along separate paths. Brigham, Jr., stayed close to Utah Territory and his church, serving in a variety of Mormon leadership positions while being viewed as an embodiment of the spiritual dedication of his father. John W. moved to New York, where he actively promoted railroad construction and sought his fortune. In the 1880s he moved to Washington, D.C., to represent church interests in the nation's capital during the time of the political crackdown against Mormonism. Constantly beseeching church leadership for money used to find favor with various members of

Congress and newspaper editors, John W. came to be viewed with increasing suspicion by church leaders and eventually was dumped from his unofficial position as chief lobbyist for the Mormon church. Using different channels, the church would continue to provide financial incentives to congressional, media, and judicial figures throughout the 1880s, resigning itself to the unofficial rules of nineteenth-century government in the United States which essentially mandated bribery as a means of leveling the playing field.

While his brothers were establishing different reputations, Joseph Don Carlos Young had emerged as a talented designer and the first formally trained Mormon architect. Serving as church architect for nearly fifty years, he took over construction of the Salt Lake Temple from the aged Truman O. Angell in 1887. He also was not reluctant to mix in the rough-and-tumble world of Utah politics, serving a term as a state legislator and having a brief run-in with the law after he took exception to a blistering attack by the *Salt Lake Tribune* and hit its editor in the nose during a streetside confrontation.

Brigham Young, Jr., c. 1885.

John W. Young, c. 1885. (all USHS)

Joseph Don Carlos Young, c. 1890.

The dawning of a new era was dramatically foreshadowed in the territory by the arrival in August 1882 of the first five-member Utah Commission. At once it instituted a voter's test oath, aimed at identifying plural-marriage practitioners. With the law loosely interpreted to lock out the largest number of voting Mormons possible, the commission estimated that 12,000 polygamists had been separated from the voting rolls after the first year of use of the oath. Despite repeated requests, however, the commission refused to suspend the voting right of women, as long as the women met the monogamous standard embraced in the test oath.

The Utah Commission brought life to the Liberal party, previously a small and ineffective political voice for non-Mormons in Utah Territory. The rise of the Liberal party indicated how deep was the divide between Mormon and non-Mormon at the start of the 1880s. While church members perceived a wholesale destruction of their guaranteed constitutional rights at the hands of a lawless federal government, the Liberal party championed and cheered each new federal initiative, including the disfranchising of their fellow citizens. A letter from the Liberal party central committee praised the Utah Commission's work and promoted the prospects for the rise of the party: "For the first time in the history of this Territory it has become possible for her free citizens to cast their votes with a certainty that they will be fairly and honestly counted."

The Liberals predicted that a new political wind would blow in the territory, and set their party sights on electing a new delegate to Congress in 1882. A remarkable campaign ensued in which P.T. Van Zile represented the Liberals and John T. Caine carried the banner for Mormon political interests through the People's party. When the votes were counted, Caine had crushed Van Zile by a ratio of six to one. The *Salt Lake Tribune* called the election a scandal, repeated a charge that Caine was a polygamist, hinted at massive voter fraud, and demanded the use of federal force to break Mormon political control. The Utah Commission investigated the charges but found the vote solid while also establishing that Caine was clearly a monogamist. The election was certified.

The Edmunds Act had set in motion a process for reordering the political climate in Utah, and it also was having a profound impact on territorial life through criminal prosecutions. The number of deputized federal marshals in

John T. Caine, delegate to Congress, c. 1890.

Unheralded, and often misconceived as merely a Mormon messenger in Washington, John T. Caine provided valuable political service to the territory during the 1880s and 1890s. Taking congressional office upon the forced ouster of George Q. Cannon on grounds of polygamy, Caine was a monogamist who tirelessly downplayed the role of plural marriage in his religion and worked diligently among Democrats in Washington—urging them to admit Utah to the Union in order that the party could reap the benefits of Mormon allegiance. Eloquent and energetic although somewhat unimaginative, Caine would later unsuccessfully seek election as Utah's first statehood governor. (USHS)

Independence Hall, Salt Lake City, 1881. (USHS)

Independence Hall interior, 1882. (USHS)

The scene of most town gatherings not affiliated with the Mormon church, Independence Hall served as everything from church house to political meetinghouse to businessmen's club during the 1880s. Brigham Young originally had been tolerant and had even encouraged some use of Mormon church buildings by other denominations in their early years in the territory; however, as those congregations joined the anti-Mormon crusade, they were soon barred from use of LDS chapels. Independence Hall served as a primary caucus site for the Liberal party of Utah as it advanced an often caustic campaign for political balance in the territory.

President John Taylor, Church of Jesus Christ of Latter-day Saints, c. 1880. (USHS)

With succession to the presidency somewhat ambiguous upon the death of Brigham Young, direction of the Mormon church fell to the collective action of the Quorum of the Twelve Apostles until John Taylor was sustained as president many months later. A survivor of the murderous shootout that killed church founder Joseph Smith in Carthage, Illinois, Taylor was a fierce and faithful defender of his faith during his life, adamantly refusing to yield any ground on the subject of plural marriage. Yet, at the same time, he showed an interest in easing church economic controls in the territory and publicly downplayed the importance of the collectivist communes known as the United Order. Still, Taylor is best remembered for his defense of plural marriage and his willingness to live his final two years in hiding "on the underground" to avoid prosecution and imprisonment for marrying fifteen wives.

the territory increased three hundred percent, with the new lawmen given a primary duty of tracking down polygamists. Frequently recruited from vocal anti-Mormon circles, the deputy marshals used paid informants and stakeouts to make their cases. Often conducting raids at night, the federal officers would burst into homes seeking to catch a man with a plural wife. Some husbands devised elaborate hiding places within their homes to evade the no-knock raids. Others took flight, losing themselves "on the underground," a Mormon network that hid polygamists during the day and guided them to the next safe house during the night. In cases where the husband had to stay to tend a family business, plural wives and children were forced to take to the underground.

The Mormon people, and their leader John Taylor, eventually sustained as president of the church in the years after Brigham Young's death, found themselves in an impossible situation. Hundreds of men were being arrested and sent to the territorial penitentiary in Sugar House. Hundreds more, including Taylor and his counselors George Q. Cannon and Joseph F. Smith, were living their lives as fugitives on the underground or simply doing their

THE MORMON UNDERGROUND

With the crackdown against polygamy fully under way by 1882, federal deputy marshals were given free rein throughout Utah to identify and arrest polygamists. Unconstrained by our contemporary understanding of constitutionally appropriate search-and-seizure requirements, the deputies used paid informants for leads, and their methods included kicking down the doors of suspected polygamists in the middle of the night in an attempt to establish unlawful cohabitation. The raids resulted in hundreds of arrests and terrified families throughout the territory.

In response, a number of small communities established a regular schedule of lookouts to watch for deputies riding into town to conduct raids. Some polygamous men went so far as to craft small hiding places within the walls of their homes to allow for a quick escape if deputies stormed the house. Mothers counseled their children to "forget your name, forget your parents, forget your home" if questioned by strangers, recognizing the federal marshals' technique of using children to point the way to their polygamous parents.

Some families, notably the upper ranks of leadership in the Mormon church, could find no adequate hiding place near their homes, businesses, or farms that would afford them safety from the reach of the deputies. These figures, including President John Taylor, literally disappeared from public view. Secreted from safe house to safe house, they lived for years at a time on the shadowy polygamy underground that stretched throughout Utah Territory into Wyoming, Idaho, Nevada, Colorado, and Arizona. With bodyguards keeping watch, Taylor managed to stay one harried step ahead of the marshals for two years, until his death in July 1887.

While men were often the focal point of arrest efforts, the women of polygamy pulled an exceptionally heavy burden through the underground. Women were left to care for their families, maintain farms and businesses, and endure constant surveillance and threats of prosecution for shielding their husbands. Some families reversed the usual process, with husbands staying to tend to business while plural wives lived a vagabond existence on the underground. The annals of the era are filled with stories of women giving birth to children under harsh conditions and of other women dying apart from their families out of fear that any form of reunion could be used in a court of law against their surviving loved ones.

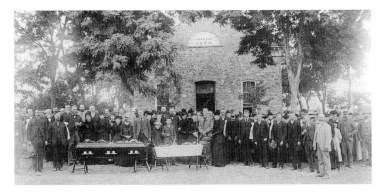

Funeral of Mrs. Francis Lyman, who died while on the underground, c. 1887. (USHS)

Edward M. Dalton, Mormon polygamist killed by federal deputies in Parowan, 1886. (USHS)

Title page, *Murder by a Deputy Marshal*, published by the *Deseret News*, 1886. (NARA)

Joseph McMurrin, future Mormon general authority who served as a bodyguard for John Taylor during the underground years, 1888. (LDS)

best to stay out of the territory. Families were suffering, the Mormon church was virtually leaderless in a traditional sense, and life in the territory was in a convulsive state of flux. Yet, for faithful church members, polygamist and monogamist alike, the point at issue was a religious principle that could not be abandoned without violating a law of God. Taylor, aged and not in good health, married another wife while on the underground and used special couriers to send messages to his followers, urging them to keep the faith, stand strong, and never shirk their responsibility to plural marriage.

Charles S. Zane, Chief Justice, Federal Territorial Court for Utah, c. 1888. (USHS)

Justice Charles Zane did not view himself as anti-Mormon, but instead believed he was charged with honestly and fairly upholding the laws of the United States, and that the law banning polygamy was no exception. Zane considered himself immensely fair in offering convicted polygamists an opportunity to renounce their plural marriages and affirm loyalty to the law as a means of easing their sentences. However, hundreds of polygamists convicted in his court took issue with his personal assessment of his evenhandedness.

Above: George Q. Cannon (seated center) and fellow prisoners, Utah Territorial Penitentiary, c. 1888. (USHS)

George Q. Cannon, a member of the Mormon church's First Presidency, served 150 days in the penitentiary toward the end of the polygamy prosecution era. Generally only changing into the standard-issue prison stripes for eager photographers of the day, Cannon was treated with some deference by the prison staff and other inmates. Standing to the left of Cannon in the photograph is James Hamilton, who reportedly was arrested seven times by federal deputies on polygamy charges.

Right: Polygamy prisoners, including Rudger Clawson, Utah Territorial Penitentiary, 1889. (USHS)

When this photo was taken in 1889, Rudger Clawson (second from right) was nearing the end of nearly four years of confinement in the penitentiary. While he would remain a vocal supporter of plural marriage to his dying day, Clawson also spoke with chilling detail about the danger, discomfort, and occasional stark terror of life behind prison bars. His letters advise those considering violation of the law to spend one night in the penitentiary as a sure preventative measure against a life of crime. There was little attempt made to segregate prisoners based on the severity of their crimes. Women were also held in separate quarters in the prison on charges of contempt of court for refusing to provide evidence regarding their polygamous marriages.

A prime player in this drama was Charles Zane, the newly appointed chief justice of the federal court for Utah Territory. Unlike his controversial predecessor Judge James McKean, Zane did not use his bench as a platform for anti-Mormon attacks, although he often was identified as an enemy by Latter-day Saints. Zane viewed polygamy as a simple issue of law and order, and he viewed polygamists as violators of the duly constituted law of the land. In what he considered a gesture of leniency, he often would present accused polygamists with the option either of going to prison or publicly swearing to abide by the federal law prohibiting plural marriage.

THE LAWS OF GOD AND MEN—THREE CHOICES

Judge Charles Zane's offer to convicted polygamists to renounce their plural marriages and promise to obey the law banning polygamy generally met with a determined rejection from Mormons facing prison sentences. But such was not always the case as federal prosecution efforts reached a fevered pitch in the mid-1880s.

Men like Rudger Clawson, who announced their proud decision to "obey God's law" over the laws of the United States, were considered heroes in the Mormon community. They received tributes in the *Deseret News* and from local pulpits for their willingness to accept prison terms rather than renounce their religious principles and turn away from plural wives and families.

When one notable Salt Lake City figure selected a different path, he caused a stir that rocked the territory and unleashed a stream of anger against him. John Sharp, Mormon bishop of the Twentieth Ward and financially secure railroad executive, was brought before Judge Zane on charges relating to his plural wives. After the routine conviction, Zane followed his standard form and offered the prisoner an opportunity to obey the law banning polygamy. To the shock of the courtroom, the Mormon church, and the entire territory, John Sharp accepted the offer, claiming he would no longer practice plural marriage in response to "the dictates of my conscience."

Church leaders then asked Sharp to resign from his church office. When he failed to act quickly, he was stripped of his title of bishop and officially distanced from the church through the process of being disfellowshipped. While the non-Mormon community cheered his decision, church leaders denounced his actions as "heartless perfidy," in the words of Apostle Abraham Cannon.

At roughly the same time, in the much different setting of Summit County, another local Mormon leader, William Cluff, was wrestling with the question of polygamy. After months of internal debate stemming from the pressure of ecclesiastical leaders for him to take a second wife, Cluff resigned his leadership position in the church. Like Sharp, Cluff said his conscience would have him live a life of monogamy as a clearer reflection of his principles.

Still, the majority of men facing prosecution under the federal law banning polygamy stayed their course and refused any and all offers to ease their sentences through publicly renouncing plural marriage. When Governor Caleb West made a dramatic visit to the prison to offer immediate release to a large group of polygamy prisoners if they would merely sign a letter promising to obey the law, Lorenzo Snow refused the offer, saying that their religious principles were sound and not to be compromised, and that the law itself was in error.

Rudger Clawson, c. 1890. (USHS)

William W. Cluff, c. 1889. (LDS)

John Sharp, c. 1885. (USHS)

Andrew Burt, Police Chief, Salt Lake City, 1883. (LDS)

Andrew Burt was a popular and respected church and civic leader in Salt Lake City in the 1870s and 1880s, and was appointed chief of the city's police force. On August 25, 1883, Burt was brutally murdered under hazy circumstances in the rough-and-tumble saloon district near the downtown area, the actual murder taking place near Smith's Drug Store during broad daylight. A number of witnesses identified a black laborer, Sam Joe Harvey, as the killer. After officers rushed Harvey to City Hall for holding, an angry mob gathered. The mob soon stormed the building, removed Harvey with little opposition, and lynched him.

Above right: Mormon wagon trains en route to Mexico, c. 1888. (AHF)

Right: Mormon settlement at Colonia Juarez, Mexico, c. 1900. (USHS)

When political efforts to ease the anti-polygamy prosecutions failed and the underground system of hiding proved too burdensome, the Mormon church pioneered new settlements just beyond the nation's borders in Mexico and Canada. While the Canadian government of Prime Minister John MacDonald was cold to the presence of polygamy, the Mexican government agreed to look away from Mormon marriage practices. For years, many of the settlements, including Colonia Juarez, thrived. Some polygamous families moved their entire households to the prosecution-free environment of Mexico; other families kept one wife in Utah while "sister wives" established homes south of the border.

To Rudger Clawson there was no choice. Brought before the court, Clawson defended his belief in plural marriage as a sacred principle and just as adamantly protested what he viewed as the unconstitutionality of the Edmunds Act. Faced with a four-year prison sentence and a fine, Clawson resigned himself to the decision of the court:

> Your honor, I very much regret that the laws of my country should come in conflict with the laws of God; but whenever they do, I shall invariably choose the latter. If I did not so express myself, I should feel unworthy of the cause I represent.

Clawson was dispatched to the penitentiary to serve the full four-year sentence, the longest sentence ever served for a polygamy conviction. Throughout the series of events, Clawson was hailed by many as a hero for refusing to turn away from God's law. He was not alone: an estimated one thousand Mormon men, and even a few women, would find themselves in the squalid confines of the territorial "pen" during the 1880s as their religious convictions ran headlong into the teeth of the Edmunds Act.

Confronted with the same dilemma, Bishop John Sharp of the church's Twentieth Ward in Salt Lake City accepted Zane's offer and promised to obey the law prohibiting plural marriage. His decision produced a sharp response in the embattled community. Sharp was treated as an outcast for agreeing to strike a deal, in effect turning away from the counsel of the leaders of the

SALT LAKE CITY NEWSPAPER "WARS"—THE 1880s

During the 1880s the newspaper "war" continued in earnest in Salt Lake City. The *Salt Lake Tribune* continued to prod and assail the power structure of the Mormon church and advance the cause of anti-Mormon political strength through its support of the Liberal party. The Mormon church responded with two information vehicles in the capital city of the territory, the *Deseret News* and the *Salt Lake Herald*.

As had been the case since its inception, the *News* was often willing to censor coverage of much of the religious controversy in the territory. Under the editorship of Charles Penrose in the 1880s the *News* offered a somewhat refined voice for Mormon church views, and only infrequently did it trade barbs with the *Tribune*. *Tribune* editors often referred disparagingly to the *News* as the "old lady." The *Herald*, on the other hand, more aggressively formed a counterpoint to the attacks and allegations that were a daily mainstay of the *Tribune*. Taking an active part in political events and coverage, the *Herald's* editors supported the candidates and principles of the Mormon's People's party in political affairs and showed

little reluctance to assail the motives of the Liberal party and the *Tribune*.

Newspapers in the territory during the 1880s captured the fervor, passions, and biases of frontier journalism at both its best and worst. It was not unusual for an editor to be followed home after publishing a particularly scathing article and be physically attacked by some of those unable to see his logic. The editorial struggle between the *Deseret News* and *Salt Lake Herald* on one side and the *Salt Lake Tribune* on the other reflected the divisive struggle that was gripping the territory and making headlines throughout the nation and the world.

Left: Charles Penrose, *Deseret News* editor and publisher, c. 1888. (USHS)

Right: Salt Lake Herald building, c. 1875. (Lee Library, BYU)

church. He was asked to resign his church offices and ultimately endured a number of years as a pariah through being disfellowshipped. Years later, Sharp would be reinstated to church membership, but his case shows the depth of conviction on both sides and how dire were the social consequences for anyone accepting the offer made by Charles Zane.

By the mid-1880s Mormon church officials had initiated a series of exploratory moves to consider steps that might be taken if the future of the church was jeopardized by the federal prosecutions. First in Mexico, then in Canada, emissaries from the church met with political leaders to gauge acceptance for Mormon colonies. In Mexico, the Mormon colonists were initially well accepted, with government officials agreeing to turn a blind eye to the practice of plural marriage in settlements such as Colonia Juarez. But in Canada the response was decidedly cooler, with Prime Minister John MacDonald telling the emissaries directly that polygamy would not be tolerated, although their settlement otherwise would be welcome. Mormon colonies that were established in both nations thrived during the nineteenth century.

Above: Eli H. Murray, Utah Territorial Governor, c. 1885. (USHS)

Left: Anti-Mormon political cartoon, c. 1885. (LDS)

Governor Eli Murray was appointed by President Rutherford Hayes in 1880 and managed to remain in his position for six years, an uncharacteristically long tenure for a Utah territorial governor. Possessing the unique background of former U.S. marshal and outspoken newspaper editor, Murray attacked Mormon political power and the practice of polygamy with a vengeance. In one of his more controversial actions, he refused to certify the election of George Q. Cannon as delegate to Congress, despite the fact that Cannon had more than ten times as many votes as his non-Mormon opponent. Murray enjoyed portraying himself, and being portrayed in the media, as the principled opponent of sinister Mormonism.

Mormon church leaders and rank-and-file members perceived the threat to their religion's existence as quite real and increasingly frenzied. On July 4, 1885, Mormons again used the national holiday as an occasion for expressing mourning over the loss of their political and religious freedoms. The flag in front of city hall was lowered to half-staff in a gesture that was read by Governor Eli Murray as an act of rebellion and a symbol of treason. A crowd quickly gathered and split angrily along religious lines; police had to be called in to prevent a riot. The trouble bolstered Murray's claim that there was a political "crisis" in the territory and that new, even more stringent, federal laws were needed to bring Utah into conformance with the nation.

Congress responded in 1887 with the Edmunds-Tucker Act, named after Senator Edmunds and Representative J. Randolph Tucker of Virginia, chairman of the House Judiciary Committee. While focusing attention on the high-profile issue of polygamy, the new law was designed to be a death blow against the Mormon church as the controlling power in the affairs of Utah Territory, and it, in fact, was viewed by many church members as an attempt to eradicate the church itself. The teeth of the bill were so sharp that representatives of the

MEMORIAL OF THE NON-MORMON PEOPLE OF UTAH.

To his Excellency, the President, and the Congress of the United States:

The undersigned your memorialists, The Territorial Central Committee of the Liberal Party of Utah Territory, respectfully represent :

That the condition of political affairs in Utah is so anomalous that the political distinction which prevail elsewhere in the United States, have no application here. The organization which we represent, comprises all those outside of and politically opposed to the Mormon Church party. We are variously styled by our opponents "Gentiles" and "Outsiders," but the name "Liberals" has been adopted by ourselves as a designation sufficiently distinctive for our purposes.

The hostility which is manifested toward us in the terms "outsider" and "Gentile" applied to us and which arises from the fact that we acknowledge the supremacy of the National authority and refuse allegiance to the rule of the Mormon Church and priesthood; and deny its right to control the citizen in his political, social and business affairs, compelled the formation of our organization.

With this preface as a reason for the manner of this memorial, and speaking as the authorized representatives of thirty thousand loyal American citizens in Utah and who, it is estimated, pay more than one third of its taxes, we proceed to a statement of the grievances to which we ask attention.

On the 7th day of November last we polled very nearly five thousand votes, and would have had a somewhat larger vote had there been a possibility of our success in the election.

On the 11th day of October last the "Liberals" of Utah held a Territorial Convention at Salt Lake City, composed of representative citizens from all parts of the Territory; most of whom are not only of the highest intelligence and respectability, but of long residence and experience in the Territory, identified with its interests and devoted to its development and prosperity. Among other declarations of opinion made by this Convention, it was unanimously resolved that:

"We arraign the Mormon power in Utah on the following grounds : It exalts the Church above the State in matters of purely administrative and political concern. It perverts the duty of the representative in official and legislative matters by demanding that the interests and wishes of that sect and of the priesthood shall be made paramount considerations. It destroys the freedom of the citizen by assuming the right to dictate his political action and control his ballot. It teaches that defiance of the law of the land when counseled by its priesthood is a religious duty. It encourages jurors and witnesses, when attempts are made in the ordinary course of law to punish the crime of polygamy, to disregard their duties in order to protect offenders who are of their faith. It discourages immigration and settlement upon the public lands, except by its own adherents, and by intolerance and gross personal outrages on non-Mormon settlers, drives them from the common domain. It restricts commerce and business enterprise by commanding its members to deal only with houses of which it approves, thus creating vast monopolies in trade in the interest of a few men, who engross the favor of its hierarchy and enjoy the income of its people. It oppresses the people by taxation, unequal and unjust, and its officers neither make nor are they required to give any satisfactory account of the disbursement of public funds. It taxes the people to build school houses and therein teaches the tenets of the sect by teachers licensed only by its priesthood—most of whom are incompetent and unlearned except in Mormon doctrines. It fills the public offices with bigoted sectarians and servants, without regard to capacity for official station or public employment. It divides the people into classes by religious distinction and falsely teaches its adherents that those not of their faith are their enemies, thus sowing suspicion and bigotry among the masses. It confers on women the suffrage and then forces her to use it under the lash of its priesthood, to perpetuate their power and her own degradation. It robs thousands of women of honorable wedlock and brands their children with dishonor, so that they may be forever deterred from any effort for relief from its grasp. In a word, it has made Utah a

Letter from an anonymous resident of Logan to President James Garfield, 1881. (NARA)

Memorial of the non-Mormon People of Utah, 1882. (NARA)
Both Mormon and non-Mormon organizations in Utah Territory attempted to sway the opinion of decision-makers in Washington with a sea of letters, protests, and memorials which portrayed their religious adversaries in the territory as dangerous and deceitful. Sometimes, such as in the letter from an anonymous woman in Logan shown above, the communication took on a deeply personal tone, recounting individual experiences that the writer hoped would demonstrate the struggle of being a non-Mormon in the territory. Others, such as the formal memorial from the Liberal party, were designed to urge the national government to come to the rescue by emphasizing the writers' loyalty to the government while decrying what was alleged to be the disloyal nature of the Mormon people. While Mormon counter-arguments were routinely drafted, arguing against the characterizations offered by their opponents, they seldom received the national exposure afforded those statements that attacked Mormon religious convictions and patriotism.

church in Washington conducted round-the-clock lobbying efforts to soften the bill or delay its passage. The efforts extended back to the territory, with church leaders grudgingly agreeing to accept a new Utah constitution that offered to make polygamy a criminal misdemeanor. The church was also active in making contributions to political leaders, and it even made outright payoffs to leading national newspapers as a means of easing the strident anti-Mormon attacks that were heavily influencing decisions affecting the fate of the territory. But all efforts failed—the Edmunds-Tucker Act became law in March 1887.

The twenty-seven sections of the Edmunds-Tucker Act swept across many aspects of civil life in the territory. The Mormon church was disincorporated, and all of its assets over $50,000 were to be seized unless the particular land, building, or property was directly used for worship. Administered by a receiver, the proceeds from the sale or distribution of the seizures were to be

BATTLE FOR THE YOUNG MINDS:

Through the 1880s non-Mormon religious organizations placed a high priority on attempting to "reform" the predominant religious culture in Utah, often by focusing their attention on the Mormon children. Recognizing that education in the territory was inconsistent under an informal system that required no teacher training, required tuition payments, and often was dependent upon a local Mormon church for its location, religious groups began offering more formal classes taught by college-trained teachers in gleaming new school buildings through-out the territory. The Methodist church alone accounted for over forty new schools in the territory.

The parochial schools, often regarded as the first dramatic step forward in public education in the territory, were generally well-received in the host communities. Thousands of Mormon children attended the schools, though there is little evidence to suggest that the campaign to change the future of Mormonism by winning the hearts and minds of the next generation ever gained its intended foothold.

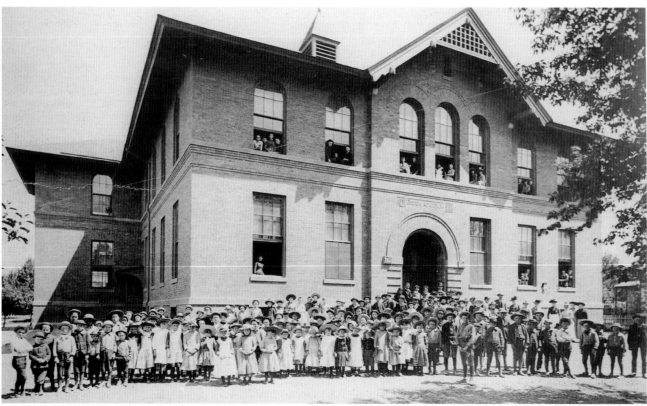

The Ogden Academy (Methodist church), c. 1885. (USHS)

Echo School, 1895. (USHS)

Seventeenth Ward School, Salt Lake City, c. 1885. (USHS)

SCHOOLS IN UTAH TERRITORY

Franklin School, Salt Lake City, date unknown. (USHS)

First Ward School, Ephraim, date unknown. (USHS)

Collegiate Institute (Presbyterian church), Salt Lake City, c. 1885. (USHS)

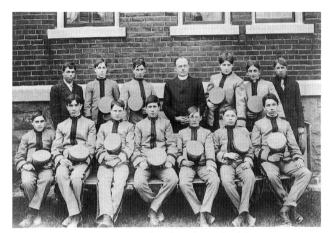

All Hallows College (Catholic church), Salt Lake City, c. 1900. (USHS)

Presbyterian church and school, Salt Lake City, c. 1890. (USHS)

Right: The Washington Monument, Washington, D.C., summer 1885. (LOC)

While a crowd gathered in the sweltering summer heat of the nation's capital to witness the dedication of the just-completed Washington Monument, Congress nearby was preparing a new legislative assault on Mormons in Utah Territory.

Senator William L. Scott, Pennsylvania, c. 1887. (USHS)

Senator Scott was nominally sympathetic to Mormon pleas for tolerance from the federal government for their deeply held religious principles. He proposed an amendment that would provide a grace period for the Mormon church to act to come into compliance with federal laws banning plural marriage. Church leadership endorsed the notion of a *political* action aimed at appeasing the federal government, and even offered a proposed new state constitution that would outlaw plural marriage in the territory. But those same leaders refused to make a definitive public statement renouncing plural marriage as a religious principle, and their constitution was viewed by many in Washington as a fraud. But, though the Scott amendment failed, it did take the first tentative steps along a path of accommodation between the Mormons and the government.

Right: Representative J. Randolph Tucker, co-author of the Edmunds-Tucker Act, c. 1887. (USHS)

J. Randolph Tucker was the chairman of the powerful Judiciary Committee of the House of Representatives. By the mid-1880s he was drafting a bill to offer a final solution to what he considered the persistent national outrage over polygamy and perceived Mormon political control of Utah Territory. After months of political jockeying, Tucker merged his effort with that of Senator George F. Edmunds, author of the 1882 Edmunds Act attacking polygamy, to fashion the Edmunds-Tucker Act. The law, a wide-ranging effort that attacked everything from women's voting rights to church immigration and included new efforts to seize church property, still stands as one of the most pointed and determined attacks ever mounted by Congress against a religious organization.

used for the support of a public school system. Women's suffrage was abolished and new test oaths were authorized for voting, holding office, and public service employment. The laws aimed at cracking down on polygamy were broadened to ease the prosecution of the accused. In a separate action, Congress appropriated $40,000 to create a "Christian Home" in the territory to provide sanctuary for the women who it was anticipated would flee polygamy in droves if given an opportunity to have a safe haven.

As leader of the Mormon church, John Taylor had balanced his public calls for adherence to the principle of plural marriage with a few modest, private acknowledgments that political solutions, clearly apart from spiritual conviction, were worthy of further study. Still, he was viewed as a rock of determination by Mormon and non-Mormon alike, and was considered unlikely to offer any concession on polygamy. "God has commanded it," said Taylor, "and man must obey." It was the view he shared with followers during his years in exile on the underground, and it was the view he took with him when he died, still on the run, on July 25, 1887.

The funeral of John Taylor, Salt Lake Tabernacle, 1887. (USHS)

"Few men have ever lived who have manifested such integrity and such unflinching moral and physical courage. He was killed by the cruelty of those officials who have in this Territory misrepresented the government of the United States."
—George Q. Cannon and Joseph F. Smith, July 26, 1887

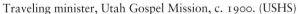

Traveling minister, Utah Gospel Mission, c. 1900. (USHS)   Sisters of the Holy Cross, c. 1890. (USHS)

Proselytizing and serving the community, ministers and members of different faiths continued to be an active presence in Utah through the end of the nineteenth century. Whether by riding a circuit sharing Bible teachings with evangelical fervor or by providing care to the sick and injured, the growth of religious diversity in the territory had a profound effect on the development of communities and services.

Within days of Taylor's death the U.S. Attorney for Utah Territory began proceedings to seize Mormon church property under provisions of the Edmunds-Tucker Act. Church temples were to be spared under the provision protecting sites of worship, but virtually all other church properties were considered fair game under the new federal law. Federal marshal Frank Dyer was selected to serve as receiver, and his first move was to seize the church's tithing office, which collected the offerings of church faithful for the support of religious efforts. He next seized the Gardo House, originally built by Brigham Young and later used by John Taylor as a primary residence. Further seizures included the record-keeping church historian's office and the Temple Block itself. Dyer would eventually allow the church to "lease" the facilities for a sum of more than $7,000 per year.

In this period of inflated rhetoric and heated emotion, Utah Territory again submitted a petition for statehood to Congress. Delegate John Caine pointed

FEDERAL SEIZURES OF MORMON CHURCH PROPERTY

Armed with the new Edmunds-Tucker Act in 1887, federal deputy marshals and prosecutors initiated a campaign to financially squeeze the life from the Mormon church—a tactic that would either destroy it or serve as a means of bringing it into compliance with national wishes on the issues of polygamy and political control of the territory. Officers were charged with going after those properties that belonged to the Mormon church but did not serve an exclusively religious purpose; however, raids were conducted by deputies with little regard to the spiritual nature of the buildings they stormed. The Manti Temple, in the final stages of construction, was raided and reportedly ransacked as deputies sought polygamists. The Endowment House, used for ceremonies held sacred by the Mormon people, was raided. The church historian's and tithing offices were raided, as was the office of the Perpetual Emigrating Fund, as federal authorities sought documentation of church assets for seizure. The Gardo House, built by Brigham Young in his last days as a special mansion for his plural wife Amelia Folsom (hence its widely-used nickname "Amelia's Palace"), was seized.

The Edmunds-Tucker Act mandated that the seized church assets would be used to fund a new public education system for the territory, a system that would be under direct federal control to avoid Mormon influence. The act also stripped Utah women of the right to vote, attacked the rights of children to inherit from polygamous fathers, and reversed the ancient common law principle of women being excused from testifying against their husbands in criminal proceedings. In its more than two dozen sections, the act also abolished the territorial militia, gave new power to the Utah Commission to control political decision-making in the territory, and targeted virtually every financial component of the Mormon church for seizure by federal authorities. The bill was so stringent that President Grover Cleveland, despite being motivated by his own strong anti-polygamy feelings, would not sign the measure, instead letting it become law without his signature.

As the decade of the 1880s neared an end, the federal government's efforts to establish control over Utah Territory had passed from a thousand prosecutions of individual polygamists to a fundamental assault on the religious structure that had defined the region for forty years.

The Endowment House, Salt Lake City, c. 1887. (USHS)

The Manti LDS Temple, c. 1887. (USHS)

Left: Looking east over the tithing office and yard toward the Wasatch Mountains with the Lion House (center, left) and Gardo House (center, right) visible along South Temple Street in Salt Lake City. (USHS)

to a population of 150,000 and a new constitution which deemed polygamy a misdemeanor as compelling reasons for granting Utah admission to the Union. In response, the House Committee on Territories tabled the admission bill. The Senate offered a more definitive statement:

> It is the sense of the Senate that the Territory of Utah ought not to be admitted into the Union as a State until it is certain beyond a doubt that the practice of plural marriages, bigamy and polygamy has been entirely abandoned by the inhabitants of said Territory, and until it is likewise certain that the civil affairs of the Territory are not controlled by the priesthood of the Mormon Church.

Wilford Woodruff, now serving at the highest level of church leadership and awaiting confirmation as church president, viewed the failure of the latest bid for statehood with dismay. One thousand of his fellow Mormons had been

Right: The Gardo House, sometimes known as "Amelia's Palace," c. 1888. (USHS)

THE DEVELOPMENT OF HIGHER EDUCATION

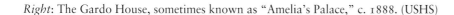

Amid the conflict and chaos born of the federal crackdown on the Mormon church, the Territory of Utah managed to take some dramatic strides forward in higher education during the 1880s. After more than thirty years of intermittent classes and no fixed abode, the University of Deseret moved into its first permanent building in 1884 at the location of present-day West High School in Salt Lake City. Two years later, the school would present its first graduating class: ten certified teachers and two graduates with bachelor degrees. The school would retain its name of Deseret until 1894, when the territorial assembly would officially change the institution's name to the University of Utah. By 1900 the school would relocate to a new site adjacent to Fort Douglas on the foothills just east of Salt Lake City.

In March 1888 the territorial legislature created in Cache Valley the forerunner of Utah State University, a land-grant agricultural and mechanical college. Interestingly, the federal land-grant program supporting the creation of a national system of agricultural colleges was itself created under the Morrill Act of 1862, the same law whose other provisions sought to end the practice of polygamy in Utah Territory.

Since 1875 the Mormon church had advanced the cause of higher education through a private academy endowed by, and named after, Brigham Young. Housed in a converted commercial building in downtown Provo until it was destroyed by fire, Brigham Young Academy took a great leap forward in 1892 when a new building was dedicated on Academy Square in Provo. In 1903 the academy would be elevated to university status, with a corresponding change in name. In 1911 the school would open new buildings on nearby Temple Hill in Provo, initiating a process that would eventually lead to the transfer of all classes to the new site.

While bearing little resemblance to the college-level education of the latter part of the twentieth century, the growth of higher-education opportunities in the territory reflected the evolution of society, the local appreciation of the arts and sciences, and an increasingly dynamic economy that needed the caliber of expertise provided to students by colleges.

The University of Deseret, Salt Lake City, 1884. (USHS)

Brigham Young Academy, Provo, c. 1896. (USHS)

The Women's Industrial Christian Home,
Salt Lake City, c. 1888. (USHS)

    The Women's Industrial Christian Home
was envisioned by a group of non-Mormon
Utah women as a gathering place for
homeless defectors from polygamy, who they
were certain would flock to a safe haven if
one were created. It was funded by Congress
in 1886. Designed to house several dozen
women and their children, it never actually
housed a population of more than one or
two dozen people. Few women chose the
dormitory living and menial-labor training of
the home over their lives in a community that
still strongly supported polygamy as a
religious principle. The home was also
hampered by restrictive federal rules that
prohibited first, or legal, wives from entry. In
the face of low use and the dramatic change
in the Mormon church's position on plural
marriage, Congress ceased funding the
project by the early 1890s.

The Salt Lake Temple, under construction, 1887. (USHS)

    A view looking south along Main Street
in Salt Lake City from a spot one block
north of Temple Square. The Salt Lake
Mormon Temple is emerging as the tallest
building in the city skyline, joining the
shining turtleback dome of the Tabernacle
as dominant features in any view of the
territory's capital city. As the decade of the
1880s came to a close, paved roads were
just starting to appear in the territory, and
new strings of telephone lines paralleled
most of the city's main streets.

sent to prison; many others remained on the underground or had relocated to
Mexico or Canada. Temporally, his church was hanging by a thread, with
property being seized and bankruptcy a distinct possibility. To compound
matters, the election of 1888 had returned to national power the Republican
party, the creator of the "twin relics of barbarism" platform plank against
polygamy more than thirty years before.

    Wilford Woodruff felt himself at the edge of an abyss. He looked for
guidance; his next decisions would determine the future of Utah Territory ...
and perhaps the fate of his church, as well.

Chapter Seven

NEW BEGINNINGS
1889–1890

The Sherman Anti-Trust Act is passed....Ellis Island immigration station opens in New York....Indians are murdered at the Wounded Knee Massacre in Dakota Territory....The United Mine Workers Union is formed....Rudolf Diesel develops an engine that he names after himself....Hollerith experiments with a computer....The nation's population is 62,947,714.

THE ARRIVAL OF A NEW DECADE found Utah, on paper, the most qualified of all the handful of territories seeking admission to the Union. The census of 1890 identified 210,779 permanent residents in Utah Territory, making it the most populous non-state area in the nation's domain. From the first pioneering settlement in the Salt Lake Valley forty-three years earlier, hundreds of cities, towns, and settlements had germinated in every corner of the state. Many prospered. By the standards of population, settlement, and political and civil order, Utah dwarfed the nearby territories of Montana, Idaho, and Wyoming.

Below: Center Street, Provo, c. 1880. (USHS)
Provo in the 1880s shows the development of the territory's cities. Telegraph poles feed wires into the telegraph office in the First National Bank building. Telephone exchanges had been installed in Salt Lake City and Ogden. Public transportation for Provo was a smoky steam locomotive pulling a single car along the unpaved streets. Gaslights atop the telegraph poles served more as beacons than as illumination.

Right: President Benjamin Harrison visits Salt Lake City, c. 1890. (USHS)

After the Civil War most presidents made a point of traveling by rail to the West, often as part of political campaigns. Often they would limit their contacts in Utah to the non-Mormon community, gaining an interesting, if lopsided, perspective on life in the territory. Benjamin Harrison was adamantly opposed to polygamy, but eased his harsh view of the Mormon church when dramatic personal events occurred during his four years as president.

Utah Territorial Governor Arthur Thomas, c. 1890. (USHS)

An audible groan likely went up in Utah Territory when Benjamin Harrison appointed Arthur Thomas to serve as governor. Thomas had been secretary to the Utah Commission, the despised political controlling board that had stripped the voting rights of thousands of Mormons because of their practice and support of polygamy. Thomas, however, proved to be more concerned with improving public education for children and managing irrigation in the semiarid territory. But he did anger Utah Mormons when he traveled to Washington in support of a bill that would strip political rights from members of the Church of Jesus Christ of Latter-day Saints.

However, in an eight-month span from November 1889 through July 1890, Montana, Idaho, and Wyoming would be swept into the Union on a wave of public opinion that meshed with a general assessment that the American frontier was now closed. Statehood was viewed as a sewing together of the quilt of the American experience. But Utah's repeated bids for statehood were pointedly and determinedly shunned and rejected by Congress.

By 1890 it was clear that Utah's failure to secure statehood was irrevocably tied to two factors: national politics and the practice of plural marriage by members of the Mormon church.

In the national election of 1888 the political landscape had dramatically turned against the Mormon church and the fortunes of Utah statehood. Benjamin Harrison had led a Republican surge that pushed the GOP to narrow majorities in the House and Senate and delivered Harrison to the White House, unceremoniously dumping Democratic incumbent Grover Cleveland. While he was far from a political ally, Mormon lobbyists in Washington had come to view Cleveland and his administration as less severe than Republicans in striking out against polygamy and the Mormon faith in general. For example, Cleveland had allowed the punishing Edmunds-Tucker Act to pass into law without his signature. While greatly disappointed that the Democrats had failed to provide a supportive environment for Utah's statehood bid, and bitter that the party's years in power had produced the Edmunds-Tucker Act, the Mormon church's political sentries were convinced that Republican control of the federal government was certain to bring even harsher treatment for the church and Utah's political fortunes. A firm stance against polygamy had been a hallmark of the Republican party since its founding in 1856.

President Harrison confirmed many of the Mormons' fears during his first month in office. Using the power of political patronage, Harrison removed the appointees of the Cleveland years from territorial office in Utah. Against protests from many citizens in the territory, he elevated Arthur Thomas from the despised Utah Commission to the office of governor. And then, in the face of even stronger pleas from Utah, he returned Charles Zane to the position of chief justice for another term. Efforts to secure statehood and increased self-determination would now face a disapproving Republican majority in Congress as well as tough "law and order" roadblocks within the territory.

PLURAL MARRIAGE IN UTAH TERRITORY

By 1890 the overt practice of polygamy had been dealt a serious blow by the fierce federal efforts to prosecute plural marriage among the Mormons. An estimated 1,000 prison sentences had been handed down in the territorial courts, many of them second or third convictions for men who insisted on visiting their plural wives and families upon their release from prison. In several instances federal deputies actually followed inmates upon their release, hoping to catch them in the company of a plural wife.

Hundreds of men and women were still on "the underground," avoiding any public contact with their families in order to avoid arrest. Mothers often were forced to move with their children just across the territory's boundaries to Colorado and Arizona or, more dramatically, to Mexico and Canada to avoid law-enforcement officers and court officers who might call upon them to testify against their husbands. Family photographs were strongly discouraged, since a glass photographic plate could be seized by deputies and used to prove "unlawful cohabitation" in the federal courts. While there were still forceful advocates of plural marriage in Mormon church leadership positions and among the rank-and-file membership, the number of new plural marriages fell precipitously in the face of the federal prosecutions.

The plural wives of polygamist Joseph W. Summerhays, c. 1880s. (USHS)

The John Nebeker residence and family members, Salt Lake City, c. 1885. (USHS)

Charles C. Rich residence, Salt Lake City, c. 1883, with one of Rich's plural wives, Sara D. Pea Rich, at front gate. (LDS)

The Utah Commission itself capped off the transition by issuing a scathing annual report chastising the territory for its failure to respond to the national will. The commission noted that there were more than 350 convictions under the Edmunds-Tucker Act during its first full year in effect, and it complained about the heroic status accorded imprisoned polygamists who were "met in the prison doors by brass bands and a procession of banners … to be toasted, extolled, and feasted as though it were the conclusion of some brilliant and honorable achievement." The commission, in effect, called for a final solution to the "Mormon question." It proposed congressional control of a public school system, lengthening prison terms for convicted polygamists, converting all territorial offices to appointive rather than elective status, and posting an outright ban on all Mormons seeking to immigrate to Utah.

In the face of such an onslaught, representatives of the Mormon church continued to pursue a quiet, politically sensitive course in Washington. George Q. Cannon emerged as a deft political spokesperson, capable of presenting the principles and convictions of the church while seeking to explore political opportunities. In the high-stakes game of partisan politics, Cannon played the Mormon membership as a political card, uncommitted but potentially ripe for association with the Republican party if that party proved to be "interested" in the future status of Utah Territory and the condition of the Mormon church. Cannon's efforts led to beneficial relationships with Secretary of State James G. Blaine and railroad baron Leland Stanford of California, and both responded to Cannon's overtures with counsel and occasional networking that later would prove pivotal for Utah's statehood bid.

Statements by Mormon church leaders often reflected the convulsive political era. Publicly, church president Wilford Woodruff would choose his words very carefully, depending on the audience. At gatherings of church members he would counsel his followers against bringing up certain sensitive subjects, notably plural marriage. At the October 1889 general conference of the church in Salt Lake City he privately expressed the hope that someone would "throw their hat" at Rudger Clawson to keep him from speaking at length of his religious convictions in light of his imprisonment for polygamy. In more intimate settings or in interviews he would offer softer, more ambiguous statements, even going so far as to tell the *Salt Lake Tribune* in October 1889 that he had "refused to give any recommendations for the performance of plural marriages since I have been President." Yet Abraham

U.S. Secretary of State James G. Blaine, c. 1890. (LOC)

"The Lord giveth and the Lord taketh away. Wouldn't it be possible for your people to find some way...to bring yourself into harmony with the law and institutions of this country?" —James G. Blaine to George Q. Cannon in the summer of 1890

The First Presidency of the Church of Jesus Christ of Latter-day Saints, c. 1890. (USHS)

The First Presidency, made up of President Wilford Woodruff and counselors George Q. Cannon (left) and Joseph F. Smith (right), accepted much of the responsibility for steering Utah's bid for statehood. They would often sign group correspondence as the "statehood committee." Woodruff's willingness to consider options and Cannon's keen political strategies were central to the events of 1890 which led to a breakthrough in the conflict between Utah and the federal government.

Cannon would write in his journal one month later that Woodruff had reported receiving a divine revelation instructing that:

> The word of the Lord was for us not to yield one particle of that which He had revealed and established....We are promised redemption and deliverance if we will trust in God and not in the arm of flesh.

For himself, Woodruff would confide in his journal that the times seemed to fulfill a prophecy offered by church founder Joseph Smith that "the whole

Left: LDS Temple, Salt Lake City, 1890. (USHS)

Federal deputy marshals and attorneys had been seizing Mormon church property since passage of the Edmunds-Tucker Act in 1887. Those seizures, however, had been stalled as the church challenged them in a case that was appealed all the way to the U.S. Supreme Court. As the church's crown jewel temple neared completion in Salt Lake City, federal agents let it be known that it was certain to be put on the list for seizure.

Bottom left: Stonecutters and artisans working on the Salt Lake Temple, c. 1890. (USHS)

An average construction worker earned about fifty dollars a month for a six-day work week in 1890. A few years later a national economic depression had spread to Utah, and many businesses and investments collapsed. The Mormon church resorted for a time to paying church workers from the food and goods of the tithing revenues, which were generally reserved for the poor.

Bottom right: An unidentified women's group, Salt Lake City, c. 1890.

Women were as dramatically split over religious issues as were men in Utah, and throughout the 1880s Mormon and non-Mormon women traded stinging speeches and editorials about life in Utah. Stripped of the right to vote by the Edmunds-Tucker Act of 1887, women on both sides of the religious chasm were active in the national suffrage movement for women's political rights, however.

CITIES EMERGE IN UTAH TERRITORY

Despite the uncertain political climate, the territory's population continued to rapidly expand. By 1890 more than 200,000 people were living in Utah, and many were choosing to establish themselves in the rapidly developing cities of the Wasatch Front. The boom in population meant a demand for services previously left to cooperative volunteers. A horrendous fire in 1883 prompted Salt Lake City to organize a professional fire department, and the growing incidence of crime led to a better organized police force. Of course, the dependence on horse power required crews to work long hours to keep the streets clean. By 1890, telephone lines were starting to link Utah towns, and the Salt Lake City telephone exchange boasted 500 telephones in operation. It was a pace of life that would seem slow and sometimes terribly unhygienic by twentieth-century standards, but which represented major leaps forward for the more "modern" Utah territory of 1890.

Main Street, Salt Lake City, 1878. (USHS)

Central Fire Station, Salt Lake City, 1884. (USHS)

Erecting telephone poles along Washington Boulevard, Ogden, c. 1890. (USHS)

Above left: Street-cleaning workers, Salt Lake City, c. 1890. (USHS)

Above right: Police officers, Salt Lake City, c. 1880. (USHS)

Left: Zion's Cooperative Mercantile Institution, Main Street, Salt Lake City, c. 1880. (USHS)

Right: Main Street, Logan, c. 1890. (USHS)

Below left: Foulger's Grocery, Salt Lake City, c. 1880. (USHS)

Below right: Flood damage, Manti, Utah, c. 1880. (USHS)

The United States Supreme Court, 1890.
(LOC)

In two far-reaching decisions, the
Supreme Court in 1890 dealt heavy blows to
the Mormon church and its political and
economic future. In *Davis v. Beason* the
Court ruled that Idaho was perfectly free to
bar all Mormons from political participation, whether they practiced polygamy or
not. In *The Late Corporation of the Church
of Jesus Christ of Latter-day Saints...* the
Court supported the seizure of church
property as a legitimate act of the federal
government—one that was not in violation
of religious freedom protections contained
in the Constitution.

Stephen Johnson Field, Supreme Court
Justice, c. 1880. (LOC)

Appointed to the Supreme Court from
California, Field was reported to be under
the control of the Washington lobby run by
railroad millionaire Leland Stanford. It has
been reported that he also may have
received money from the Mormon church as
part of its campaign to ease the crackdown
on polygamy. It was Field, however, who
was selected to write the 1890 *Davis*
decision which upheld an Idaho law denying
the vote and political office to all Mormons.

nation would turn against Zion." As 1889 drew to a close, he wrote: "The
nation has never been filled so full of lies against the Saints as to Day [sic]. 1890
will be an important year with the Latter-Day Saints & the American nation."

The Supreme Court quickly confirmed Woodruff's prediction. In two
closely spaced decisions in 1890 the Court upheld attempts to financially
control the Mormon church and to strip its membership of many American
civil rights. In *The Late Corporation of the Church of Jesus Christ of Latter-
day Saints v. United States* the Court upheld the seizure of church property
under federal law, freeing federal marshals to begin confiscating church assets
in the territory. Of even greater consequence, in *Davis v. Beason* the Court
confirmed the right of the Territory of Idaho to strip Mormons of virtually all
political and civic involvements, and restrict further political activity whether
or not they personally practiced plural marriage.

The decisions were devastating blows for Mormon leaders seeking to effect
political change, and, when they were coupled with the *Reynolds* decision of
1877, members of the Mormon church began to believe that the Supreme
Court had declared an open season on their faith. Within weeks the Cullom-
Struble Bill was introduced in Congress; it sought to nationalize the Idaho law
disfranchising all members of the Mormon church. In Utah Territory deputy
marshals continued to study records, looking for additional church assets that
could be seized.

The local political scene had also undergone a dramatic change. First in
Ogden in 1889, then in Salt Lake City in 1890, the anti-Mormon Liberal party
swept to its first significant election victories in races for city offices. Each side
leveled angry charges against the other, claiming widespread voter fraud.
Mormons claimed that the gentile interests had conspired with the railroads
to ship in large numbers of non-Mormon miners and railroad workers from
Wyoming to vote for the Liberal party candidates. The Liberal party responded by accusing the Mormon People's party of concocting municipal
public-works projects just prior to the election in order that large numbers of
Mormons could be temporarily hired and thus be inclined to vote for the
People's party candidate. The Utah Commission became the final arbiter; it
declared the Liberal party candidates the winners in the contested elections.

In the midst of the rancorous pitched struggle for political control of the
territory, a small but significant movement emerged to bridge the yawning
chasm between Mormon and non-Mormon. The first glimmers of reconcili-

The Ogden City Council, 1890. (USHS)

A political earthquake shook Utah Territory in 1889, and its epicenter was Ogden's municipal government. In a stunning political victory, which Mormons claimed was due entirely to fraud and a government conspiracy, non-Mormons won control of city offices in Ogden. Followed by a similar Liberal party victory in Salt Lake City in 1890, the elections represented a dramatic setback for the political dominance of the Mormon church in the territory and added to the deluge of events flooding against the church. The events almost certainly can be attributed to the efforts of the Utah Commission to remove thousands of Mormons as registered voters.

Senator Shelby Cullom of Illinois, c. 1890. (LOC)

When word of the Supreme Court's decision in the *Davis* case reached Utah, a group of non-Mormons raced to Washington to plead for a new law based upon the Idaho model that would strip all Mormons of their political rights. They found a willing ally in Shelby Cullom, who had first proposed anti-Mormon laws twenty years before. Cullom viewed his bill as the hammer set to strike against the anvil provided by the Supreme Court to crush the Mormon church.

ation came from an infant chamber-of-commerce movement. Using a lofty though difficult to practice motto of "leaving religion and politics at the door," the Salt Lake City Chamber of Commerce brought together an unheralded, low-profile group from the midsection of the business community who were uncomfortable with the animated struggles and the extreme viewpoints that had dominated Utah life since the 1870s. Much to the surprise of the antagonists, the group members found that Mormons and non-Mormons could do business together, could speak the same language, and could harbor similar hopes and fears for the future of the territory once they side-stepped the vexing religious problems and the political posturing that had hitherto hindered cooperation.

Progress toward mutual understanding in the business community led to some mild accommodations in the political process. The People's party, long viewed as the partisan sledgehammer of Mormon political interests, broke new ground when it invited a few non-Mormon businessmen to run as candidates for local office. Mormon and non-Mormon women shared mutual interests in the suffrage movement, which was hampered in Utah by the restrictions of the Edmunds-Tucker Act, and others transcended their religious beliefs to support a fledgling child-welfare movement that mirrored national concerns over child labor abuses and victimization. Literary and arts organizations began to cross cultural and religious lines with greater frequency. And, when all else failed, baseball could serve as a great equalizer uniting neighborhoods, industries, and communities in support of their local team.

But the accommodations were not enough to stem the tide of increasingly intrusive government measures aimed at breaking the practice of polygamy and the perceived hold of the Mormon church on real political power in Utah Territory. The Cullom-Struble bill was already making its way through

Congress, promising another blow against church membership. An intense Mormon lobbying effort aimed at killing the bill was losing ground. In a private conversation with George Q. Cannon early in 1890, Secretary of State James G. Blaine assured the church's representative that there would be no easing of the federal enforcement effort until polygamy was ended. As

Walker Opera House, Salt Lake City, 1882. (USHS)

A symbol of the financial success of the Walker brothers and an indicator of their philanthropic support for an emerging arts culture in Utah, the Walker Opera House was considered the non-Mormon alternative to the Salt Lake Theatre, and it attracted top national talent during its heyday. The building, located on Second South between Main and West Temple, burned down under mysterious circumstances in July 1890.

Salt Lake City policemen, c. 1890. (USHS)

The city's police department was locally controlled, and therefore was often seen as a countervailing force to the federal deputy marshals. On several occasions, the police department would find itself on one side of a disturbance, while federal agents were on the other. The police department became embroiled in controversy in 1890 when control of Salt Lake City government passed to non-Mormon officials. Within a year, local non-Mormon religious groups were complaining to city government that law-enforcement officers had been told to lay off saloons, brothels, and gambling houses, leading to a "depraved environment," according to one Methodist protest.

recounted later by the Mormon leader's son Frank J. Cannon, Blaine forecast that there would be no progress toward statehood until the Mormons brought themselves into harmony with the laws of the nation:

> Believe me, it is not possible for any people as weak in numbers as yours to set themselves up as superior to the majesty of a nation like this. We may

The Salt Lake Red Stockings baseball team, 1878. (USHS)

With conflict gripping almost every aspect of life in Utah Territory as the federal crackdown against polygamy escalated, baseball was a saving grace. Neighborhoods, towns, churches, and mining camps fielded teams to do spirited and generally friendly battle with opponents. The games often would provide an opportunity for Mormons and non-Mormons to interact more peacefully. The Salt Lake Red Stockings were an outstanding team of their day, claiming the 1878 local championship. While his batting average has been lost to the ages, the club included a wiry second baseman, Heber J. Grant (seated, middle row, center), who would gain greater notoriety years later when he served as president of the Mormon church.

Bicycling club, Salt Lake City, c. 1890. (USHS)

While the first bicycles appear in Salt Lake City photographs in the 1870s, an organized club featuring the classic large-wheel vehicles was not formed until 1890. Utah's unpaved streets were generally unfriendly terrain for the unwieldy bikes, and it is probable that more than one cyclist took a nasty spill on Main Street in the middle of horse traffic when the rider wedged a wheel in the trolley tracks.

The Salt Lake Theatre group, 1890. (USHS)

A theatre group supported the productions of the Salt Lake Theatre as actors and behind-the-scenes stage members. This photograph earns a footnote in history because of the handsome young thespian seated on the left. His dramatic training might have aided Heber M. Wells's successful campaign to serve as Utah's first state governor six years later.

succeed this time in preventing your disfranchisement, but nothing permanent can be done until you get into line.

On the heels of Blaine's warning came another report from the Utah Commission. It indicated that President Wilford Woodruff had made refer-

---

26 REPORT OF THE UTAH COMMISSION.

Indictments pending in which no arrests have been made for the reason that "the defendants are either in hiding or have been sent out of the country as missionaries" are as follows:

Polygamy 4
Unlawful cohabitation 30
Adultery 4
Fornication 1
                                                                                ——
    Total 39

The number of cases reported from the United States commissioners for the same period is as follows:

	Complaints.					Held to bail.				
	Polyg-amy and bigamy.	Unlaw-ful co-habita-tion.	Adul-tery.	Forni-cation.	Total.	Polyg-amy and bigamy.	Unlaw-ful co-habita-tion.	Adul-tery.	Forni-cation.	Total.
J. W. Greenman, Salt Lake	8	27	10	13	53	3	19	7	11	40
A. G. Norrell, Salt Lake...	....	2	1	4	7	....	....	1	3	4
H. Pratt, Salt Lake	....	4	4	....	8	....	1	4	....	5
C. C. Goodwin, Logan	....	45	13	3	61	....	45	13	3	61
E. P. Johnson, Corinne..	....	2	....	....	2	....	....	....	....	
J. M. Cohen, Park City..	....	....	1	....	1	....	....	1	....	1
C. K. Norris, Beaver	....	15	1	1	17	....	10	1	1	12
G. C. Viele, Fillmore....	....	4	2	....	6	....	3	2	....	5
J. T. Leonard, Salina....	....	15	5	2	22	....	15	3	2	20
R. W. Cross, Ogden	....	12	2	6	20	....	11	2	2	15
W. Zabriskie, Mount Pleasant	1	3	1	....	5	....	1	1	....	2
Total	4	129	40	29	202	3	93	31	22	149

The Commission has heretofore made recommendations for further legislation in support of the existing laws designed to stamp out this evil, and respectfully refers to the recommendations to be found on page 18 *et sequitur*, of its report for 1889, to which it requests the attention of the law-making power of the Government, as being in its opinion necessary and proper legislation to more effectually accomplish the desired ends.

In addition it recommends that the powers of the Utah Commission be so enlarged as to authorize and enable it to issue instructions which shall be binding upon the registrars of its appointment in the performance of their legal duties.

Utah Commission Annual Report, 1890. (USAR)

The annual report of the Utah Commission released in September 1890 produced intense controversy in Washington. President Wilford Woodruff of the Mormon church had made public assurances that he was refusing to authorize new plural marriages among the Mormons. The report, in effect, branded Woodruff and the Mormons as liars, claiming that dozens of new polygamous marriages had been sanctioned in the past year. The report, while deeply flawed and apparently based on little more than old newspaper obituaries, prompted members of Congress and newspaper editors to call for even more aggressive measures against the Mormons in Utah Territory.

Mormon church leaders in San Diego, c. 1890. (USHS)

To avoid a subpoena in a legal action designed to seize the Mormon temples, church president Wilford Woodruff (seated, left) and counselor George Q. Cannon (seated, second from right) traveled to California in the late summer of 1890. While in San Francisco they met with ranking leaders of the national Republican party to consider ways to ease the federal attacks on the Mormons. Told that nothing could be done until his church finally and formally ended the practice of polygamy, Woodruff returned to Utah knowing his next public directive could drastically affect the fate of his church and forty years of work in building the Territory of Utah.

ences to the church ending an endorsement of plural marriage but that, in fact, more than forty new polygamous marriages had taken place while Woodruff was offering reassurances to the contrary. The August 22, 1890, report was flawed, drawing some of its conclusions on polygamous unions from information in obituaries in the local papers, but it sparked a flurry of activity and outrage.

Partly to evade the probe of a federal inquisition into church property holdings, and partly to explore a possible eleventh-hour political solution, Wilford Woodruff and George Q. Cannon made a quick trip to California. In San Francisco they turned to Isaac Trumbo, a former railroad lobbyist who had been assisting the church in making political contacts with the Republican administration. Through Trumbo they met with Leland Stanford, now a United States Senator, as well as with Republican party national committee chair Morris Estee and at least one representative of the *San Francisco Examiner*. Each conversation yielded the same conclusion: the noose around the church was certain to tighten further unless polygamy was ended.

Dispirited, Woodruff and Cannon returned to Utah only to receive information that the Utah Commission's report had created a furor in Washington. The allegation that polygamy was continuing while Woodruff spoke otherwise infuriated members of Congress, adding fuel to a drive by some congressional representatives to disfranchise all Mormons once and for all. On September 25 Wilford Woodruff wrote in his journal:

I have arrived at a point in the History of my life as the President of the Church of Jesus Christ of Latter Day Saints where I am under the necessity of acting for the Temporal Salvation of the Church. The United States

Isaac Trumbo, Washington lobbyist, c. 1890. (USHS)

The son of a Mormon mother and Catholic father, Isaac Trumbo was born in Utah and grew up in Salt Lake City. Deciding against joining the Mormon church, Trumbo made his way to California to seek his fortune. He proved his usefulness to railroad millionaire Leland Stanford, and soon was recognized as being talented at working behind the scenes of government to get things done. Genuinely supportive of the Mormons, Trumbo saw the political future of Utah Territory as a great personal opportunity. He opened doors in the Republican party for Mormon representatives, encouraged church leaders to follow the standard political practice of the day by attempting to buy influence in Congress and the courts, and helped orchestrate a campaign of bribes and gifts to help quiet the most strident anti-Mormon newspapers in the nation's larger cities.

Left: Wilford Woodruff, c. 1898. (USHS)

Returning to Salt Lake City from his trip to California, Woodruff confronted the storm of criticism facing the Mormons as a result of the Utah Commission's annual report for 1890. Diaries of fellow church authorities recounted that Woodruff entered a period of intense prayer and personal reflection in mid-September. When he met with his counselors and the twelve apostles, he presented them with a document that he said was the result of his prayer. The statement, soon to become known as the Woodruff Manifesto, announced his intention to obey the national laws regarding polygamy and added that he would counsel his fellow Mormons to do the same.

Leland Stanford, railroad magnate, governor, and U.S. senator, c. 1890. (USHS)

A primary figure in the Central Pacific Railroad in California, Stanford is recognized as a pivotal force in linking the nation with the transcontinental railroad. A U.S. senator as well as governor of California, Stanford was adept at working government for his own financial interests. He viewed Utah as a likely spot to extend his influence and secure substantial financial benefit for his railroads, so he offered the service of his lobbying team, including Isaac Trumbo, to the Mormon church. Stanford wanted to see Utah swing to the Republican party if it was admitted to the Union.

Right: Portion of a letter from John T. Caine to the Secretary of the Interior, October 1, 1890. (NARA)

No one was more relieved to hear of the Woodruff Manifesto than was John T. Caine, Utah's delegate to Congress. Caine distributed the proclamation to Congress, the White House, and newspaper offices in Washington, claiming that the Manifesto was exactly what the federal government had been demanding from the Mormon church for nearly thirty years. This letter to Interior Secretary John Noble, whose department administered territories of the United States, reflects the role of the Utah Commission's annual report in bringing about the Manifesto, quoting from the report before offering the full text of Woodruff's message in rebuttal.

HOUSE OF REPRESENTATIVES, U. S.,

WASHINGTON, D.C., October 1st, 1890.

Hon. John W. Noble,

Secretary of the Interior,

Washington, D.C.

Dear Sir:

The Utah Commission in its report to you, dated August 22, 1890, gives considerable space to the Mormom Church and to the alleged or intimated continuance of the practice of polygamy. Without troubling you by means of a lengthy controversy on the points raised in the report, I quote the following sentence therefrom:

"The Commission is in receipt of reports from its registration officers, which enumerate forty-one male persons, who, it is believed, have entered into the polygamic relation, in their several precincts, since the June revision of 1889."

And beg leave to call your attention to the following unequivocal declaration of Wilford Woodruff, President and highest authority of the Church:

SALT LAKE CITY, UTAH, Sept. 24, 1890.

To whom it may concern:

Press dispatches having been sent from Salt Lake City, which have been widely published for political purposes, to the effect that the Utah Commission, in their recent report to the Secretary of the Interior, allege that plural marriages are still

2

being solemnized, and that forty or more such marriages have been contracted in Utah since last June or during the past year; also, that in public discourses the leaders of the church have taught, encouraged, and urged the continuance of the practice of polygamy:

I, therefore, as President of the Church of Jesus Christ of Latter-Day Saints, do hereby, in the most solemn manner, declare that the charges are false. We are not teaching polygamy or plural marriage, nor permitting any person to enter into its practice; and I deny that either forty or any other number of plural marriages have, during that period, been solemnized in our temples or in any other place in the Territory.

One case has been reported in which the parties alleged that the marriage was performed in the Endowment House in Salt Lake City in the spring of 1889, but I have not been able to learn who performed the ceremony. Whatever was done in this matter was without my knowledge. In consequence of this alleged occurence the Endowment House was by my instructions taken down without delay.

Inasmuch as laws have been enacted by Congress forbidding plural marriages, which laws have been pronounced constitutional by the Court of last resort, I do hereby declare my intention to submit to those laws, and to use all my influence with the members of the church over which I preside to have them do likewise. There is nothing in my teachings to the church, or in those of my associates, during the time specified which can reasonably be construed to inculcate or encourage polygamy, and when any elder of the church has used language which appeared to convey such teaching he has been promptly reproved; and I now publicly declare that my advice to the Latter-Day Saints is to refrain from contracting any marriage forbidden by the laws of the land.

WILFORD WOODRUFF,

President of the Church of Jesus Christ of Latter-Day Saints.

Inasmuch as the Commission's claim is based upon what "is believed" and upon what is readily susceptible of other construction, I submit that the explicit and authoritative declaration of President

Government has taken a Stand & passed Laws to destroy the Latter Day Saints upon the Subject of poligamy [*sic*].... After praying to the Lord & feeling inspired by his spirit I have issued the following Proclamation ...

What followed was, in a sense, a press release. Wired to the Associated Press bureau in Chicago, Woodruff's message was a clear effort finally to draw the curtain on the controversy and conflict plaguing his church. It included the following words to that effect:

Inasmuch as laws have been enacted by Congress forbidding plural marriages, which laws have been pronounced constitutional by the court of last resort, I hereby declare my intention to submit to those laws.... And now I publicly declare that my advice to the Latter-day Saints is to refrain from contracting any marriage forbidden by the laws of the land.

Church representatives in Washington quickly produced one thousand copies of the document, which was soon called the "Manifesto," and distributed the copies to every corner of the federal government. Immediately there was second-guessing and suspicion. In Washington and among territorial officials acceptance of the Manifesto was hindered by nagging questions. Was the announcement to be viewed as a directive from God superseding the earlier directive instituting plural marriage? Could the content be trusted? Was the document filled with loopholes that would enable Mormons to keep plural wives in Mexico and Canada? In Utah the Manifesto was accepted by the

---

WILFORD WOODRUFF AND PLURAL MARRIAGE

Historian Thomas G. Alexander has called Wilford Woodruff the third most important leader in the early history of the Church of Jesus Christ of Latter-day Saints, ranking him just behind church founder Joseph Smith and colonizing giant Brigham Young. Conversely, other writers have characterized Woodruff as merely an easygoing, sometimes doddering figure who was often manipulated by others.

While he was clearly influenced by the strong personalities and abilities of his counselors George Q. Cannon and Joseph F. Smith, there is no doubt that Woodruff considered himself uniquely and personally responsible for the survival of his church and the well-being of its members. A man of unquestioned spiritual faith and integrity, Woodruff had served at high levels of church leadership for fifty years prior to assuming the presidency in the late 1880s.

Accepting plural marriage as a divinely inspired institution, Woodruff married five wives and fathered more than thirty children. His first wife, Phoebe, harbored private reservations about plural marriage but would never publicly question its role in her faith. Many historians believe that Woodruff would have resisted change longer had it not been for the efforts of federal authorities to seize the Mormon temples, which he treasured and considered sacred.

Historians, political scientists, and theologians have argued about the roots of the Woodruff Manifesto for more than 100 years. The basic conflict stems from trying to determine whether spirituality or political realism was the deciding motivator in the issuing of the proclamation. Such a dialogue, in its own way, resembles the classic "chicken and egg" dilemma. Any attempt to divorce politics from the Manifesto would be naive, while any attempt to deny the spirituality of Wilford Woodruff in fashioning the statement would be blind.

Left: Wilford Woodruff and plural wife Emma, c. 1890. (USHS)

Right: Phoebe W. Woodruff, first wife of Wilford Woodruff, c. 1890. (USHS)

reasons for its promulgation contained in its text are not the reasons given by its author and his first councilor to the conference.

President Wilford Woodruff said to the conference:

I want to say to all Israel that the step which I have taken in issuing this manifesto has not been done without earnest prayer before the Lord.

His first councilor, George Q. Cannon, said:

We have waited for the Lord to move in the matter; and on the 24th of September President Woodruff made up his mind that he would write something, and he had the spirit of it. He had prayed about it and had besought God repeatedly to show him what to do. At that time the Spirit came upon him, and the document that has been read in your hearing was the result.

The document itself attributes the occasion of "the Spirit" coming upon him to "press dispatches having been sent for political purposes from Salt Lake City" in regard to the statement in the Utah Commission in its last report upon the subject of the solemnization of plural marriages; in substance, that forty or more such marriages had been reported to it by its officers during the preceding year.

A great part of the manifesto is devoted to a vigorous assertion that the report of the Commission is false, a general and specific denial of the facts stated therein, and but a small space is devoted to President Woodruff's declaration of his personal intention "to submit to the laws," and "to use his influence with the members of the church to have them do likewise." The most important part of the manifesto is contained in the closing words:

And I now publicly declare that my advice to the Latter-Day Saints is to refrain from contracting any marriage forbidden by the law of the land.

How much weight could be given to the declarations of a man who dares to assert that the Spirit of God came upon him and moved him to charge that the Utah Commission was the retailer and peddler of falsehoods, and by reason of that fact he was to declare to the world that the church he commands will now change front completely and abandon the ordinance of God, which has heretofore been so delightful a work for them to perform, can be judged to a degree from the declaration itself. Some further light may be thrown upon his character and the weight to be given his utterances by a perusal of the following, which fell from his lips at the same conference, as officially reported for

Portion of Utah Commission Annual Report, 1891. (USAR)

One year after the publication of the Woodruff Manifesto, the Utah Commission was urging the federal government not to put full faith in the document. The commission spent much of its report defending its members' view that polygamy was continuing in Utah, and urging federal decision-makers to maintain the intensity of the prosecutions for plural marriage. The report scoffed at Mormon beliefs of divine inspiration, and attempted to assail the character of Wilford Woodruff by making light of his recounted dreams in which he claimed to have spoken with Mormon church founder Joseph Smith.

SIR:

SINCE I FORWARDED MY RECENT REPORT ON THE AFFAIRS OF UTAH, AN EVENT HAS OCCURRED WHICH I BELIEVE WILL VITALLY AFFECT ITS FUTURE, AND I DEEM IT OF SUFFICIENT IMPORTANCE TO JUSTIFY A SUPPLEMENTAL REPORT.

ON THE 24TH OF LAST SEPTEMBER A PROCLAMATION, SIGNED BY THE PRESIDENT OF THE MORMON CHURCH, WAS GIVEN TO THE COUNTRY BY TELEGRAPH, WHICH IN EFFECT ANNOUNCED SUBMISSION TO THE LAW, AND ADVISED THE MEMBERS OF THE CHURCH TO NOT CONTRACT MARRIAGES FORBIDDEN BY THE LAWS OF THE LAND.

MANY DOUBTS EXISTED, AND DIVERSE OPINIONS WERE GIVEN BY NON-MORMONS AS TO THE PURPOSE AND EFFECT OF THIS PROCLAMATION, AND TO A GREAT EXTENT DEFINITE OPINIONS WERE SUSPENDED UNTIL THE GENERAL CONFERENCE OF THE CHURCH APPOINTED FOR THE FOURTH OF OCTOBER LAST, SHOULD BE HELD. AT THE CONFERENCE THE PROCLAMATION WAS RATIFIED BY A UNANIMOUS VOTE AND ADDRESSES TO THE PEOPLE IN REFERENCE TO THE SUBJECT, WERE MADE BY THE PRESIDENT OF THE CHURCH AND THE LEADING APOSTLES. THE PRINCIPAL ADDRESSES SHOULD BE READ IN CONNECTION WITH THE PROCLAMATION, IN ORDER TO UNDERSTAND THE FORCE OF THIS ACTION IN PRESCRIBING A RULE OF CONDUCT.

Part of a letter from Governor Arthur Thomas to the Secretary of the Interior, November 6, 1890. (NARA)

"I think the ultimate effect of this act will greatly benefit the territory. It may lead in time to the formation of political parties. Legitimate politics will be discussed. Individuals will vote according to their personal interests and opinions, instead of the interests of an organization. Social and business relations will be extended." —Arthur Thomas, Utah Territorial Governor

Amid the speculation and arguments about the veracity of the Woodruff Manifesto, territorial governor Arthur Thomas offered one of the more thoughtful and surprisingly farsighted assessments in a letter he wrote to Interior Secretary John Noble. Thomas, never known for his support of the Mormons, urged Washington to accept the Woodruff Manifesto in good faith, and recognize its ability to open a new political era in Utah.

majority of church members with a mixture of relief, sadness, and some confusion. Were all plural marriages now to be null and void? What would happen to the women and children of polygamous unions? Was this only a temporary solution, or was it an enduring new principle?

Although doubts and confusion would linger in many quarters for decades, the Woodruff Manifesto is regarded as a breakthrough event in Utah's quest for statehood. The open conflict between the church and the government eased dramatically in the months following the September 1890 release of the message. No issue had impeded the territory's progress to statehood as had plural marriage.

But polygamy was not the only issue needing to be resolved before the final barriers to statehood could fall. The territorial legislature followed the strong urging of national political leaders and began to fashion a new public school system that was supported by fair taxation and was free from sectarian control. The Mormon church quickly set about disbanding its political People's party, and it actively encouraged its members to join either the national Democratic or Republican parties. In fact, church leaders had to strongly encourage Mormons to consider membership in the Republican party, given its history of tough anti-Mormon stances. The non-Mormon

PUBLIC EDUCATION AND UTAH TERRITORY

The Woodruff Manifesto may have helped Utah Territory over the hurdle of polygamy, but a number of other obstacles had to be overcome before statehood could be achieved. One of the most pressing concerns was with the shoddy public-education system in the territory.

The notion of a collective responsibility for educating the next generation had produced only a spotty, often substandard, response in the territory. With the legislature virtually silent on the subject, and with no funds provided for school buildings or materials, Utah's public-school system was in terrible shape by 1890. Classes often were held in Mormon wardhouses as the only appropriate public meeting place. There were no requirements for teacher training and there were no standard textbooks. Students often learned their vocabulary by being led through the *Book of Mormon*. Funding was even more chaotic, with some areas providing local funds to support schools while others relied on a tuition system in which the tuition was often paid in crops or livestock.

The emergence of the so-called "missionary schools"— opened by Christian denominations coming to Utah to serve the increasingly diverse population while they attempted to convert Mormons—had a profound impact on education in the territory. Faced with the choice of their children going to a poorly equipped and staffed local ward school or attending a new, professionally run parochial school, many Mormon families decided to accept the missionaries' invitation for their children to attend the church-run schools. In response, many communities started to upgrade their local schools to more effectively compete with the missionary schools.

Congress was joined by crusading groups outside of the territory in demanding that the Mormon church be separated from the public-school system and that a funding mechanism be devised to ensure the viability and independence of schools to which the majority of children had access. In 1890 the territorial legislature passed the Free Public School Act, starting Utah down the road to development of a high-quality public-education system. At the time, however, that education did not extend past the elementary-school years.

Left: All Hallows College, Salt Lake City, c. 1900. (USHS)

Right: Quaker School, Clear Lake, 1890. (USHS)

Presbyterian church, Smithfield, c. 1895. (USHS)

It was not unusual for non-Mormon churches in Utah Territory to fly the flag as a determined sign of their parishioners' patriotism and to distinguish their house of worship from Mormon gathering places. In fact, some of the most pointed attacks against the Mormon church were offered by clerics from other denominations who challenged the national loyalty of the territory's predominant faith. Mormons, professing a deep love of the Constitution and the national experience, were often afforded no opportunity to respond to the charges in the forum where they had been presented.

First South and Main Street, Salt Lake City, 1890. (USHS)   Plum Alley, Salt Lake City, c. 1900. (USHS)

Downtown Salt Lake City had two faces at the end of the nineteenth century. The business district presented a well-ordered, well-maintained center of economic life for the territory; but, just steps away, down an unlit side street, was Plum Alley, one of the ghetto and slum areas that had developed in Salt Lake as in other cities throughout the nation. Plum Alley served as part haven and part ghetto for Chinese laborers who had remained in the territory after the years of railroad construction. City police often left the Asian population to police themselves, and merchants and pedestrians were constantly on guard against muggings and robbery.

Right: New York City, 1890. (LOC)

National public opinion against po-lygamy and Mormon political dominance in Utah was a powerful influence on the federal government's crackdown on the Mormon church. In the mid-1880s the church hierarchy, at the urging of non-Mormon lobbyists including Isaac Trumbo and Alexander Badlam, spent more than $150,000 in "gifts" to influence newspapers on the east and west coasts to soften their rhetoric against the church. The diary of church official Hiram B. Clawson mentions $25,000 paid in 1887 alone to three New York City newspapers—the *New York Times*, *New York Sun*, and the *New York Evening Post*. Another $30,000 was promised to the same papers after Utah was admitted as a state. Badlam often would serve as the bag man for the payments, confirming in letters to church authorities that certain editors in the east "had been handsomely taken care of in a most eco-nomical fashion." The strident tone of the anti-Mormon campaign in newspapers eased dramatically in 1890—due in large part to the Woodruff Manifesto and in no small part to the strategic "investments" made by the Mormon church.

Liberal party would follow suit and disband a few years later. Care was also taken to eliminate any public vestige of the old economic divisions and boycotts that had pitted Mormon against non-Mormon business interests.

Advocates of statehood marveled at the progress. Polygamy had been set aside as the nation's lengthiest, most legislated religious issue. Schools, the economy, and the political process in the territory had been assured relative freedom from sectarian control. The territory had made friends in the Republican administration and felt itself to be in compliance with every prerequisite for admission to the Union. Statehood boosters predicted Utah's admission in a matter of months. However, it would take nearly six additional years.

Chapter Eight

ACCOMMODATION
1890–1896

The *Plessy v. Furgeson* Supreme Court decision allows "separate but equal" facilities for black Americans....A national economic depression (the Panic of 1893) causes many banks to fail....Langley creates the first experimental airplane....Freud explores psychoanalysis....Roentgen discovers the x-ray....Sun Yat-sen leads a movement to end Manchu rule in China.

THE ANNOUNCEMENT OF THE WOODRUFF MANIFESTO effectively ending plural marriage among the Mormons had an immediate impact in Congress and on public opinion. A handful of anti-Mormon bills ground to a halt in the national legislative process as members studied the declaration from Utah Territory. "Polygamy in Utah is a dead issue," promised territorial delegate John Caine, who used the Manifesto to beat back bills extending disfranchisement efforts and proposing further restrictions on the Mormon church and its members.

Opinion in influential eastern seaboard newspapers swung dramatically behind Utah's renewed bid for statehood in the wake of the Mormon church's announcement. "The Territory of Utah is knocking at the door of the Union and demanding statehood," wrote the *Boston Globe* in the summer of 1891;

Below: The Capitol Building, Washington, D.C., 1890. (LOC)

The Woodruff Manifesto apparently ending Mormon plural marriage did not immediately produce a dramatic change in national policy. Delegate John T. Caine was kept busy trying to delay several pieces of anti-Mormon legislation. President Harrison said he would not support Utah's bid for statehood until it was beyond dispute that the territory was serious about ending polygamy, and he refused a plea from church leaders for amnesty for men convicted under the anti-polygamy laws.

LIFE IN UTAH TERRITORY OUTSIDE SALT LAKE CITY

While some aspects of life in the Salt Lake Valley were dominated by the stalemate over polygamy and Utah's political future, much of the rest of the territory was dealing with the less complex but equally challenging dilemmas of life in a society just emerging from the frontier. Ogden had to dramatically bolster its police force to deal with the drifters and toughs associated with the booming railyards of Weber County. Park City, Bingham, and other mining towns had incredibly diverse populations drawn from migrants not associated with the Mormon church seeking economic opportunity. The first signs of union activity started to appear among miners in the territory during the 1890s. Communication also was changing—a handful of telephone owners in Salt Lake City, Ogden, and Provo were able to place long-distance calls to each other on a system that rapidly was rivaling that of the telegraph lines. Other areas of the territory, however, still relied on older methods of communication but looked forward to sharing the new technologies.

Right: Miners' union parade, Main Street, Park City, c. 1895. (USHS)

Ogden policemen with city judge S.M. Preshaw, 1891. (USHS)

Park City, c. 1895. (USHS)

Pond on Center Street, Provo, c. 1890. (USHS)

Saloons in Bingham Canyon, c. 1895. (USHS)

"The demand should be granted." The *New York Times* expressed a similar view, predicting that death for plural marriage meant political life for the state of Utah.

In 1891 the national political parties made their first significant appearance in Utah ballot boxes, signaling another important step forward in Utah's national integration. The Democrats, still viewed by many observers as heir to the political power of the now-disbanded Mormon People's party, secured two-to-one majorities in both houses of the territorial legislature. Their closest rival, the anti-Mormon Liberal party, was hampered by the first inroads of the Republican party and the lingering stain of municipal scandals that had gripped Salt Lake City and Ogden after Liberal candidates had been elected to office in those cities.

The legacy of years of distrust still lingered in many influential circles, however, forming an internal barrier to Utah's bid for statehood. The Utah Commission, backed by the *Salt Lake Tribune*, continued to oppose the movement toward admission and publicly challenged the integrity of the political and social revolution that seemed to be gripping the territory:

> This Commission cannot recommend that the "protecting" and fostering hand of government be withdrawn, and is most emphatic in expressing its opinion that it would not at this time be safe to entrust to this people the responsibilities and duties of statehood.

The future of Utah soon became wed, once again, to national politics as President Benjamin Harrison tiptoed around the "Mormon question" as the election of 1892 loomed large. His Democrat opponent was Grover Cleveland, returning for a third bid for the presidency. Both men tried their best to avoid saying anything positive about Utah's lingering request for statehood, wanting to appear tough to an uncertain public, and claiming the territory needed to demonstrate a willingness to police itself regarding future plural marriage before it could be granted the increased control of its own affairs that statehood would bring.

Harrison actually went so far as to pocket a request from Utah Territory for an amnesty declaration, which would authorize the release of prisoners still held in the territorial penitentiary on polygamy charges and restore their full citizenship rights. The amnesty request as well as statehood bills presented by both the Democratic and Republican parties were quietly ignored as the political season increased in intensity.

Benjamin Harrison, twenty-third president of the United States, 1890. (LOC)

Generally considered an able president hamstrung by a dull and sometimes offensive personality, Harrison initially was very reluctant to warm to the actions of the Mormon church to conform with the nation on the issues of polygamy and politics. But powerful Secretary of State James G. Blaine believed in constructive engagement with Mormon leaders and provided important suggestions as the Mormons sought a path to statehood. The illness and subsequent death of his wife shook Harrison in the months leading to the 1892 election, and he made small gestures to church representatives demonstrating a softening of his position, including granting a limited amnesty to convicted polygamists as one of his last acts before leaving office.

Telegram to President Harrison from Mormon church officials on the death of Harrison's wife, 1892. (LOC)

"*The death of your beloved companion comes home to us individually as if it were our private loss. We sincerely and deeply sympathize with you and appeal to the Supreme Being who holds the destiny of us all in his hands to bless, comfort and sustain you in this your hour of great trial and sorrow.*" —Wilford Woodruff, George Q. Cannon, Joseph F. Smith

Below: Capstone ceremony, Salt Lake LDS Temple, April 1892. (USHS)

For forty years the construction of the centerpiece Mormon temple in Salt Lake City seemed to symbolically represent the political fortunes of Utah Territory. Born of deeply felt spiritual commitment in the earliest days of settlement, the temple had advanced in surges of stonecutting and building. Construction also would stall for extended periods, often coinciding with the times of harshest anti-Mormon sentiment in the federal government. By the spring of 1892 the Salt Lake LDS Temple achieved its crowning glory with the placement of the last stone in the structure, to the approval of a large crowd at an impressive ceremony.

An indication of dramatic change in the political environment, demonstrating how the relationship between Utah Territory, the Mormon church, and the federal government was smoothing, came in October 1892, less than a month prior to the presidential election. Benjamin Harrison's wife had been suffering through a long illness, clearly losing ground in a fight for life. In a gesture that touched his guests, Harrison had asked representatives of the Mormon church, visiting his office to argue for statehood and amnesty, to pray for his wife's health and well-being. When his wife died in the last week of October, hundreds of telegrams poured in to the White House expressing condolences. One telegram carried the signatures of the First Presidency of the Church of Jesus Christ of Latter-day Saints: Wilford Woodruff, George Q. Cannon, and Joseph F. Smith. Just five years earlier the same level of church leadership had been dodging federal marshals on the Mormon underground. Now some of them had been guests in the Oval Office and they were caring sympathizers for a distraught president.

Harrison apparently did not forget the gesture. After losing in a landslide to Cleveland, Harrison took the request for amnesty for polygamists out of his pocket and on January 4, 1893, signed into effect a limited, carefully worded amnesty proclamation. It was decidedly less than Mormon representatives had hoped for, since it failed to clearly restore voting and office privileges to people convicted under anti-polygamy laws, but it was accepted as another step along the path of putting the pitched battle of polygamy behind the Republican party and the Territory of Utah.

RECREATION IN UTAH TERRITORY—THE GREAT SALT LAKE

"We consider the Great Salt Lake one of the wonders of the world." —Wilford Woodruff, 1847

From the earliest days of pioneer settlement the Great Salt Lake had charmed the people coming to live on the land east of the lake's shoreline. Salt works had been developed on the shore, but residents of the territory also recognized the lake's potential for recreational development as early as the 1870s. Brigham Young enjoyed making the nearly day-long trip to Black Rock beach to "float like a cork," and the church president also liked camping with a large entourage on the cool sands during the summer months. The 1880s brought new swimming pavilions on the lake and health spas opening near the shoreline to take advantage of natural hot springs. In 1893 the Mormon church built Saltair on the southern shore of the lake—a magnificent amusement center and recreational resort. For years Saltair boasted the largest dance floor in the world, and special trains would deliver carloads of bathers to the resort for a day of swimming and an evening of dancing under the ornate dome.

Black Rock Beach, Great Salt Lake, c. 1880. (USHS)

Lake Park Bathing Resort, Great Salt Lake, c. 1895. (USHS)

Beck's Hot Springs, near Salt Lake City, c. 1890. (USHS)

Garfield Beach, Great Salt Lake, c. 1895. (USHS)

Saltair Resort, Great Salt Lake, c. 1900. (USHS)

The inauguration of Grover Cleveland to a second, non-consecutive term as president was viewed as the gateway to the final stage of Utah's admission to the Union. Coincidentally, the Mormon church dedicated its just completed Salt Lake Temple the same week in April 1893 that Cleveland swept the territorial offices of Harrison holdovers, replacing them with a group of appointees clearly inclined to advance Utah's statehood bid. Even the Utah Commission relaxed its stance, advocating the return of the vote to previously disfranchised polygamists, and presenting an annual report that, for the first time, failed to identify plural marriage as a continuing crisis in the territory. Property seized from the Mormon church slowly was being returned by the federal receivers, easing a financial crisis that had gripped the Mormon church since the Edmunds-Tucker Act was passed in 1887.

In this emerging era of good will Utah scored a national public-relations triumph. Responding to an invitation from event organizers, the territory and

Above: Grover Cleveland, twenty-second and twenty-fourth president of the United States, 1893. (LOC)

The only president ever elected to non-consecutive terms of office, Cleveland returned to the White House after all doubts about Utah statehood had vanished. In 1894 he completed the process started by Harrison and granted a complete amnesty and pardon to men convicted under the anti-polygamy laws, returning voting rights to hundreds of Utah residents. Cleveland's second term, however, would prove to be a political disaster. A national financial panic that gripped the country early in the decade had grown into a full-blown economic depression by 1893. Cleveland's efforts to calm the panic by rejecting federal silver purchases and staying with the gold standard outraged western political interests, and his policies were repudiated by some members of his own party.

Above right: The Utah Pavilion, Chicago Exposition, 1893. (USHS)

Right: Brigham Young Statue, Chicago Exposition, 1893. (USHS)

"*The crowd at the fair today was estimated to be nearly 250,000. Honors have fallen thick on Utah's head.*" —special correspondent, *Salt Lake Tribune*

The Chicago Columbian Exposition, organized to celebrate the 400th anniversary of the exploration of the Americas by Christopher Columbus, was a breakthrough event for Utah Territory. The Utah Pavilion, stressing themes of patriotism and industry, attracted as many as two million curious visitors, who heard both the Mormon and non-Mormon guides talk about the new path away from polygamy, shattering many presuppositions about Utahns. A bronze statue of Brigham Young was commissioned for the exposition and dominated the pavilion's grounds. The Mormon Tabernacle Choir took second place in the fair's international choral competition.

the Mormon church joined to send a full delegation and exhibit to the Chicago International Exposition in the summer of 1893. Housed in their own building, representatives from Utah met hundreds of thousands of visitors from throughout the United States, often shaking hands and greeting visitors well into the night. The Utah pavilion extolled the success of mining and agriculture in the territory, played up patriotic themes, and, through exclusion, downplayed the controversy surrounding polygamy. A new bronze statue of Brigham Young, stressing his role as a model pioneer, graced the grounds, and the Mormon Tabernacle Choir took second place in an international chorale competition. Looking and sounding like the embodiment of the nation's values, the Utah exhibit received international publicity.

In September 1893, forty-four years after the first petition for statehood had been drafted by a handful of pioneers hoping to create the State of Deseret, the House of Representatives acted to bring a bill to the floor enabling Utah's admission to the Union. The Committee on Territories, the killing field for so many previous statehood bids, printed an eloquent endorsement of Utah as a state, concluding simply: "Your Committee recommend that the bill does pass." On December 13 the clerk of the House read to a half-full chamber House Resolution 352, an enabling act for drafting a state constitution and forming a state government in Utah. Without ceremony, the bill was quickly passed with only minor opposition.

The enabling act now made its way to the Senate, where political gamesmanship slowed the bill as national parties jockeyed for position. Through their agents in Washington, Utah and the Mormon church had often represented themselves in various political shades, depending on the party in power. Members of the Senate now turned a close eye on Utah to see how its admission as a state might impact the narrow balance of power in their body. Recent elections in Utah had shown an emerging strength in the local Republican party, and Senate Democrats balked at creating a state that would send two new Republicans to the chamber and swing majority status back to the GOP. In the early months of 1894, back-room negotiators worked at a compromise. Finally, the enabling act was amended to ensure that Utah would not be formally admitted as a state until the current term of Congress came to a close at the end of 1895.

Portion of Utah Presbyterian protest letter opposing statehood, 1893. (NARA)

As Utah's bid for statehood gained momentum in Congress during 1893, a number of groups in the territory tried to delay admission. In this protest to President Cleveland, Presbyterian church officials argued that federal oversight of the territory was the only protection the non-Mormon population of Utah had against a domineering Mormon majority. Such protests were relatively few in number, however. The House of Representatives approved the Utah Enabling Act in December 1893; the Senate followed suit the following summer, and President Cleveland signed the act into law on July 16, 1894.

Left: City and County Building, Salt Lake City, 1894. (USHS)

Passage of the Utah Enabling Act set the stage for the territory to hold a seventh constitutional convention to draft a formal constitution for the new state when it would be admitted to the Union in 1896. Without a capitol building, the 107 constitutional convention delegates used the recently constructed Salt Lake City and County Building to hold the convention. Originally scheduled to use a large civil courtroom for the meeting, delegates attending the first day of the proceedings in March 1893 found themselves escorted into a room labeled "Criminal Courtroom"—which produced more than a few pointed jokes among the delegates.

LIFE IN SALT LAKE CITY IN THE "GAY NINETIES"

Life in Salt Lake City as Utah neared statehood appears more familiar to twentieth-century readers looking back in time. The major streets were now paved, and electric streetcars had arrived in 1895 to replace the old system of horse-drawn public transportation. The sky overhead was a tangled mass of wires as telegraph lines competed for space with newly strung telephone wires. The new communication marvel was attracting more and more customers; however, each phone call required an opera-tor to plug in wires to make the connection. The city still had a strongly rural flavor, however, and it was not unusual for heavily laden farm wagons to slowly make their way through the heart of the city. Weary laborers could spend a night in a flop house for ten cents. You could have a new set of false teeth installed by the Red Cross dentists for four dollars, if you were sufficiently brave. And Rieger and Lindley would sell you cigars handrolled in a Salt Lake City factory, two for five cents.

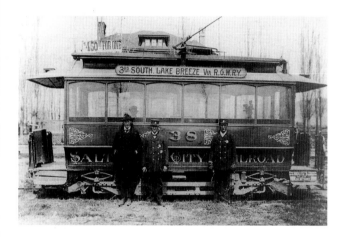

Above left: Early electric streetcar, Salt Lake City, 1895.
Left: Main Street and Second South, c. 1890.
Above right: Salvation Army and the Workingmen's Hotel, Salt Lake City, c. 1900. (all USHS)

Left: Main Street and Second South, c. 1890. (USHS)

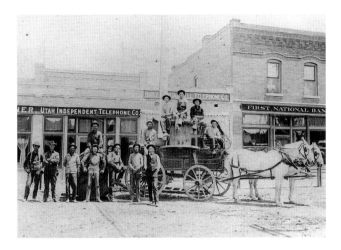

Above left: Rieger & Lindley Liquor Store, Salt Lake City, c. 1900.
Above right: Telephone line crews in front of competing company offices, Salt Lake City, date unknown.
Right: Telephone exchange and operators, Utah Independent Telephone Company, c. 1900.
Below: Business scene, Salt Lake City, c. 1900. (all USHS)

William Jennings, mayor of Salt Lake City in the 1880s, c. 1890. (USHS)

The national economic depression of 1893 reached deep into Utah, closing mines, rocking banks, and wiping out many businesses and investments. Even with the slow return of federally seized property, the Mormon church was in dire financial straits. The church was unable to meet its payroll on several occasions and was forced to pay workers with tokens for food and goods at the tithing store, generally reserved for the church's poor. Former Salt Lake City mayor William Jennings, a once prominent merchant, was devastated by his financial losses and took his own life at the peak of the depression in 1893.

On July 10, 1894, the Senate passed the enabling act for Utah with only two dissenting votes.

On September 17, 1894, President Grover Cleveland, citing his personal conviction that Mormons were obeying the law and refraining from contracting new polygamous unions, signed a comprehensive presidential amnesty and pardon for those convicted under the anti-polygamy laws, and he ordered the full restoration of their civil rights.

In Utah, attention now turned to drafting yet another state constitution. Forty years of conflict and repeated prior attempts had resolved most of the issues that Congress felt must be addressed in Utah's constitution: polygamy would be forever banned; a free market economy would be embraced; there would be an absolute separation of church and state, most keenly noted in the political arena and public schools.

The state constitutional convention convened in March 1895 in the recently completed City and County Building in Salt Lake City. For sixty-five days more than 100 delegates would wrestle with hammering out a blueprint for Utah. The most contentious battle surfaced over women's suffrage. Thought by many to have been resolved in principle with the previous granting of the vote to women in the 1870s, the battle over suffrage dominated convention debate and led to some angry splits at the constitutional convention. Brigham Roberts voiced strong opposition to granting women the vote in the constitution, claiming it would only set up a new battle with Congress over Utah's future. Proponents pointed to the legacy of voting rights already established for women in Utah, and claimed suffrage was a simple act of justice. A strong majority finally voted to approve Article IV, Section 1, which read in part: "Both male and female citizens of this state shall enjoy all civil, political and religious rights and privileges."

Above left: John Henry Smith, Mormon apostle and president of the constitutional convention, c. 1895. (USHS)

John Henry Smith was an unabashed Republican at a time when the Mormon church was keenly interested in building political diversity among its largely Democratic membership. Saying he was "doing the Lord's work," Smith campaigned in the territory to convince the Latter-day Saints that it was "possible to be a good Mormon and a good Republican." In 1895 he sat as president of the convention which drafted the constitution—the territory's seventh—that enabled Utah to enter the Union.

Above right: Joseph Rawlins, constitutional convention delegate and delegate to Congress, c. 1894. (USHS)

Joseph Rawlins was an important delegate in the Utah Constitutional Convention of 1895. After the Manifesto by Wilford Woodruff had overcome the hurdle of federal opposition to plural marriage, Rawlins had the relatively easy task of shepherding Utah's admission to the Union through Congress. Facing only token opposition in both the House and Senate, and bolstered by an extraordinarily effective lobbying campaign in government and the media, Rawlins was given credit by some as the "Father of Statehood" when the Utah Enabling Act was signed into law in 1894. That is a gross overstatement; the bulk of the difficult and important political work had been undertaken by George Q. Cannon and by Rawlins's predecessor as delegate, John T. Caine.

UTAH WOMEN ON THE EVE OF STATEHOOD

By the 1890s women in Utah Territory had moved into important positions of leadership in arts, health care, and public welfare, and they continued to advance the cause of their political empowerment. Women were the driving force behind the establishment of the Mormon church's first venture in modern medical care, Deseret Hospital, when it was opened in 1882. Key figures like Ellis Shipp and Martha Hughes Cannon returned to the territory after receiving advanced medical training, and then mentored hundreds of women learning techniques of medical care and midwifery. At the same time, the women of the territory continued to press both locally and nationally for political rights. Representatives from Utah participated in the major women's rights and suf-

frage gatherings of the late nineteenth century, and they were forceful advocates for including women's suffrage in the 1895 Utah constitution. Although barred from service as delegates to the convention because of their disfranchisement under the Edmunds-Tucker Act of 1887, they nonetheless successfully lobbied the convention to grant women full and equal political rights in the new Utah state constitution. Sarah Anderson of Ogden would wage a determined fight for the right of women to vote on approving the state constitution, only to lose an election-eve decision by the Utah Supreme Court.

Left: Hilda Erickson (right), midwife and circuit-riding care provider, c. 1895. (USHS)

Zina Diantha Young, plural wife of Brigham Young, c. 1890. (USHS)

Ellis R. Shipp, M.D., c. 1890. (USHS)

Zina Williams, politically active women's leader, c. 1885. (USHS)

Martha Hughes Cannon, M.D., c. 1890. (USHS)

Maude Adams, celebrated actress, 1892. (USHS)

Sarah Anderson, political rights activist, c. 1895. (USHS)

Brigham H. Roberts, Mormon church general authority and politician, c. 1895. (USHS)

Moses R. Thatcher, Mormon church apostle and politician, c. 1895. (USHS)

In 1895 Roberts and Thatcher were Democratic candidates in the election to fill Utah's first political offices after statehood—Roberts running for the House of Representatives and Thatcher for a U.S. Senate seat. While both held high positions in the Mormon church, they were viewed by some other church leaders as mavericks who were not in "harmony" with church political principles. When they announced their candidacies without consulting the highest ranks of church leadership, First Presidency counselor Joseph F. Smith lashed out at the men during a church meeting on Temple Square. Smith's comments were widely read as an attack on the Democrats by the church and touched off a storm of controversy over perceived church control of the political process. The church offered a flurry of denials and explanations, but Republicans steamrolled to victory in the election. While Roberts later would return to good favor, gain election to Congress, and even serve as official church historian, Thatcher would be removed from his position as an apostle due to erratic behavior and an increasingly strained relationship with church leaders.

George Sutherland, constitutional convention delegate, c. 1900. (USHS)

A young Salt Lake City attorney when he was selected to serve as a delegate to the constitutional convention, Sutherland later would achieve national prominence during his lengthy career. Serving two terms as a U.S. Senator, Sutherland was also the first person from Utah to serve as president of the American Bar Association. He was appointed to the U.S. Supreme Court in the 1920s and would serve for sixteen years until he resigned in 1938, becoming part of the "court packing" controversy involving President Franklin D. Roosevelt and older Republican members of the Court.

Passage of the suffrage clause did not end debate. Delegates also exchanged sharp words over the growing national temperance movement toward prohibition. With a number of Mormon and non-Mormon delegates voicing concern that a constitutional clause embracing prohibition of liquor might be viewed as a religious position, in the final days of the convention, by a three-to-one majority, the delegates quietly killed the move to make Utah a dry state.

Their work completed, the constitutional convention voted itself out of existence, endorsing the new constitution on May 6 by a vote of 72 to 0.

On November 5, 1895, the proposed constitution went to the voting public in an all-or-nothing, approve-or-defeat election. By a four-to-one margin voters approved the constitution, with women and convicted polygamists still unable to vote under the lingering provisions of the Edmunds-Tucker Act. Women would not resecure the vote until the constitution went into effect with statehood, and polygamists would need to reregister as voters without the test oaths of the Utah Commission as a deterrent.

Other critical components on the ballot were the election of the first state officers and a congressional representative. Despite the inroads made by the Republican party in recent years, local newspapers were forecasting Democratic victories in the races for governor and Congress. All of that changed in October when Joseph F. Smith of the First Presidency of the Mormon church used a church meeting to direct some caustic comments toward the candidacies of two Mormon leaders who had not sought formal church clearance for their political campaigns. The candidates, Brigham Roberts and Moses Thatcher,

Above left: The White House, 1896. (LOC)

Left: Oval Office, the White House, c. 1895. (LOC)

Before a final signature could be affixed to the executive proclamation making Utah a state, Utah's new constitution had to be submitted to Washington for review by Congress and the White House to ensure that it complied with the stringent requirements of the enabling act. Approval was a foregone conclusion, however, since the constitutional convention had followed the federal directives to the letter and had scrupulously avoided entering into controversial areas such as prohibition of alcohol. By Christmas 1895 Grover Cleveland had indicated that he would sign the proclamation immediately after the first of the year, complying with congressional deal-making that forced Utah to remain outside of the Union until 1896. On January 4, Cleveland, beleaguered by the national economic depression and criticism of his policies for controlling its devastating effects, signed the two-page document making Utah the nation's forty-fifth state.

Frank Cannon and Caleb West rushed to the White House on the morning of January 4, 1896, to be present when President Cleveland signed the statehood proclamation. They had already devised a plan with Western Union to telegraph news of the signing to the new state so that a celebration could begin. As they paced in the waiting room outside of the Oval Office, Cleveland emerged with the proclamation already signed and quickly walked away to attend to pressing business. Crestfallen, Cannon and West were offered Cleveland's pen as a consolation gift. The two men then sent word to the former territory that the deed had been done and that Utah was now a state.

Frank J. Cannon, U.S. Senator, photograph c. 1910. (USHS)

Caleb West, Utah's last territorial governor, c. 1895. (USHS)

were both Democrats. Through trumped-up media coverage and loose rumors, Smith's remarks were soon commonly viewed as an attack upon the candidates and their party. This touched off a storm of controversy, with newspapers attacking the church for meddling in political affairs, and Demo-

BY THE PRESIDENT OF THE UNITED STATES OF AMERICA.

A Proclamation.

WHEREAS: The Congress of the United States passed an Act which was approved on the sixteenth day of July, eighteen hundred and ninety four, entitled "An Act to enable the people of Utah to form a Constitution and State Government and to be admitted into the Union on an equal footing with the original States," which Act provided for the election of delegates to a Constitutional Convention to meet, at the seat of government of the Territory of Utah, on the first Monday in March eighteen hundred and ninety-five, for the purpose of declaring the adoption of the Constitution of the United States by the people of the proposed State and forming a Constitution and State Government for such State ;

And whereas, delegates were accordingly elected who met, organized and declared on behalf of the people of said proposed State their adoption of the Constitution of the United States, all as provided in said Act ;

And whereas, said Convention, so organized, did, by ordinance irrevocable without the consent of the United States and the people of said State, as required by said Act, provide that perfect toleration of religious sentiment shall be secured and that no inhabitant of said State shall ever be molested in person or property on account of his or her mode of religious worship, but that polygamous or plural marriages are forever prohibited ; and did also by said ordinance make the other various stipulations recited in Section Three of said Act;

And whereas, said Convention thereupon formed a Constitution and State government for said proposed State, which Constitution, including said Ordinance, was duly submitted to the people thereof at an election held on the Tuesday next after the first Monday of November, eighteen hundred and ninety five, as directed by said Act;

And whereas, the return of said election has been made and canvassed and the result thereof certified to me, together with a statement of the votes cast and a copy of said Constitution and Ordinance, all as provided in said Act, showing that a majority of the votes lawfully cast at such election was for the ratification and adoption of said Constitution and Ordinance;

And whereas the Constitution and Government of said proposed State are republican in form, said Constitution is not repugnant to the Constitution of the United States and the Declaration of Independence; and all the provisions of said Act have been complied with in the formation of said Constitution and government;

Now, therefore, I GROVER CLEVELAND, President of the United States of America, in accordance with the Act of Congress aforesaid and by authority thereof, announce the result of said election to be as so certified and do hereby declare and proclaim that the terms and conditions prescribed by the Congress of the United States to entitle the State of Utah to admission into the Union have been duly complied with, and that the creation of said State and its admission into the Union on an equal footing with the original States is now accomplished.

In testimony whereof, I have hereunto set my hand and caused the seal of the United States to be affixed.

DONE at the city of Washington this fourth day of January in the year of our Lord one thousand eight hundred and
[SEAL.]   ninety six, and of the Independence of the United States of America the one hundred and twentieth.

GROVER CLEVELAND

By the President:
RICHARD OLNEY
Secretary of State.

Utah Statehood Proclamation (reprint), 1896. (NARA)
"The creation of said State and its admission into the Union on an equal footing with the original States is now accomplished."
—President Grover Cleveland

crats desperately trying to downplay the significance of Smith's comments. It was all to no avail. In the November 5 vote Republicans swept every statewide office and secured two-to-one majorities in the new state legislature.

All that remained between Utah and the forty-fifth star was ceremony. Shortly after nine a.m. on the fourth day of 1896, Grover Cleveland slipped his ample girth behind his desk in the Oval Office, picked up a fountain pen, and affixed his signature to a proclamation declaring Utah a state. Cleveland

Mormon Tabernacle, Salt Lake City, January 1896. (UU)

Preparations were made for a celebration of statehood and the inauguration of Utah's first elected state officials in the tabernacle in Salt Lake City on January 6, 1896. Evan Stephens wrote a special hymn for the occasion, "Utah, We Love Thee," which would be selected as the state's official song twenty years later. A 1,000-voice choir, built around the acclaimed Mormon Tabernacle Choir, gave the song a resounding debut.

did not know that Utah's final territorial governor, Caleb West, and Senator-designate Frank Cannon had traveled to Washington to be part of the historic event and were in his waiting room while he signed the document. He gave them the pen as a consolation.

The *Salt Lake Herald* of January 5, 1896, told what happened next:

> The click of the telegraph instrument conveyed to Manager Brown of the Western Union the news for which the people of Utah had been hoping the past 45 years. The "flash" indicated the signing of the Statehood Proclamation. Mr. Brown then started the excitement by firing two shots on Main Street in front of the Western Union Office. Bedlam broke loose … the swarming crowds filled the streets shouting and laughing.

On January 6, 1896, some 15,000 spectators jammed the flag-draped Tabernacle on Temple Square in Salt Lake City for the noontime swearing-in of Utah's elected leaders. Wilford Woodruff, eighty-nine years old and in failing health, asked George Q. Cannon to deliver the invocation Woodruff had dictated earlier. Included were these words:

Statehood celebration decorations, Mormon Tabernacle, Salt Lake City, January 1896. (USHS)
  Draped with an enormous flag and adorned with red, white, and blue bunting at every corner, the tabernacle offered an imposing patriotic backdrop for the celebration of statehood and the inauguration of Utah's first elected state officials. Braving the cold of a blustery winter day, the crowd filled every seat and overflowed onto the pathways of Temple Square during the ceremony.

And may the privileges of free government be extended to every land until tyranny and oppression shall be broken down to rise no more ... and the voice of strife hushed.

Cleveland's pen was then displayed to the cheers of the crowd. A special 1,000-voice choir sang patriotic songs. Then Heber M. Wells, son of Daniel Wells, the defiant general of the Nauvoo Legion, stepped forward to take the oath of office as governor, administered by Justice Charles Zane, who for so many years had firmly enforced the anti-polygamy laws in his courtroom. Wells stepped to the podium of a structure that had been a symbol of religious principle, defiance, and struggle for the people of Utah Territory for decades. He now spoke to the people as the governor of their state:

We have been received into the great sisterhood of states.... We are now endowed with self-government in state and local affairs.... Our patriotism must never falter. Our allegiance to the national government will ever remain supreme.

DESERET EVENING NEWS.

12 PAGES · **5 O'clock EDITION**

UTAH A STATE

The Proclamation Issued by President Cleveland.

ONE OF THE AMERICAN UNION.

Official Message That Arouses Joyous Enthusiasm in the Hearts of the People.

Above: Heber Manning Wells, first Governor of the State of Utah, 1896. (USHS)

Heber Wells was only thirty-six years old when he took the oath of office as Utah's first state governor. His father, Daniel H. Wells, had been the commander of the territorial militia when it was called to arms to repel the federal army during the Utah War of 1857. When he stepped to the podium in the Tabernacle, Wells took the oath of office from territorial chief justice Charles S. Zane, the federal judge who earlier had sent hundreds of Mormon men to prison on polygamy-related charges.

Deseret News, January 4, 1896. (USAR)

The "5 O'clock Edition" of the *Deseret Evening News* carried the story of the morning's celebration after Grover Cleveland signed Utah's statehood proclamation. Announced on a Saturday, the event was celebrated on the following Monday by decision of government and church leaders. The event was so well anticipated that one of the last acts of the territorial legislature as it ended in 1895 was to declare Monday, January 6, a holiday to celebrate statehood.

Statehood celebration parade, Salt Lake City, January 6, 1896. (LDS)

Early on the morning of Monday, January 6, 1896, with temperatures hovering near freezing and snow packed firmly on the downtown streets, crowds started to assemble for the day-long celebration of Utah's admission to the Union. Bands and military units marched through the heart of the city, turned west on South Temple, and continued past Temple Square, where the inauguration ceremonies would be held.

UTAH CELEBRATES ITS STATEHOOD

January 6, 1896, was a day of celebration throughout the new state of Utah. Some towns planned parades, others just enjoyed spontaneous gatherings of the local populace in the heart of the particular town. After forty years of conflict, there were still some hard feelings in public opinion: a small group of Mormons publicly questioned whether statehood was worth all that was sacrificed during the years of federal prosecution. Similarly, some non-Mormons feared that statehood meant the end of their protection under the Constitution. But for the vast majority it was a long-anticipated day of deliverance from territorial status. The spirit of celebration was so strong that many cities, including Salt Lake City, staged another round of parades and parties that July.

The summer celebration of statehood provided Utahns both ample time to prepare and better weather for festivities and decorations. Army units from Fort Douglas, sporting new hot-weather helmets, marched south down

Above: Statehood celebration crowds, Main Street, Salt Lake City, January 6, 1896. (LDS)
Right: Carriage decorated for statehood celebration, West Temple and Second South, Salt Lake City, 1896. (USHS)
Below: Chinese dragon, summer statehood parade, Salt Lake City, 1896. (LDS)

Main Street past the Mormon Temple. Telephone poles and store fronts sported patriotic bunting, and the parade featured dozens of decorated wagons, colorful participation by ethnic groups representing homeland cultural traditions, and even a float sporting an elegantly dressed young woman above the banner "The Flower of Our State." Men in straw "boaters" and women with parasols stood in groups of up to ten deep to watch the parade, many clutching small flags bearing forty-five stars.

Above: Floats, summer statehood parade, Salt Lake City, 1896. (LDS)

Left: Celebration, Spanish Fork; reported as January 1896. (USHS)

Below: Army units, summer statehood parade, Salt Lake City, 1896. (LDS)

Flag-draped Mormon Temple, Salt Lake City, 1896. (UU)

Flag protocol in 1896 was not nearly as well defined as it has become by the late twentieth century. Determined to make a patriotic gesture in celebration of Utah's admission to the Union, leaders of the Mormon church ordered an enormous forty-five-star flag to be prominently displayed on the south side of the Temple in Salt Lake City. Observers today might question why the flag was displayed backwards; however, in 1896 it was not considered backward and not questioned—it was merely accepted as the gesture of celebration it was intended to be.

FORTY-FIVE STARS
1896–

NEARLY FIFTY YEARS HAD ELAPSED from the beginning of the Mormon westward trek to the affixing of the signature of Grover Cleveland on the statehood proclamation for Utah. In 1847 the Great Basin had been the cherished but demanding homeland of a few Native American tribes living in delicate balance with the forces of nature. By the dawn of 1896 about a quarter of a million people lived in the new state of Utah, creating emergent urban

Mormon Tabernacle Choir, c. 1900. (UU)

After its performance at the Columbian Exposition in 1893, the Mormon Tabernacle Choir emerged as (and has remained) one of the nation's premiere choral groups. Many trappings of the statehood celebration remained in the Tabernacle for years.

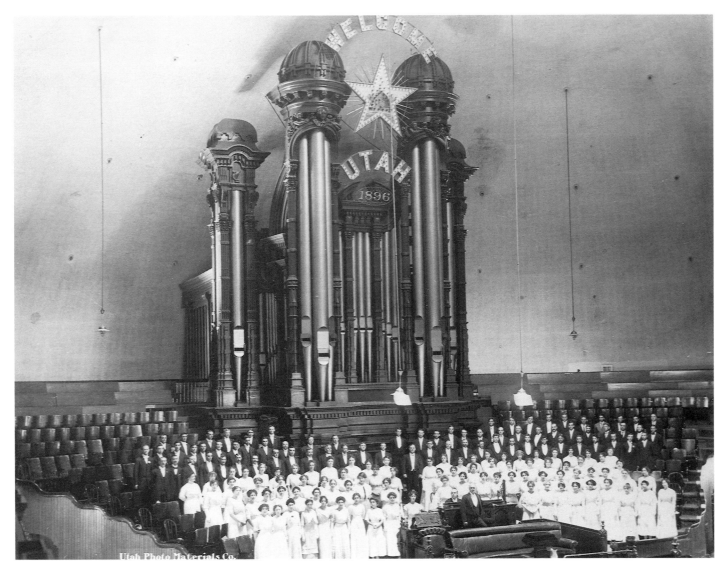

cultures and reordering the landscape with their determined agricultural and mining activities. The early Mormon utopian vision of the Kingdom of God had been transformed; there was in its place a stronger sense of membership and partnership in the American union and experience.

But the men and women experiencing the events of the mid-1890s would soon realize that their political struggles were far from over. Lingering suspicions about plural marriage were confirmed when evidence surfaced indicating that Mormon church leadership had secretly continued to support a very limited practice of polygamy after the announcement of the Woodruff Manifesto. Disclosure of polygamy's enduring presence triggered outrage in Washington, prompted exhaustive confirmation hearings for Utah Senator-elect Reed Smoot, and threatened renewed congressional action against the Mormon church. Church president Joseph F. Smith finally resorted to a second, highly publicized, manifesto in the early years of the twentieth century to close the controversy and distance the Mormon church from plural marriage once and for all.

While Smoot's case captured the national spotlight, other early representatives to Washington from the state of Utah had even rougher experiences in the nation's capital. Arthur Brown and Frank Cannon, selected by the legislature

Members of the Typographical Union in front of *Salt Lake Tribune* offices built in 1892, Labor Day, c. 1910. (USHS)

The *Salt Lake Tribune* maintained a vigilant watch on Mormon compliance to end polygamy. With editor and former U.S. Senator Frank Cannon leading the way, the *Tribune* printed numerous stories at the turn of the century attempting to document the secretive continuance of polygamy among the Mormons. The reports caused a furor, prompted lengthy congressional hearings in Washington, and ultimately contributed to the Mormon church taking steps to definitively end plural marriage among the Saints in 1904.

Below right: LDS Church President Joseph F. Smith with family, c. 1910. (USHS)

A supporter and practitioner of plural marriage, Joseph F. Smith became president of the Church of Jesus Christ of Latter-day Saints in 1901. When the election of his fellow Republican Reed Smoot to the Senate was contested, Smith was called to testify before Congress on political practices and the continuation of polygamy in Utah. In response, he issued a detailed and firm declaration against plural marriage (often described as the "second manifesto") in 1904, which plainly stated that polygamy was not part of the Mormon church and vowed excommunication for any church member who attempted to sustain the practice. In a dramatic showdown shortly thereafter, church leaders Matthias Cowley and John W. Taylor were excommunicated when they were deemed out of compliance with the newly detailed church position.

to serve as the state's initial senators in Washington as part of the local Republican landslide of 1895, both had short, embattled careers on Capitol Hill. Elected representative Brigham Roberts was actually denied his seat as a member of Congress.

Arthur Brown, a transplant to Utah after a scandalous love affair in Michigan in the 1870s, would serve a short two-year term before returning to the state amid controversy that he had spent more time chasing women in Washington than protecting Utah's interests. He was shot and killed by a disgruntled mistress in the nation's capital in 1906.

Frank Cannon, a son of church leader and political strategist George Q. Cannon, would serve one shortened term in the Senate before being unceremoniously dumped by the people of Utah for his opposition to high tariffs that might protect the state's industries. Cannon drifted away from membership in the Mormon church, joined Thomas Kearns's *Salt Lake Tribune* as an editor, and began a new career attacking the church and its leadership. His book *Under the Prophet in Utah* reopened old wounds concerning church political involvement and control.

Brigham H. Roberts, on the other hand, took his lumps for staying too close to his religion and the people and practices of Utah. Defeated in his 1895 bid for Congress after the controversial comments by fellow church leader Joseph F. Smith, Roberts rode his enduring personal popularity to a resounding victory in an 1898 rematch. But Roberts's involvement with polygamy, including his 1889 conviction for unlawful cohabitation and his ongoing relationships with his three wives, triggered a national media attack against his character. After long and heated hearings in Washington, Congress voted to deny B. H. Roberts his seat in the House of Representatives.

This was one example of the cauldron of partisan politics, and it was one of many signs that Utah was fully engaged in the gamesmanship and responsibilities of governance at the turn of the century. Another, more poignant, indicator came in 1898 with the outbreak of the Spanish-American War. A short conflict that served to elevate the United States to major-player status in world events, the war also provided the first opportunity for Utah volunteers to fight for their country. Artillery units made up of Utah native sons fought in the Philippines under the leadership of Captain Richard W. Young, a grandson of Brigham Young and the second Mormon graduate of West Point. Staying after the war to battle Philippine insurgents seeking political independence, the Utah units suffered fifteen deaths. The military

Arthur Brown, Utah's first U.S. Senator, c. 1896.

Senators were actually "elected" by state legislatures until passage of the Seventeenth Amendment to the Constitution in 1913. In Utah there was an unwritten agreement between political and civic leaders at the time of statehood to the effect that one of the two U.S. Senators would be Mormon and one would be from the non-Mormon community. Arthur Brown, a non-Mormon attorney who relocated to Utah after a somewhat checkered career in Michigan, and Mormon Frank Cannon were selected as Utah's first two senators. Rumors of philandering followed Brown in Washington and his political travels, and he served only one twelve-month term before leaving office in March 1897. Brown died in 1906 at the hands of a woman who claimed he had fathered her illegitimate child and had refused to honor his promises of marriage.

Left: Members of the first Utah State Senate, 1896. (USHS)

Gathered in front of the Salt Lake City and County Building prior to an early session of the first state legislature, members of the Utah State Senate pose with support staff. There were no women members of the legislature, in part due to the ban on their political participation through the Edmunds-Tucker Act, which had remained in effect until after the election that selected the first legislature. Physician Martha Hughes Cannon won election to the state senate late in 1896, and would serve two terms in the body as Utah's, and the nation's, first woman state senator.

Troop formation during Spanish-American War at Fort Douglas, Utah, c. 1898.

At the outbreak of war with Spain in 1898 the government called upon each state to provide a complement of volunteers to bolster the army. Utah was asked to provide about 500 volunteers, but more than 800 men ultimately volunteered to serve their country. While most of the Utah volunteers spent much of their enlistment fighting the war and a subsequent insurrection in the Philippines, other units with Utah ties earned heroic acclaim in Cuba. African-American regiments from Fort Douglas and Fort Duchesne—the legendary "buffalo soldiers"—took part in the dramatic fight at San Juan Hill with future president Theodore Roosevelt.

service of 800 Utah enlistees, just a few short years after the political exile of their territory had ended, was viewed nationally as a distinguished act of patriotism and service. Utah's commitment to the defense of the nation would never again be questioned.

Some observers, however, would remain uncomfortable with the nature of society, politics, and religion in Utah as the state entered the twentieth century. Correspondents occasionally would offer accounts of the powerful role of the Mormon church in the affairs of the state, or note with curiosity the passing of the vestiges of polygamy from the scene. Dubious barometers were employed to gauge the progress of the "Americanization" of the newest and oddest state. Lost amid most of the accounts was a sense of the history that had shaded each page of the Utah story.

Any account of Utah, then or now, struggles to find an objective solid ground that still does justice to a distinctive place inhabited by people imbued with a rare sense of purpose. Utah was a place settled with a vision that transcended economics and even the notion of "home." Settled by people joined through a spiritual purpose, the land played host to experiences that carved a unique place in the legends, lore, and history of the West. A singular spiritual purpose, and its resulting sense of social unity, had sustained the people through unprecedented targeting by their government, an opposition ironically triggered by the people's beliefs. An emerging diversity that at first appeared to threaten the spiritual experience actually strengthened it by revealing a shared love of the land and an understanding of common bonds to the nation. The necessary changes that were eventually effected were not a breaking faith with the past as much as an aim at securing the future. The history and lessons of the struggle for statehood would be certain to trouble, inform, and grace the days that would follow. To deny or diminish any contribution to that story would be to deny the history itself.

In 1911 Judge Orlando Powers stepped forward to offer an after-dinner speech in honor of President William Howard Taft's visit to Salt Lake City. Powers had been one of the most passionate combatants in the last days of Utah Territory, firmly applying the law against polygamy and lashing out against the political actions of the Mormon church. In return, he was reviled by many Mormons as a bigoted, power-hungry political animal. If anyone

UNCLE SAM:— "NOW THERE'S A MERGER THAT WILL STAND LOOKING INTO."

Left: Anti-polygamy political cartoon, 1907. (LOC)

R.T. Richards's spoof of Mormon married life depicting Uncle Sam's lingering anger with polygamy reflected the slow-to-fade suspicion that Mormons were not being entirely honest in their claims that plural marriage had ended. In reality, Utahns and federal government officials knew that an appearance of plural marriage would endure for a number of years since there was no intent or effort to break up families that had been created during the years of church-sanctioned polygamy. Those families would quietly carry on, and wives from the years of sanctioned plural marriage lived in Utah well into the 1950s. By the 1930s, however, the Mormon church began to actively support law-enforcement efforts to crush the continuing practice of polygamy by individuals and Mormon splinter groups claiming that the principle remained a true Mormon doctrine that should continue to be practiced.

Orlando Powers, judge and politician, c. 1900. (UU)

Orlando Powers came to symbolize the convulsion, change, and reconciliation that characterized Utah's joining with the national mainstream. A determined and often outspoken judge, Powers had sent a number of Mormon men to prison during the years of the anti-polygamy crackdowns. A strongly partisan Democrat, he also had vehemently protested Joseph F. Smith's criticism of Brigham Roberts and Moses Thatcher in the 1895 election. Although still somewhat suspicious of the Mormons, he nonetheless urged "a new spirit" for Utahns after statehood admission, one that would build upon mutual tolerance and a sense of shared purpose.

could harbor ill will against methods or motives, it was certain to be Judge Orlando Powers. Instead, he offered words of counsel and hope:

> In the fierce conflicts that have at times shaken the state as by an earthquake, I have seen Utah emerge each time a little more like the rest of the union. And from the experience in which I have been schooled I declare and I believe that Utah can work out her own salvation. What we need now more than all else is a spirit of toleration. Out of the flames of the conflict that has caused us such sorrow and filled our hearts with bitterness, there is certain to rise a new Utah ...

Prophetic words, indeed. For out of the flames of conflict a new Utah did emerge: a state that continues to tread a unique path among its fellows, but whose differences enrich the American experience as certainly as the lessons of its history touch the lives of its people to this day.

Brigham Young Monument, Temple Square, c. 1898.

After serving as the centerpiece in the triumph of Utah's participation in the 1893 Chicago Exposition, the bronze statue of Brigham Young was freighted back to Salt Lake City and erected in the heart of Temple Square. Years later, the statue was removed from the religious confines of the Square to a location in the heart of Salt Lake City. The move carried a much larger message: the years of pioneering struggle and colonizing leadership embodied by Young were a legacy for all of Utah and all Utahns.

UTAH CHRONOLOGY
1846–1896

c. 10,000 B.C. The first ancient Native Americans come to the Great Basin and Colorado Plateau regions.

c. 1000 B.C. The Anasazi and Fremont cultures populate the region, a presence that continues through the thirteenth century A.D.

c. A.D. 1400 Ancestors of Utes, Shoshonis, and Navajos are in the region.

1540 Conquistador Francisco de Coronado sends expeditions to explore the northern reaches of "New Spain." They venture as far as the Colorado River.

1760 Juan María Antonio de Rivera explores the area near present-day Moab.

1776 The Domínguez-Escalante expedition seeks a route to Monterey, California, venturing as far north as Utah Lake.

1824 James Bridger reportedly reaches the Great Salt Lake.

Trapper Etienne Provost reaches Utah Lake.

1825 William Ashley leads a contingent of fur trappers to the area. His Rocky Mountain Fur Company will be a steady presence in the area for the next few years.

1826–27 Jedediah Smith explores the Great Salt Lake and associated salt flats.

1830s Roving trapper/trader Denis Julien probably follows the Green River to its confluence with the Colorado River. Antoine Roubidoux also is active trapping and trading in the region.

1841 The Bartleson-Bidwell party is the first wagon train to traverse Utah bound for California.

Jesuit missionary Jean-Pierre DeSmet travels in the region.

1843 John C. Frémont, accompanied by Kit Carson, leads an exploration through Utah, navigating the Great Salt Lake. Frémont publishes his account in 1845.

1844 Joseph Smith discusses a westward move by the Church of Jesus Christ of Latter-day Saints (Mormons) in order to "have a government of our own." Smith is murdered in Carthage, Illinois, on June 27.

1845 Lansford Hastings publishes his *Emigrants Guide*, presenting a short cut to California through the Salt Lake Valley and Great Salt Lake Desert.

Denis Julien inscription, near Green River in Grand County, Utah; photo 1909. (USHS)
 A little-known trapper and trader, Denis Julien was an early white explorer of the Green River, most likely following the river to its confluence with the Colorado River near present-day Moab. He carved numerous inscriptions—this one dated May 3, 1836. The trapper-trader era was crucial to early exploration in the American West, and led to government expeditions, such as that of Captain John C. Frémont, to more accurately map the land that would become Utah.

Samuel Brannan, c. 1850. (USHS)

Selected by Brigham Young in 1846 to lead a contingent of Mormons to California by way of sailing around Cape Horn, Brannan landed at Yerba Buena, later to be renamed San Francisco. Brannan and his group thought the area a perfect final destination for the Mormon migration, and he traveled overland to attempt to convince Brigham to continue on to California. The two met near Green River in present-day Wyoming, but Young rejected California as a destination because it did not afford the isolation he desired for his people. Brannan returned to the coast, eventually broke with the Mormon church, and went on to live a prosperous life in California.

The Mormons evacuate their Nauvoo headquarters, their leaders suggesting several final destinations including Vancouver Island, California, and a location in the Rocky Mountains.

1846   The nucleus of the Mormon church is in a temporary settlement on the banks of the Missouri River in present-day Nebraska.

Negotiations with President James K. Polk lead to the creation of the Mormon Battalion to join United States forces battling Mexico. The Battalion begins a long march through the unexplored Southwest.

The Donner party follows the Hastings Cutoff through the Salt Lake Valley.

1847   With a fixed destination of the Salt Lake Valley, the great Mormon westward trek begins.

Samuel Brannan, sent by sea to San Francisco with a contingent of Mormons, urges California as a preferred destination; but he is rebuffed by church leader Brigham Young.

July 21: Orson Pratt and Erastus Snow are the first Mormons to enter the Salt Lake Valley.

July 24: Bedridden due to illness, Brigham Young arrives in the Salt Lake Valley and confirms it as "the right place."

1848   A grasshopper plague decimates the first major crops in the valley.

The Mexican War ends. Mexico transfers huge tracts of land, including the present-day state of Utah, to the United States in the Treaty of Guadalupe Hidalgo.

Gold is discovered by members of the Mormon Battalion near Sacramento, touching off the great California gold rush of 1849.

A harsh winter (1848–49) leads to much suffering in the Salt Lake Valley.

1849   Church leaders organize a legislative assembly which crafts a constitution for the "State of Deseret" to submit to Congress with a petition for statehood.

The Stansbury-Gunnison survey party studies the region of the Great Salt Lake and also records observations of the people.

Colonization of the region is well advanced.

1850   Population of the area is 11,300 Mormon settlers.

Congress authorizes territorial status for "Utah," rejecting "Deseret" as a name.

The *Deseret News* is first published as a church newsletter.

The University of Deseret offers its first classes, but soon closes.

1851   Brigham Young is appointed first territorial governor by President Millard Fillmore.

First non-Mormon federal officials arrive in the Salt Lake Valley.

1852   Migration of Latter-day Saints from Illinois and Nebraska deemed complete.

First federal officials leave the valley, complaining of church control.

Orson Pratt offers a public announcement and defense of plural marriage as an aspect of Mormon faith.

1853   Captain John Gunnison's survey party is killed by Indians.

The Walker War erupts, pitting the Nauvoo Legion against Ute Indians led by Chief Wakara.

Brigham Young orders the arrest of trader Jim Bridger under charges of conspiring with Indians against the Mormon people.

Ground is broken for the Salt Lake LDS Temple.

1854   Colonel Edward Steptoe clears Mormons of complicity in Gunnison's death but refuses to accept appointment as governor.

1855   Territorial Assembly moves the seat of government to Fillmore for a more central location, but the idea is soon abandoned.

Chief Wakara dies.

1856   Fights between settlers and raiding parties are dubbed the "Tintic Indian War."

Another constitution is drafted with another petition for statehood; both are rejected by Congress.

The Willie and Martin handcart companies are trapped by an early blizzard in Wyoming. Hundreds die before relief efforts reach them.

The Mormon Reformation peaks; it is a call for spiritual recommitment and dedication.

Associate Judge W.W. Drummond flees Utah. His resignation letter is filled with charges against the Mormons.

The Republican party fashions its first national platform, decrying slavery and polygamy as the "twin relics of barbarism."

1857   President Buchanan appoints new territorial officials and orders 2,500 army troops to effect their installation in Utah.

Brigham Young declares martial law on August 5.

The Baker-Fancher party from Arkansas enters the territory and is massacred at Mountain Meadows in southern Utah on September 11.

Lot Smith and other Mormon guerillas attack army supply trains.

The army under Colonel Albert Sidney Johnston camps for the winter near Fort Bridger.

Thomas Kane arrives to negotiate between Brigham Young and the federal government.

1858   A peace commission negotiates a final settlement, seating Alfred Cumming as governor of the territory, with Johnston's Army stationed forty miles away from the capital at Camp Floyd.

1860   Population of the territory is 40,273.

The Pony Express begins operation; it ends in 1861.

Abraham Lincoln's election triggers a secession movement.

1861   The transcontinental telegraph is completed, linking Utah to east and west coasts. Brigham Young sends the first message, vowing loyalty to the Union.

The handcart era ends.

The Civil War begins at Fort Sumter, April 12.

Governor John Dawson serves one month before attempting to flee

Kanosh and sub-chiefs, Pahvant Band, Ute Indians, c. 1860. (LDS)

Kanosh (seated, second from right) was the leader of a band of Ute Indians who based their life in the Pahvant Valley of central Utah, near present-day Fillmore. The Pahvant band was blamed for the attack on Captain John Gunnison and his survey party in 1853 that resulted in the deaths of the popular Gunnison and seven others. A subsequent investigation by the army dispelled the rumor that Mormon leaders had orchestrated the attack; it concluded that the attack was most clearly a reprisal for a brutal attack against Kanosh's people by non-Mormon emigrants passing through the Pahvant Valley.

Telegraph line construction, Weber Canyon, 1868. (USHS)

As the transcontinental railroad crews raced toward completion of the tracks in Utah, additional crews followed the tracks of the Union Pacific Railroad and erected telegraph poles for use by the rail lines. Telegraph connection with the world had already come to Utah in 1861.

the territory after a sexual indiscretion. He is severely beaten on his way out of Salt Lake City.

1862   Congress passes the Morrill Act, outlawing polygamy, disincorporating the Mormon church, and calling for property seizures.

General Albert Sidney Johnston, wearing the uniform of the Confederate States of America, dies at the Battle of Shiloh, April 6.

The Morrisite War: followers of Joseph Morris are arrested following a brief but violent standoff in which Morris is killed.

Colonel Patrick Edward Connor and the California Volunteers establish Camp Douglas in Salt Lake City to protect the overland routes to the Pacific Coast.

1863   The Battle of Bear River: Connor's men kill 250 men, women, and children of the Northwestern Shoshoni Tribe in a one-sided, four-hour firefight on the present-day Utah-Idaho border, January 29.

The "Josephites" (missionaries from the Reorganized Church of Jesus Christ of Latter Day Saints) claim 300 converts in the Salt Lake Valley. They leave, claiming persecution.

1864   Nevada is admitted to the Union. Congressional recognition of other states and territories has reduced Utah to its present configuration, with the exception of a disputed area near Fort Bridger.

1865   The Black Hawk War erupts. It is a lengthy series of battles between Mormons and Indian parties under the leadership of Chief Black Hawk in central Utah. Connor refuses to intervene with his troops.

1867   The Utah Territorial Assembly demands repeal of the Morrill Act, leading to a series of new "anti-Mormon" bills being debated in Congress.

The Salt Lake Tabernacle is completed.

1868   The creation of Wyoming Territory carves the final shape of Utah, delivering the Fort Bridger area to Wyoming control.

1869   The transcontinental railroad is completed with a celebration at Promontory Point, Utah, May 10.

John Wesley Powell conducts his first exploration of the rivers and canyons in eastern and southern Utah.

Vice-president Schuyler Colfax visits Utah on a fact-finding tour of the West.

The "Godbeite" movement emerges. William Godbe and others urge less communitarianism among the Mormon people and more diversity in social, political, and economic life.

1870   Population of the territory is 86,780; a majority of adults are foreign-born immigrants.

Mormon women stage massive protests against the Cullom Bill, which proposes new restrictions on the Mormon people.

The territorial assembly authorizes women's suffrage.

The "Wooden Gun Rebellion": the territorial militia (Nauvoo Legion) flaunts an order by Governor J. Wilson Shaffer banning their drilling with weapons.

1870s   Throughout the decade, a mining boom, encouraged by Colonel Connor, will grip the territory, leading to the arrival of thousands of new, non-Mormon residents to the area.

Throughout the decade, the cooperative and United Order movements will grow. They are in great part efforts to preserve the integrity of internal economics in the face of dramatic changes brought by the mining and railroad booms; the movements emphasize communitarianism and a strict "buy Mormon" creed. By the end of the decade, many United Order communities will have faded.

Throughout the decade, Christian missionaries will arrive in Utah as part of evangelical crusades to "redeem" the Mormon people; they will establish churches, schools, and hospitals.

1871   Chief Justice James B. McKean indicts Brigham Young on charges of illegal cohabitation.

John Wesley Powell begins his second exploration of the Green and Colorado rivers.

1872   Through the Englebrecht decision the U.S. Supreme Court throws out the methods used by Judge McKean to form juries and prosecute the Mormons. Brigham Young's indictment is thrown out.

Another constitution and bid for statehood is prepared; it is subsequently rejected.

President Ulysses S. Grant denounces Mormonism and polygamy in a major address to Congress.

1873   The *Salt Lake Tribune* passes from William Godbe to a politically active group dedicated to reining in the power of the Mormon church.

1874   The Poland Act passes Congress, vesting all criminal authority in the district courts and limiting the probate courts (and Mormon judges) to estate and divorce proceedings.

Brigham Young's secretary, George Reynolds, is selected as a test case to challenge the constitutionality of the Morrill Act.

"The Republic of Tooele" has a brief fling with local government that is not controlled by Mormons.

1875   Twenty years after the tragedy, John D. Lee is tried for murder in the case of the Mountain Meadows Massacre. The first trial produces a hung jury, the second a conviction. Lee is executed by firing squad at Mountain Meadows in 1877.

Corinne, a new town on the rail line, is promoted as the "Gentile Capital" of Utah. Non-Mormons actually lobby Congress to move the territorial capital to Corinne.

Ann Eliza Webb Young ("The Twenty-seventh Wife") files for divorce from Brigham Young. Judge McKean arrests Brigham on a contempt charge.

Church leader George A. Smith, counselor and close personal friend of Brigham Young, dies.

1877   Brigham Young's marriage to Ann Eliza Webb is declared null and void.

The St. George LDS Temple is dedicated by Brigham Young.

Brigham Young dies, August 29. The Quorum of the Twelve assumes group leadership of the church, with John Taylor to be confirmed later as president.

In the first thirty years of territorial settlement, eighty thousand LDS converts have migrated from Europe to Utah.

Construction of the St. George Mormon Temple, 1875. (USHS)

Jesse Tye, an early photographer in southern Utah, captured the construction of the St. George LDS Temple as it neared completion in 1875. Seated in the group in the extreme foreground is construction supervisor Miles Romney. The first temple completed in Utah, the St. George Temple was dedicated by Brigham Young just months before his death in 1877.

Three hundred settlements have been established in the West under Brigham Young's direction.

1878   As Congress debates new restrictions on the Mormons, women in the territory hold competing rallies and letter-writing campaigns. Non-Mormon ("gentile") women urge tough laws, while Mormon women urge a respect for religion and the granting of statehood.

1879   The U.S. Supreme Court hands down its decision in *Reynolds v. United States*. Acknowledging a protected right to religious *beliefs*, the Court says it is perfectly legal for Congress to control religious *actions*, such as polygamy. The Morrill Act is upheld. Through its practice of polygamy, the Mormon church is now deemed outside of the law of the land.

Mormon groups in Utah Territory organize funerals for the Constitution.

1880   The territorial population is 143,963.

1881   James A. Garfield is inaugurated president and promises a dedicated crackdown on Mormons and polygamy. He is assassinated two hundred days into his administration. Chester Arthur takes office and renews the anti-Mormon pledge.

Noted author Harriet Beecher Stowe (*Uncle Tom's Cabin*) personally finances a series of published letters in the eastern press denouncing polygamy and theocratic control in Utah.

1882   Senator George Edmunds of Vermont travels to Utah on a fact-finding mission.

Another drive for statehood is made in Washington, and ignored.

Congress passes the Edmunds Act, denying Mormon polygamists the right to vote, hold office, and sit on juries. As part of the new law, President Arthur appoints the Utah Commission to take charge of the political process in Utah.

Dozens of new federal deputy marshals are hired to investigate polygamy.

George Q. Cannon is denied his seat as Utah's delegate to Congress because of his practice of polygamy.

1883   More than 12,000 people have been disfranchised under the Edmunds Act.

The Denver and Rio Grande Railroad comes to the territory, providing new economic opportunity and development.

Delegate John T. Caine delivers another petition for statehood to Congress.

After a major fire destroys several downtown businesses, Salt Lake City creates a professional, full-time fire department.

1884   Rudger Clawson is arrested and begins serving the longest sentence (three years and one month) for polygamy at the territorial penitentiary in Sugarhouse. He is viewed locally as a hero and a "prisoner for conscience."

Mormon Bishop John Sharp is arrested and accepts a court offer of leniency if he will obey the law on plural marriage. Sharp is stripped of his church position and is treated as an outcast.

1885   Much of the leadership of the Mormon church, including the entire First Presidency, is on the run from federal marshals, living in a shadowy "underground" network.

Salt Lake City Fire Department, 1883. (USHS)

Pictured here is the first unit of the professional fire department, created in Salt Lake City in 1883 after a fire and explosion caused substantial damage in the downtown area. The fire unit worked out of a building adjoining Salt Lake's City Hall, the brick building with the clock tower in the photograph.

A near riot takes place on July 4 when Mormons lower their flags to half-staff in Salt Lake City to protest their persecution.

The first local telephone exchanges open in Salt Lake City.

Mormon colonies are founded in Mexico as a haven for polygamists against prosecution. These colonies, including Colonia Juarez, flourish through the remainder of the nineteenth century but begin to be abandoned by Mormons due to political troubles in Mexico in the twentieth century.

1886   Congress funds a "Utah Women's Industrial Christian Home" to serve as a refuge and sanctuary for women fleeing plural marriage. Senator George Edmunds and Representative J. Randolph Tucker promise tough new bills aimed at the Mormon church.

1887   The Edmunds-Tucker Act becomes law, without President Cleveland's signature. It eases prosecution standards for plural marriage, and provides for escheating church property.

A new constitution from the territory outlaws polygamy for the first time, identifying it as a misdemeanor. This constitution, and references by church leaders to a "period of transition," are viewed as the first indications that polygamy might be subject to change.

Mormon church president John Taylor dies, July 25.

The U.S. Attorney in Utah begins legal action to seize Mormon church property. Marshals eventually seize the tithing office, Gardo House, and the Perpetual Emigrating Fund office, among others.

Marshals raid the Endowment House on Temple Square.

1888   Mormon church representatives meet with Canadian Prime Minister John MacDonald, seeking approval for a settlement in Alberta. MacDonald is adamant that polygamy is not welcome in Canada.

Church leader George Q. Cannon serves time in prison for plural marriage.

The Mormon church's People's party offers the first non-Mormon candidates on its slate. Prominent banker William McCornick is elected to Salt Lake City government on a so-called "fusion" ticket.

Continuing a pattern of political donations and payoffs, the Mormon church funnels $25,000 to President Grover Cleveland's re-election campaign. He loses to Benjamin Harrison.

Harrison promises new efforts against Mormonism unless polygamy is abandoned.

1889   The Liberal (non-Mormon) party wins municipal elections in Ogden, a major reversal for Mormon political interests.

The Utah Commission reports 357 polygamy-related convictions in the past year. By the end of the decade, 900 Mormon men will serve prison sentences under polygamy convictions; many will have multiple convictions and prison terms.

The "gathering of the Saints" continues with the founding of Iosepa in Skull Valley to house Hawaiian converts to the church.

1890   The population of the territory is 210,779.

The U.S. Supreme Court upholds the legality of seizing Mormon church property (*The Late Corporation of the Church of Jesus Christ of Latter-Day Saints...*) and the Idaho law disfranchising all Mormons who follow church teachings (*Davis v. Beason*).

McCornick and Company, Salt Lake City, c. 1885. (USHS)
William McCornick (seated, center) was a non-Mormon businessman and banker who generally refused to take an antagonistic course with the predominant religion in Utah Territory. Respected by Mormons for his approach, diametrically opposed to general anti-Mormon sentiment, McCornick became an important figure in the early attempts at religious reconciliation and coexistence in the territory during the 1880s. McCornick agreed to run as a non-Mormon on a slate of muncipal candidates assembled by Mormons to serve in Salt Lake City government. His election to local office represented a political first, as Mormons crossed over to vote for a non-Mormon candidate.

The Struble-Cullom Bill is introduced in Congress, seeking to extend the Idaho test oath and disfranchisement of Mormons.

The Liberal party wins the Salt Lake City municipal elections.

Federal officials announce their intention to begin seizing Mormon temples.

Church President Wilford Woodruff and counselor George Q. Cannon hold meetings with Republican party contacts in California and are assured nothing will change until polygamy is gone.

President Woodruff issues a manifesto, September 24. The document declared the intention of the church president to obey the laws forbidding plural marriage, and urged church members to do the same.

1891　An "Americanization" drive is under way. A public school system free from sectarian control is instituted. The Mormon church disbands its political party and endorses membership in either the national Republican or Democrat parties.

With property still being seized, the Mormon church teeters on the brink of bankruptcy.

With prosecutions and imprisonment continuing, the territory petitions President Harrison for amnesty for convicted polygamists.

1892　Benjamin Harrison loses the presidential election to Grover Cleveland. As a lame duck, Harrison delivers a limited presidential amnesty for polygamists.

Some of the "escheated" property is returned to church control.

1893　The Salt Lake LDS Temple is completed.

The Utah Commission allows previously disfranchised polygamists to vote under a new test oath.

At the Chicago World's Fair Utah enjoys widespread acclaim and acceptance for its exhibit and its willingness to adapt.

An enabling act for statehood is passed in the House of Representatives.

1894　Cleveland grants a more complete amnesty and pardon for people convicted under the polygamy raids.

The Senate passes the enabling act for Utah statehood. A political compromise mandates that statehood not be granted until after the current session of Congress.

Cleveland signs the enabling act, July 16.

1895　The Utah Constitutional Convention opens March 4, with John Henry Smith as convention president. While most provisions have been mandated by events of the previous ten years, the convention becomes embroiled over women's suffrage, which is ultimately embodied in the constitution. The convention adopts the constitution on May 6.

Future Mormon church president Joseph F. Smith creates a furor about church intervention in the election for new state officers when he criticizes Democratic party candidates.

Voters ratify the new constitution by a four-to-one margin, and deliver a landslide victory for Republican candidates.

1896　President Grover Cleveland signs the document designating Utah as the nation's forty-fifth state, January 4. In Salt Lake City thousands of

Letter to Interior Department, 1895. (NARA)

In 1895 a Salt Lake City woman who identified herself as a person who knew the Mormon church inside and out wrote Secretary of the Interior John Noble to plead with him to find a way to deny Utah admission as a state. Claiming the Mormons could not be trusted and were merely making meaningless concessions to secure their political control of Utah, the woman asked that her name be closely guarded to protect her against the "treacherous designs" of the Mormons if they learned her identity. In forwarding the letter for processing, the Interior Department prominently listed the name of Mrs. Caroline Wellock of Salt Lake City and stamped the date on the letter—February 8, 1896—one month and four days after Utah had been admitted to the Union.

people brave mid-winter temperatures and snow to celebrate the news and Utah's final attainment of success in its struggle for statehood.

Heber M. Wells is sworn in as Utah's first governor in a ceremony at the Salt Lake Tabernacle, January 6.

Statehood celebrations are held throughout the territory during the year, especially in midsummer—often in conjunction with Pioneer Day but also on the Fourth of July, now more ardently celebrated by area residents than had been the case in the years before.

Below: George Cotterell, c. 1850s. (USHS) Cotterell was a member of Lot Smith's guerilla fighters, harassing and frustrating the federal army as it marched on Utah during the "war" of 1857–58. Members of the Nauvoo Legion played a pivotal role in delaying the army and avoiding an open armed conflict. For years afterwards they were revered as heroes among Mormons in Utah, and symbolize Utahns' fortitude and determination to establish their homeland.

Pioneer Day parade, Salt Lake City, 1872. (USHS)

   At first celebrated simply and quietly with prayerful remembrance, the anniversary of Brigham Young's arrival in the Salt Lake Valley—July 24—soon evolved into a special day of celebration for Utah. As early as 1857 the pioneers used the date for daylong picnics, dancing, and celebration. By the 1870s towns throughout the region were staging parades to celebrate the pioneers. In 1872 Salt Lake City used the Pioneer Day parade to show off its newly acquired steam-powered pump wagon, used by the volunteer fire department that served Utah's largest city.

— ☆ —

SELECTED BIBLIOGRAPHY

Alexander, Thomas G. *Things in Heaven and Earth: The Life and Times of Wilford Woodruff, a Mormon Prophet.* Salt Lake City: Signature Books, 1991.

Allen, James B., and Glen M. Leonard. *The Story of the Latter-day Saints.* Salt Lake City: Deseret Book, 1976.

Anderson, C. LeRoy. *Joseph Morris and the Saga of the Morrisites.* Logan: Utah State University Press, 1988.

Arrington, Leonard J. *Great Basin Kingdom: An Economic History of the Latter-day Saints, 1830–1900.* Cambridge: Harvard University Press, 1958.

———. *Brigham Young: American Moses.* New York: Alfred A. Knopf, 1985.

Arrington, Leonard J., Feramorz Y. Fox, and Dean L. May. *Building the City of God: Community and Cooperation Among the Mormons.* Salt Lake City: Deseret Book, 1976.

Bancroft, Hubert Howe. *History of Utah, 1540–1886.* (Reprint) Las Vegas: Nevada Publications, 1982.

Beecher, Maureen Ursenbach, and Lavina Fielding Anderson, eds. *Sisters in Spirit: Mormon Women in Historical and Cultural Perspective.* Urbana: University of Illinois Press, 1987.

Brodie, Fawn M. *No Man Knows My History: The Life of Joseph Smith the Mormon Prophet.* New York: Alfred A. Knopf, 1945.

Brooks, Juanita. *The Mountain Meadows Massacre.* 2d ed. Norman: University of Oklahoma Press, 1962.

Bunker, Gary L., and Davis Bitton. *The Mormon Graphic Image, 1834–1914.* Salt Lake City: University of Utah Press, 1983.

Burton, Richard F. *The City of the Saints, and Across the Rocky Mountains to California.* Fawn M. Brodie, ed. New York: Alfred A. Knopf, 1963.

Embry, Jessie L. *Mormon Polygamous Families: Life in the Principle.* Salt Lake City: University of Utah Press, 1987.

Firmage, Edwin Brown, and Richard Collin Mangrum. *Zion in the Courts: A Legal History of the Church of Jesus Christ of Latter-day Saints, 1830–1900.* Urbana: University of Illinois Press, 1988.

Foner, Eric, and John A. Garraty, eds. *The Reader's Companion to American History.* Boston: Houghton Mifflin, 1991.

Furniss, Norman. *The Mormon Conflict, 1850–59.* New Haven: Yale University Press, 1960.

Gove, Jesse Augustus. *The Utah Expedition, 1857–1858: The Letters of Captain Jesse A. Gove, 10th Inf., U.S.A.* Otis Hammond, ed. Concord: New Hampshire Historical Society, 1928.

Hansen, Klaus J. *Quest for Empire: The Political Kingdom of God and the Council of Fifty in Mormon History.* East Lansing: Michigan State University Press, 1967.

Heywood, Martha Spence. *Not by Bread Alone: The Journal of Martha Spence Heywood.* Juanita Brooks, ed. Salt Lake City: Utah State Historical Society, 1978.

Hill, Marvin S. *Quest for Refuge: The Mormon Flight from American Pluralism.* Salt Lake City: Signature Books, 1989.

Kimball, Stanley B. *Heber C. Kimball, Mormon Patriarch and Pioneer*. Urbana: University of Illinois Press, 1981.

Larson, Gustave O. *The Americanization of Utah for Statehood*. San Marino, CA: Huntington Library, 1971.

Lyman, Edward Leo. *Political Deliverance: The Mormon Quest for Utah Statehood*. Urbana: University of Illinois Press, 1986.

Milner, Clyde A., Carol A. O'Connor, and Martha A. Sandweiss, eds. *The Oxford History of the American West*. New York: Oxford University Press, 1994.

Mulder, William, and A. Russell Mortensen, eds. *Among the Mormons: Historic Accounts by Contemporary Writers*. Lincoln: University of Nebraska Press, 1958.

Poll, Richard D. *Quixotic Mediator: Thomas L. Kane and the Utah War*. Ogden, UT: Weber State College Press, 1985.

Powell, Allan Kent, ed. *The Utah History Encyclopedia*. Salt Lake City: University of Utah Press, 1994.

Quinn, D. Michael. *The Mormon Hierarchy: Origins of Power*. Salt Lake City: Signature Books, 1994.

Roberts, Brigham H. *Comprehensive History of the Church of Jesus Christ of Latter-day Saints, Century I*. 6 vols. Salt Lake City: Deseret News Press, 1930.

Schindler, Harold. *Orrin Porter Rockwell: Man of God, Son of Thunder*. 2nd ed. Salt Lake City: University of Utah Press, 1983.

Shipps, Jan. *Mormonism: The Story of a New Religious Tradition*. Urbana: University of Illinois Press, 1985.

Smith, John Henry. *Church, State and Politics: The Diaries of John Henry Smith*. Jean Bickmore White, ed. Salt Lake City: Signature Books, 1990.

Stout, Hosea. *On the Mormon Frontier: The Diary of Hosea Stout, 1844–1861*. Juanita Brooks, ed. 2 vols. Salt Lake City: University of Utah Press/Utah State Historical Society, 1964.

Tullidge, Edward W. *A History of Salt Lake City and its Founders*. Salt Lake City: Edward W. Tullidge, 1880.

Van Wagoner, Richard S. *Mormon Polygamy: A History*. Salt Lake City: Signature Books, 1986.

Winn, Kenneth H. *Exiles in a Land of Liberty: Mormons in America, 1830–1846*. Chapel Hill: University of North Carolina Press, 1989.

INDEX

UTAH:
The Struggle for Statehood

Book design by Richard Firmage, Salt Lake City, Utah.

Composition by Richard Firmage in Adobe Sabon typeface family.

Printed on Warren's Patina, an 80-pound acid-free paper,

by Publishers Press, Salt Lake City, Utah.

Bound by Mountain States Bindery, Salt Lake City, Utah.